PRAISE FOR *CREATING MICRO-S(*
FOR COLORFUL MISMATCHED

In telling the story of LEADPrep, Maureen O'Shaughnessy makes the clear case and provides a how-to guide for micro-schools. But it's much more than that. She issues a clear challenge and call for all schools to imagine how much more they could be.

—**Mark Crotty**
Executive Director, Northwest Association of Independent Schools

Maureen's passion as an educator, parent, and thought leader is abundantly clear as she provides step by step guidance to furthering the micro-school movement. As a parent of a colorful mismatched kid, I am so grateful to have found Maureen and LEADPrep. We are no longer suffering through school avoidance, long nights of useless homework, and the feelings of inadequacy that were prevalent under the traditional education model. In our micro-school, every staff member knows my child's strengths, weaknesses, and preferred method of learning. The confidence I have seen grow in my child as a student and as an individual as a result of this program is truly incredible.

I implore you to read on and discover what micro-schools can do for your child and your community.

—**Kristin Stay**
LEADPrep parent of 10th grader

Micro-schools: an educational breakthrough whose time has come. O'Shaughnessy blazes through ineffective, traditional education with a unique creative approach. She brings a creative freshness to youth who struggle with traditional norms. Colorful, mismatched kids are offered a ray of hope with an educational design that meets their needs!

—**Dr. Marianne LaBarre**
Founder of Executive Leadership Program,
Professor Emerita, Seattle University

Everything you need to know to create your own micro-school and change the learning experience, life, and future of students.

—**Bea Rosner**
Former LEADPrep Board President

Maureen is the best person to introduce you to the concept of micro-schools. She is living micro-schools every day, and Maureen has a unique perspective on how we can create the future of education one micro-school at a time. I recommend this book to any parent who wants the best education for their child, or to any educator who wants to become part of the micro-school revolution.

—**René Bouw**
Chief Architect at Risk Management Services, and
Software engineering leader, former serial intrapreneur at Microsoft
Founding Board President of LEADPrep

This book begins with a great summary of the problem—middle and high schools just don't serve most young people well. It makes a compelling case for micro-schools and includes a step-by-step process for how to start one of your own.

—**Tom Vander Ark**
Author of *Better Together: How to Leverage School Networks*
For Smarter Personalized and Project Based Learning
CEO and Partner of *Getting Smart*

Maureen is incredible to work with! I have been consulting with her during my endeavors to form STRIDE. Not only is she extremely knowledgeable, but is kind, passionate, and encouraging. I am amazed and inspired by all she has accomplished with her own successful micro-school, LEADPrep, and how she desires to help others be successful, too.

—**Whitney Sapp**
Founder of STRIDE Christian Academy

As an educator in a small, progressive elementary school, I was excited to find a similar middle/high school for our outgrowing students. Now, thanks to LEADPrep as a model, more 'tweens and teens can have the educational setting they deserve and in which they can thrive. Thanks, Maureen, for so clearly sharing your vision for micro-schools so that more children and their families can benefit from, and build on, your experience.

—**Joyce Kidd-Miller**
Early Childhood and Elementary Teacher,
At an Independent, Progressive School for 30+ years
Voted Eastside Best Teacher of the Year

Maureen's "think outside of the box" methods for creative, amazing, intuitive children is beyond refreshing! Her tactical, practical tools give you a roadmap to take your children and create an educational plan directly for them! Read this book if you need a plan to start a school that matters!

—**Jessica Butts**
CEO Front Seat Life

In 2007, I collaborated with a "tribe" to start our own private school focused on individualized learning experiences for neurodiverse students. At that time, there were very few resources available for help. This book is full of a wealth of information and tons of practical advice for anyone thinking about opening a micro-school. A passionate parent, educator, and entrepreneur, Maureen not only thought about what it would be like to create a new normal for colorful learners, she successfully achieved it!

—**Alison Moors Lipshin, MA, LBA, BCBA**
Founder of The Academy for Precision Learning,
Owner of "Precision Learning Solutions," a company that provides educational and
behavioral solutions for neuro-diverse learners and those who love them

Maureen has taken the proverbial bull by the horns in creating a relevant, viable, and effective solution for every student, every parent, every teacher—everyone who is sick and tired of the one-size-fits-all, traditional, factory-model school system. Her creative and tenacious spirit lives in the success of every student in her school. I am going to insist that my entire faculty and Board of Trustees read this book—it is that compelling and brilliant! A blueprint for creating 21st century schools.

—**Dr. Jorge O. Nelson**
Director of Balboa Academy, Panama City, Panama

Dr. O'Shaughnessy's passion for each student attending her school is truly remarkable, distinguishing her school and approach from traditional and other independent schools. Her approach is so well articulated in this text, paving the way for educational leaders to engage in the micro-school process and new paradigm for educating and preparing our youth for the quickly changing cultural and vocational climate of our country. This is a must-read for educators looking for inspiration to break out of the box and revisit the love of learning. It is a must-read for parents to learn there is hope for our educational system to meet the needs of their unique learner. It is a must-read for students looking for a new window to learning and a place for them to grow and flourish.

—**Julie Burgess-Dennis, MS, CCC-SLP**
Speech Language Pathologist
Co-founder of Under the Umbrella, Seattle, Washington
Specializing in social communication and learning

As a parent of two beautiful children who, by all appearances, seemed just like every other kid on the block, our son's sudden plummet into academic failure upon entering middle school took us by complete surprise. We just couldn't understand why the public school system that seemed to work so well for his older sister, was failing him completely despite our best efforts. Max's downward spiral caused us to step back, question "the system" and wonder, "Was there something better out there that would meet his unique style of learning?" Surely there were other kids out there who didn't fit the mold, right? Thus began our sojourn to find something better for our sweet boy before we lost him entirely. Little did we know this would open our eyes to the array of learning needs, teaching styles, and academic opportunities that exist today. There was hope after all and we found it at LEADPrep.

Maureen O'Shaughnessy not only is a micro-school expert, but she has a love for children and learning that exceeds all expectations for a school administrator. She recognized a need in the American public school system and found a way to fill it. She saw the variety of children, personalities, learning styles, and basic need to be accepted and created a learning environment that would benefit everyone, not just those who "fit the mold." As the future of our country is more and more frequently called into question, it is more important than ever before that we find a way to help every child be successful and go on to become a contributing member of society. Consequently, we need a wider variety of schools to address the needs of our youth if we want to contribute to the longevity of our way of life. We need to act now. We need to arm our children with the tools they will need to support themselves, their community, and their country or we are doomed to fail and go the way of other great civilizations that fell prey to the social norms and neglected to expand and explore their horizons. Enter LEADPrep and this amazing book, written by someone who has lived on both sides of the fence as a parent and a school administrator.

If you have found yourself struggling with the one-size-fits-all mentality and are looking for an alternative, then this book is for you.

—**Phyllis A Pierce**
Parent of a brilliant, funny, personable, and very capable teenager
for whom the public school system *did not work*

If you are a parent of a child struggling to "fit" into the generic education system, a teacher longing for a way to meet the diverse needs of your students, or an aspiring educator interested in shifting the school system to enable true learning, this book is for you. Inspiring, informative, and beautifully written, Maureen O'Shaughnessy exquisitely lays out a comprehensive seven-step plan to build a powerful micro-school of your own. *Creating Micro-Schools for Colorful Mismatched* Kids is filled with stories and a clear roadmap that will embolden you to take up the micro-school mantle today! I wish I had gone to this school!

—**Patti Dobrowolski**
Author of *Drawing Solutions: How Visual Goal Setting Will Change Your Life*

If it's true that a calm mind is one that is open to learning, then it is easy to see how a quieter, smaller school environment is one that can offer this kind of safe space for curious exploration to grow, especially for students with a complex neurophysiology. In her book *Creating Micro-schools for Colorful Mismatched Kids*, Maureen O'Shaughnessy outlines the need for this exact kind of learning environment that only a micro-school can provide. We read how a strengths-based approach can then re-ignite our complicated learners back into a sense of agency and a passionate interaction with life. Sometimes, it is these basic, fundamental shifts in a smaller learning environment like LEADPrep that can reorient a student's trajectory toward openness with an inclination of a positive interaction with the world.

Thank goodness for school options, especially ones that consider the particular needs of our creative thinkers who can easily slip through the cracks of the mainstream school system.

—**Heather Rudin**
LEADPrep mother of a fantastic 2E student

Since that earliest flicker of life, our collective rate of change has accelerated from billions of years to millions to millennia to centuries to decades. Today, calculations that once required decades are completed in minutes; communications that once required months occur in seconds. The rate of change experienced over the previous 20 years will be duplicated in the next 10 and we have every reason to believe that this exponential acceleration will continue.

Perhaps more so than ever before, humanity finds itself faced with the staggering necessity and moral imperative to address all crusty, irrelevant and outpaced systems, chief among them being those which would purport to prepare our youth to navigate this world we now pass into their care.

I celebrate Dr. Maureen O'Shaughnessy for championing such a timely call to evolution.

—**Dr. Richard Loren Held**
Senior Minister/Spiritual Director at Unity in Lynnwood
Award-winning college educator and K-12 teacher

CREATING
MICRO-SCHOOLS
for
COLORFUL
MISMATCHED KIDS

A Step-by-Step Process that Empowers
Frustrated Parents to Innovate Education

Maureen O'Shaughnessy, EdD

With Contributing Editor Kester Limner

ISBN-13 (print book): 978-1-7334736-0-6
ISBN-13 (ebook): 978-1-7334736-1-3

Library of Congress Number: 2019912608

Cover design by Joelle Chizmar
Photo by Tara Gimmer

Printed by Gorham Printing in the United States of America

*Note: The information provided in this book does not, and is not intended
to, constitute legal advice; instead, all information, content, and materials
available on this site are for general informational purposes only.*

This book is dedicated to
Jadrian, Giana, and the kids of LEADPrep.

I see your amazing potential,
and will never stop supporting you
and celebrating your uniqueness,
kindness, and bravery.

CONTENTS

Part One · 1

Demand Change: Why Our Colorful Mismatched Kids Need Micro-Schools to Thrive

Part Two · 55

You Can Do It: Seven Steps for Creating a New Micro-School

Part Three · 127

How We Did It: Opening LEADPrep's Doors to Serve Happy Colorful Mismatched Kids

Appendices · 219

MESSAGE TO PARENTS

Hello, Parents!

My name is Dr. Maureen O'Shaughnessy. I'm a career educator who has studied and worked in educational leadership for more than 25 years. I'm also the mom of two wonderful unique adult daughters, who each grew up with very different educational needs.

As a mom, let me be honest with you—I'm frustrated with the education system in this country. And maybe you're frustrated, too. Maybe your kid is a little bit different and doesn't fit into the "normal" or "average" box. My kids certainly didn't. One of my daughters has a chromosomal variation with a diagnosis of autism spectrum disorder (ASD) and attention deficit hyperactivity disorder (ADHD), and my other daughter is considered academically "gifted." I raised both girls in international schools as I traveled around the world as an overseas school administrator. When I brought them back to the US as teenagers, it was difficult to find a school that worked well for either of them. We found ourselves piecing together a patchwork of alternative education, Catholic schools, all-girls schools, homeschooling, online education, dual enrollment with college, and International Baccalaureate.

Trying to find the right kind of education was exhausting. Every option for high school seemed inhumane and outdated. These schools weren't preparing my children for the world. They were just a painful purgatory of assembly-line learning that made my children feel invisible and turned them away from the joys of learning.

Many children are rendered invisible or damaged by the conventional school system. When I see other kids set on this trajectory of pain and despair, I choose to say *no*. It is *not* acceptable for these children to be ignored or traumatized by their education. This determination was the catalyst for me to start LEADPrep, an innovative micro-school in Seattle. Drawing on my experience at other micro-schools, international school administration, and advanced degrees in alternative learning and school systems, LEADPrep became the school I wish my daughters could have attended. Each child brings a unique learning profile of abilities, needs, and preferences. Children are deserving of schools that see, value, and nurture them in ways that encourage (not stifle!) their one-of-a-kind uniqueness.

If your kid is a little bit different, and is struggling with school, I hope this book provides support and empowerment. Conventional schooling is an option that works for some children, but not all. As new research emerges on how teen brains work and learn and grow, we need to stand up for the implementation of new education models. We need to question the rigid tenets of school models created in the 1800s, and demand a flexible, humane school system that is relevant to today's youth. We love our kids, with all their quirks and differences. If you're feeling frustrated, that's good! Frustration can be turned into passion and action. The LEADPrep model and the Micro-School Coalition can be resources for your advocacy. I invite you to learn from our journey and be inspired to take practical, real-life steps today.

Our challenge, as caring adults, is to become the change we wish to see in the world. Every school year, kids are waiting, giving up, and being lost. There is an urgency here...let's start now!

Your ally in supporting our colorful, mismatched kids,

Maureen O'Shaughnessy, Ed D

WELCOME TO OUR MICRO-SCHOOL

*There's a world of difference between
insisting on someone's doing something and
establishing an atmosphere in which that
person can grow into wanting to do it.*

—Fred Rogers

Welcome to Leadership Preparatory Academy! At LEADPrep, we love having visitors. Come in and take a look at what we're doing here. If you're in the Seattle area, you can visit us in person, but until then let me take you on this "virtual tour" of our real-life, fully operational micro-school.

It's morning, and the students are arriving. The first thing you might notice is the kids saying hi to each other, and the teachers saying hi to each kid. Every person is noticed when they come in the door. That's because there's not very many of them—there's no crush of bodies in the hallway, no long, crowded rows of desks. Instead, it's just a handful of tweens and teens walking freely around the room and gathering at tables.

The kids range in age, from around ten to nineteen. Some are loud and some are quiet. Some kids seem "nerdy," and some seem "cool," but they all talk with each other and nobody is ignored. Shy kids are invited into conversation with a few other peers. Kids who prefer to be alone with a book are greeted by a teacher and asked about their weekends. Younger kids are greeted kindly by some of the older teens they admire. There are some loud, happy kids who are joking around with each other, but the overall noise level of the room is pretty low because there are only 15, maybe 20, students. Is that it? It's pretty small, right? And, wow, there are four adults in the room—three teachers and a visiting occupational therapy specialist. One of the students is excited to talk with the English teacher about the honors-credit essay they've* been working on. The English teacher has time to join in that student's enthusiasm, while the co-teachers continue greeting and engaging the kids coming in.*

The next thing you might notice is that the students are not carrying heavy backpacks. There are no textbooks, no binders, no paperwork. These kids seem to stand up straighter without a load of stuff on their backs. They've brought their lunches and a pair of headphones, and that's it. Well, some of them have also brought a basketball or a deck of Magic cards for their student-led club activities. You notice that kids are checking their phones into the pocket of a hanging plastic shoe organizer that's labeled "phone jail," and some of them check out their school-issued laptops to share a video with friends. A high-school junior comes in with an anxiety therapy dog and it causes quite a stir—lots of kids want to greet the dog!

One of the three teachers quickly responds to the situation and moves into a leadership role, calling the morning meeting into session. This leading teacher goes over the official class agreements regarding the therapy dog, while the other two teachers move around the room helping the students settle down or encouraging them to focus. When a troubled high-school-age student comes in late, one of the co-teachers discreetly steps aside for a personal conversation to find out why the student is late and to make sure everything is okay at home.

Meanwhile, the students are each sharing two emotions they experienced over the weekend with the help of a school-designed Emotion Awareness Board. The teachers remind them that they have to choose one negative emotion and one positive emotion. Choosing a positive emotion is a challenge for some of the grouchy kids, but they seem genuinely interested in each other's stories and excited to share their feelings. Some of the kids who like to give long, rambling answers are gently reminded to keep it short so that everyone gets a chance to be heard.

You look at the color-coded class schedule taped to the wall. There are a lot of subjects—Spanish, Civics, Math, English, STEM, Chemistry, clubs, Toastmasters—but you notice the schedule is laid out in a block schedule with only three long classes per day. The students have started in on their Civics class, but it's not a lecture. A different teacher has moved into the leadership role

---

* When referring to individual students in this book, we often use gender neutral pronouns of "they" and "them."

and is giving a short introduction to a hands-on activity. These students seem to be in the middle of an elaborate project that involves pretending to be a staffer for a Seattle city council member, and today's work involves collecting data and citizen input about where to locate a new homeless shelter. The kids are divided up into groups, and the goal of the activity is written clearly on the board. For the next 30 minutes the kids are up out of their seats, talking, negotiating, planning, and writing on big sheets of butcher paper. Instead of standing in front of the class, the teachers are shoulder-to-shoulder with the students, helping them work. When a group gets stuck, one of the co-teachers encourages them to ask different kinds of questions and experiment with new ideas. It's noisy and active!

As you walk around the classroom from group to group, you realize that the kids who finished quickly are getting an extra challenge question from the teachers. Likewise, kids who are struggling get a simpler version of the same work. You notice one of the high school students getting discouraged, but a teacher stops to help the student break the task down into smaller steps so they can catch up with some of their peers. You notice that one or two of the younger students are working well above their grade level, and their passion is encouraging the other junior high kids to focus and dig deeper. In a small group, enthusiasm is contagious!

At the end of the activity, the teacher invites each group of students to share what they produced. The students present their findings, review their efforts, and learn from other groups. The Civics teacher guides the discussion and weaves together the threads of the activity into a conclusion that fits into the larger project. After a student speaks, the teacher reflects their words back to them, to let them know that they've been heard, and to clarify the point for the other students. The teacher even accepts student critiques of the activity and collects feedback about what they'd like to do for the next class session. The students and the teacher seem to be in a dialogue where the curriculum is a collaborative work, proposed by the teacher, but influenced and guided by the needs and interests of the students.

As you watch the LEADPrep students learn interactively and personally, perhaps you think back to your own school years, when you were required to sit still at a desk for hours, passively receiving information, just another face in the crowd. Maybe you think, "I wish my younger self could have gone to a school like this one!"

The good news is, this school is real. LEADPrep is not a wishful-thinking, pie-in-the-sky fantasy, but an actual, functioning micro-school with a wide variety of students who are benefiting right now from innovative, flexible, humane education. We currently have 37 students attending on two campuses, with 11 full-time faculty and four part-time teachers. The two campuses provide classes that are small enough for personalized learning, with shared staff and communal time together on Fridays.

LEADPrep is able to serve kids with dyslexia, autism, sensory processing disorders, and ADHD. We also serve kids who are incredibly intelligent and bored to tears by regular school. We serve kids who are determined and argumentative, and kids who struggle with anxiety and shyness. We have kids who went through cancer treatment or have epilepsy. We have kids who have come out of foster care or residential therapy programs. We have transgender and gender-creative kids. We serve kids with multiple labels and kids with no labels at all. We have one high schooler who is taking college-level science classes at a local university. On the same day this student gets to run around on our campus and act like a kid at break time, being silly and making close friends for the first time in their life. Because LEADPrep is small and nimble, we can flex to meet the needs of each group of students, each year. We have the privilege of getting to know each kid for who they are.

One day, as our diverse, multi-age student population poured out of school at pickup time, a parent named Victoria commented, "What a happy, colorful group of mismatched socks we have!"

I will always remember and treasure Victoria's insight, because it gets to the heart of what we have accomplished at LEADPrep. Our students feel valued and safe in sharing their uniqueness. They know that it's a myth that there's a "normal way" to be a teenager. They don't feel pressure to conform to some outside standard. When they need extra help, it's always available. When they have questions or comments, their voice is heard. They feel accepted for who they are, and when each mismatched sock feels accepted, they in turn are accepting of their fellow mismatched classmates. A group of kids who used to feel stressed out or excluded are now happy and exuberantly showing their unique colors.

INTRODUCTION

Today's unique and varied youth need innovative and humane educational options that will support them in reaching their potential and becoming leaders in our world. Unfortunately, teens rarely have access to humane education. At both public and private schools, children are bored, disengaged, stressed out, or even traumatized by their school experiences. Anxiety[1] and depression[2] have skyrocketed in our teens and young adults. Dropout rates[3] are high in my home state of Washington, especially for minority students and students with learning differences. Parents are reporting "failure to launch"—a phenomenon where students who do graduate are unable to take the next step towards college[4] or a career[5]. As we will discuss in chapter two of this book, more and more teen "outliers" are being acknowledged, including LGBTQIA+ youth, autism-spectrum kids, hands-on learners, sensitive learners, reluctant learners, kids with ADHD and executive function challenges, and children with serious health or trauma backgrounds. Some of what we share in Part One will be upsetting. Many kinds of children suffer and struggle in the one-size-fits-all conventional education system. I wrote this book because I believe micro-schools are the answer. We must create small, innovative, community-based schools that see our students as whole people. This is a call to action!

In my 30+ years of work in education, I've come to know hundreds of wonderful kids and families, and worked at all kinds of schools. I've observed firsthand the types of barriers kids face and witnessed amazing success stories. As part of this journey, I've started three micro-schools and overseen a fourth. One of the micro-schools I started was a small learning community within a large public high school, for alternative learners and at-risk kids. Two other micro-schools were international community-based schools—one high in the Andes and one in the jungles of the Philippines. Today, I'm happy to be running LEADPrep, a two-campus progressive micro-school in North

Seattle and Kirkland. Students with a wide range of learning styles and backgrounds are included in our quirky group of kids. I've been there, I've done it, and I'm here to tell you that starting a micro-school is totally possible.

So, how do we get from here to there? In order to move secondary education into the 21st century and add humanity to the experience of learning, we need to do three things:

First, we all must acknowledge and embrace our colorful, mismatched socks. We can't be in denial about this issue. When unique, varied students are pressured into the traditional model of passive learning, they suffer distress and are unable to reach their full potential. But collectively, these colorful mismatched learners are the majority of students in school. We can all raise our voices together and be heard. Parents, have hope. You are not alone.

In this book, I often refer to teens and tweens as "our kids." From my perspective, all the kids in our town, city, or neighborhood are "ours." When a kid is excluded or falls through the cracks, it breaks my heart. As parents, we care about our own unique children and try to understand them. When we create a micro-school community, we are extending that care and understanding to other people's children as well.

Second, we must demand that humane methods drive our students' learning. Let's ask some tough questions! Do hours of homework really result in more life-ready adults? Are kids being held to a high standard of learning, or are they just being held to a high standard of compliance? Does the large school model need to be predominant? One of our local school districts offers small, specialized choice schools by lottery, and the waiting list for these schools is in the hundreds—at each school! Families know how beneficial it is to join smaller schools where students are seen, heard, and valued, and they deeply desire this kind of education for their children. These smaller schools do not have to be the exception. We can create many new, vibrant learning communities that combine the latest scientific breakthroughs with our deepest beliefs that each student has value and worth.

Third, each parent and educator (and vocal student) who wants to see more options for secondary learning communities must be an active part of the solution. This change cannot happen in isolation. We are strongest when we are working together. The shared resources and synergy we bring as a collective can be harnessed to create something bigger than ourselves. Starting a micro-school is like starting a snowball at the top of a hill. The snowball may start off tiny, but as it starts rolling, it collects more and more snow. When more people join the effort, momentum builds. With determination, we can create a tribe of caring adults who demand alternative learning options for all middle and high school students. (My focus in this book is on secondary learning, where I've seen the greatest need. There are frequently more inclusive and creative options for younger students. Of course, the micro-school design process could also apply to a new elementary school.)

A micro-school doesn't have to be big or elaborate. Start small and start now. If you have kids, start a conversation with some other families, and see if they have similar goals for their own kids. Team up with a few teachers to create pilot versions of a school-within-a-school. Network with young educators who have hopes and dreams about what school could be. Start a parent-led co-op. Collaboration in community is the place where ideas become reality.

Here's a story about a student named Skye. (Well, that's not his real name. All the students mentioned in this book are real people, but their names have been changed for privacy purposes.) Skye has always loved animals, and this year he asked if LEADPrep could have a class pet. In the past, Skye has been a reluctant learner, and it can be challenging to get him engaged in an assignment. But Skye's love of animals motivated him to write me a formal letter requesting a specific type of pet, with supporting arguments and a detailed financial breakdown of all the costs involved. As an educator, I was thrilled! On his own initiative, this student combined personal interests with English, math, and social skills. Skye had the confidence to submit his request because he knew the staff of the school would take time to listen and respect his voice. That's just one of the many real-life stories we have to tell, so keep an eye on these sidebars for more personal anecdotes.

We'll talk about community in the first part of this book. Why is there a need for micro-schools in our society and neighborhoods? Which students can benefit? How can parents create tribes of support to demand change? What is a micro-school, and how do they help our students and families thrive?

The second part of the book will lay out a seven-step plan for establishing a micro-school, including design, funding, staffing, and other practical considerations. Each step will include "start now" actions your community can take to create and sustain momentum for your own micro-school.

In the third part of the book, I'll walk you through our own journey in creating LEADPrep, and how we applied the seven-step process. You will be able to learn from our trials, setbacks, discoveries, breakthroughs, and successes. Every school is different, and we are an ongoing work in progress, but in this third section you will be able to see how LEADPrep used the seven-step plan to open its doors in 2013.

We love our kids, so let's demand more for them: more learning, more happiness, more understanding. Blaze a trail in your community! Join the progressive micro-school movement, and together we'll learn how to create a new kind of school for our colorful, mismatched kids.

Part One

DEMAND CHANGE:
Why Our Colorful Mismatched Kids
Need Micro-Schools to Thrive

Chapter One

WE HAVE A PROBLEM IN SECONDARY EDUCATION

Every day, in a 100 small ways, our children ask,
"Do you hear me? Do you see me? Do I matter?"
Their behavior often reflects our response.

—L R Knost

"MY SON IS SUPER-SMART and loves learning. So why is he getting F's in half his classes?"

"My daughter gets good grades, but she's so stressed out and worried. She cries every day. Something just doesn't seem right."

"My son says school is torture. He spends all day staring out the window, waiting for it to be over."

"Things were going well in elementary school, but when we got to junior high, everything just...fell apart."

At LEADPrep, we receive a lot of mid-year phone calls from worried parents. Some of their children attend public schools, and some attend expensive private schools, but the conversation is the same. My child is unhappy. My child is not learning.

Many of these parents have sixth or seventh graders who did very well in elementary school, but as soon as they were dropped into the chaotic world of secondary education, they started to flounder and sink. Some of these distressed kids are crying or complaining every day, but many kids show their distress with dysregulated behaviors or drastically lowered grades. Many kids have outbursts, or panic attacks. Some children withdraw, suffering in silence because they don't know how to express their emotions, or because they feel like they are trapped without another choice.

At LEADPrep, we LOVE getting last-minute, mid-year applications because we know that they come from compassionate, tuned-in parents who have received their kids' S.O.S. signals and are determined to get them into a better situation.

As parents and educators, we know that our traditional middle/high school model is not serving students. If you've picked up this book, you probably already agree. Dropout rates, bullying, sleep deprivation, and teen depression and anxiety are high. Students' sense of direction and self-knowledge after graduation is low. Many parents are desperate, angry, and deeply concerned. Recent solutions from the government exacerbate the problem by increasing testing mandates without increasing funding. Teachers are getting burned out, and the ones who stay are being asked to do more and more with less and less; caring for kids in spite of the system, not because of it. And sure, some kids may "succeed" in conventional middle/high school, but even the ones who do well are getting through it with white knuckles and gritted teeth. Many kids are just miserable.

One of our LEADPrep parents was consulting a leading pediatric neuropsychologist at Seattle Children's Hospital who stated, in all seriousness, "Junior high is developmentally inappropriate for all children." Wow! If our society's best scientists, doctors, teachers, parents, and students are all sounding the alarm bells, why are we still following the old models?

The limits of our present school model are creating three major problems:

1) The needs of many students are going unmet by our impersonal, one-size-fits-all approach to education.

2) As the education system creates stress, parents and students experience increasing anxiety and despair.

3) The voices of parents and students are not being heard.

Let's address the first and most obvious point, which is that many students are falling through the cracks of our conventional junior and senior high schools. The Washington State dropout rate has hovered around 25% for many years. Officially, our dropout rates[6] for 2017 are 17.4 percent for girls and 23.7 percent for boys, but there is evidence that many dropouts are not actually being reported. My home state prides itself on being the birthplace of Amazon, Boeing, and Microsoft, yet almost one quarter of our youth are not completing their high school education. For kids with a public school special education plan called an individualized education plan (IEP), the official dropout rate is even higher[7], at 40.6 percent! With high school graduation a foundation to future success, our youth in today's school system are in crisis.

Our impersonal, one-size-fits-all approach to education is not meeting the needs of many students. In the conventional school system, children are sorted by age only, regardless of their individual development. Because of overcrowding, underfunding, and state-mandated testing, we have developed an assembly-line model of education. This approach does not take into consideration different learning styles, prior knowledge, interests/passions, or psychological needs. This problem is not just found in public school. Well-funded private schools often have entrenched systems and traditions that only serve a narrow band of the student population. If a student doesn't fit the model, they are asked to leave. When individual differences are ignored, our children feel rejected, invisible, and dehumanized.

So why does this feeling of invisibility and dehumanization get so much worse in junior high? Why do so many students see their grades drop and their stress levels rise when they enter secondary school? Quite simply, it's a breakdown in relationships. No one is seeing our kids as whole people.

In elementary school, kids stay in the same class, with the same teacher, for all their academic subjects. Over the course of the year, the teacher gets to know a small population of students well. This teacher knows which kid needs help with organization, and which kid needs more time to grasp a concept. They start to notice which kids need help making friends, and which kids need extra learning to stay motivated. In a single classroom, the needs of each student are seen across different subjects and through multiple lenses. Even if the teacher is unable to solve a specific problem, they still have a complete picture of the entire school day. That holistic perspective can help the child's parents and support team understand a child's learning and behaviors in context.

In middle and high school, this level of personal attention is absent from the system. Beginning in junior high, a 12-year-old student must find their own way to and from seven or eight different classrooms throughout campus. The schools themselves are much larger and more chaotic, with a thousand kids or more all changing classes at once. Nobody is making sure the students are keeping their backpacks or lockers organized and bringing what they need to class. Nobody is making sure a child is making friends or treating others with kindness. Students are suddenly asked to prioritize and manage all aspects of their academic and social lives without a consistent, guiding adult presence. Surrounded by a shifting kaleidoscope of hundreds of peers and a dozen teachers, a student must ask himself many times a day, "Do I recognize this person, or are they a stranger? Is this person kind, or mean? Are they a potential friend, or an enemy? Are they joking, or serious? Should I ask a question, or be quiet? What does this person expect from me? Where do I need to be right now? What do I need to bring? What is required of me in this hour?"

With hundreds of shallow relationships and multiple academic expectations to sort through and keep track of, it's no wonder our children are irritable, distracted, anxious, and exhausted. Some students are able to form a meaningful, supportive relationship with at least one of their seven teachers, but many kids end up falling through the cracks completely.

I always tell parents to imagine going to work, and instead of having one boss, you had seven different bosses! Each of these seven bosses has a different management style, and gives you different work to do, and wants you to prioritize their assignments. And what if, instead of working at one desk, you were assigned seven desks, all in different parts of the office building. It sounds like a nightmare, right? Very few adults would tolerate these working conditions, and yet we are requiring our 12- and 13-year-olds to survive them on a daily basis.

The transition to middle school was especially difficult for one of my daughters, Jadrian. She didn't get the extra help she needed in sixth grade. Gone was the loving elementary teacher to help her navigate her day. With so many different teachers and expectations, and peers at lunch with whom to fit in, making it through a day of middle school exhausted all her energy. She would often fall asleep in the car on the way home from school. Sometimes she would fall asleep after school and not wake up again until the next morning! As a mother, this was heartbreaking to see. One of the toughest parts of school for Jadrian was dealing with her locker. When school ended, she was unable to sort out what she needed to bring home, and what she needed for middle school volleyball practice, and pull it all together to be at practice on time. She was so sad and felt hopeless. Thankfully, being overseas, we were attending a K-12 school with a tight-knit community of support. I was able to turn to the high school volleyball coach for help. The gracious high school coach mentioned this concern to her team. Three older girls volunteered to meet Jadrian at her locker after school and help her with this transition. Jadrian was introduced to all three girls and got to pick one to be her "transition buddy." This cool buddy added the help Jadrian needed to shift gears at the end of a long day of school. For the high school girls, this was an opportunity to learn the power of compassion. When there is a sense of community in our schools, there are solutions to meet the needs of our precious children.

This extra mental burden is being placed on our children during the very years when adolescent hormones are surging. Teens are having sudden, strong emotions and a keen desire to meet peer approval. It is also when our children begin to establish themselves as separate from mom and dad, taking the natural developmental step of pushing away from their parents. Thus, parental support and teacher support are both lessened while the human needs of our adolescents are increasing.

By the time high school comes around, the students who are working behind their age cohort are embarrassed and discouraged, and the students who are working ahead of their age cohort are only succeeding at the cost of intense pressure and hours of extra study and homework. As a secondary education specialist, I speak to high schoolers all the time, and I witness the negative self-talk that will follow them into adulthood. Frustrated students say things like, "I guess I'm just stupid," "I'm too lazy," "I don't care about anything." Successful students confess, "If I get a bad grade, everyone will see that I'm not really that smart," and "People only like me because I work really hard to earn their approval."

The challenges of creating an identity, fitting in, having friends, and being liked are all magnified and transformed by social media. Teens report intense amounts of pressure to be "always on," managing friendships and identity across multiple app platforms. At school, they are judged with grades, and on social media they are judged with likes, followers, and subscribers. Screen use reduces the amount of face-to-face connection our children receive, which in turn increases the feelings of dehumanization and alienation. It's not just the teens who choose technology over personal interaction. We adults are often just as culpable, checking our phones instead of checking in with our kids. Our social norms haven't adjusted to handle the flood of information and entertainment at our fingertips. At the same time, our students are intensely interested in technology. They are developing valuable new skills and interests online. Without responsive innovation, the academic parts of school feel old-fashioned and irrelevant, and are rarely aligned with a student's personal interests.

Apart from academics and social pressure, it's the logistical pieces of life that can cause the most problems. Students today are getting less sleep[8], nutrition[9], and exercise[10] than any generation before—deficits that increase stress and psychological disorders. At school, kids have to deal with long lunch lines, time pressures getting from class to class, problems seeing the board or hearing the teacher, and no time or privacy to use the bathroom. For the average

American high schooler, time spent on homework averages about one hour a day[11], and for students in higher-achieving school districts, that number jumps up to more than three hours a day[12], compromising health and family relationships. Without holistic support, no one is seeing our students' whole day and how all the pieces fit together. Practical concerns are the invisible burdens that often make school intolerable.

Parents and children are feeling increased anxiety and despair as the education system creates stress and doesn't work. In the United States, student anxiety has climbed to epidemic proportions. One-third of high school students experience anxiety as a debilitating mental health condition. According to Pew Research[13], 70% of teens say that anxiety and depression are the number one issue facing their peers. *Time Magazine*[14] reported on this crisis in 2016's "Teen Depression and Anxiety: Why the Kids Are Not Alright." (Content warning: self-harm and eating disorders.) The article speaks of one girl who started cutting herself in eighth grade: "The pain of the superficial wound was a momentary escape from the anxiety she was fighting constantly, about grades, about her future, about relationships, about everything. Many days she felt ill before school. Sometimes she'd throw up, other times she'd stay home. 'It was like asking me to climb Mount Everest in high heels,' she says."

The article goes on to explain that her parents did not understand the depths of her depression until after high school. The statistics *Time* cites by the National Institute of Mental Health (NIMH) supply the data to confirm this epidemic: "In 2015, about 3 million teens ages 12 to 17 had had at least one major depressive episode in the past year, according to the Department of Health and Human Services. More than 2 million report experiencing depression that impairs their daily function. About 30% of girls and 20% of boys–totaling 6.3 million teens–have had an anxiety disorder."

Sadly, the damage started in secondary school continues to impact our children after high school. Since teen anxiety and depression are rarely addressed fully, the condition follows the youth to college, where college counseling directors are alarmed by the growing number of students with significant psychological problems[15].

From where is this anxiety and depression coming? We'll talk more about teens with mental illness in the following chapter, but for now let's focus on how school affects our kids' well-being. The *Washington Post* reports[16] that teens list school as the top source of stress: fully 83 percent of teens said that school was "a somewhat or significant source of stress." Twenty-seven percent reported "extreme stress" during the school year, though that number fell to 13 percent during summer. Ten percent felt that stress had a negative impact on their grades. In a poll[17] from NPR and the Harvard School of Public health, almost 40 percent of parents say their high-schooler is experiencing a lot of stress from school.

When new students come into our micro-school, we often witness the effects of this stress first-hand. A ninth-grader, Jane, began compulsively pulling out her eyelashes after attending a huge public high school with too much noise and activity for her sensitive nature. Jane was very intelligent and academically capable, but was suffering from the sensory and social demands of a conventional school system. Another student, 11th grade Chris, came to us from a residential boarding school. His specialized boarding school helped him deal with his extreme anxiety. Chris completed the therapy and needed to return home, but there was no way he'd agree to go back to the large public high school where he had begun to feel so overwhelmed. Our school, with 26 students, was a sanctuary for Chris and he quickly became a happy, confident leader. Mischa and Kai came to us with eating disorders—drastically seeking clarity and autonomy in a world full of conflicting expectations. Chances are, you know many teens and tweens in your community who self-harm, have disordered eating, or suffer from panic attacks. Perhaps this even describes your own experience in middle school and high school.

My other daughter—bright, passionate, empathetic Giana—spent a few months attending a well-respected all-girls private school. The academic culture was highly competitive, and these driven students felt the strain. Giana was surrounded by classmates ignoring their physical well-being fueled by pursuit of impossibly high academic goals. After a while, she began having severe headaches. We went to several doctors and specialists who couldn't discover the cause. Finally, one specialist felt Giana's face and gave us an answer: she was suffering from severe jaw muscle tension caused by stress, and the pain from her tense facial muscles was radiating into her head. We were given a referral to a physical therapist who specialized in intra-oral massage. Giana had been literally gritting her teeth to get through high school. Even for gifted students without learning difficulties, school can cause a lot of suffering.

Research has also shown that most teens with autism experience significant anxiety during adolescence. This research also suggests that kids with autism often keep their anxiety a secret or display it in ways that are hard for parents and teachers to understand. In my experience, the best way to find out how an autistic student is doing is to get to know them and ask them to share their feelings. At LEADPrep, I have had the privilege to build close relationships with many students with autism, and to speak with them about their fears and desires for school. Many have told me about how hard and stressful school has felt for them in the past. With as many as 1 in every 152 children being diagnosed with autism or sensory processing disorders, it is more important than ever to make sure these kids feel safe at school and are effectively screened for stress and anxiety.

When school, the largest part of a child's life, isn't working out, parents become frustrated and concerned. An unhappy child translates to an unhappy home. Of course, all parents want their child to be served and happy. They want learning to work. And they want to be heard by their school and by their communities when they express concern.

This brings us to the third problem I see so often in our current secondary school system: **The voices of parents and students are not being heard.** As parents, it's difficult to know how to advocate for our children in the present secondary school system. Do we speak to the principal? Each teacher individually? Is there some kind of guidance counselor? While an IEP offers extra learning resources, setting one up is arduous, and often the IEP agreements are not followed by each individual teacher, who sees hundreds of students a day. Many students do not even qualify for an IEP. To help our children, we are forced to assemble a patchwork team of therapists, tutors, doctors, coaches, administrators, and single-subject teachers. Help is fragmented, and none of these caring adults is able to see the whole child in context.

Where else can a parent turn for support? Our society has created a culture of shame around adolescent struggles, and parents feel very alone navigating their child's middle and high school challenges. When my children were babies and young grade-schoolers, I felt comfortable asking for suggestions on things like breastfeeding, potty-training, snack ideas, helping a child learn to read, etc. Just like receiving hand-me-down clothes, I could get hand-me-down advice from parents who had made it through the developmental phase I was tackling with my child. But, by middle school, this collaborative paradigm shifts—parenting difficulties are now a private affair. Just when our children are becoming exposed to the dangerous or drastic dimensions of drugs, alcohol, sex, and peer pressure, mutual parent support is withdrawn. Parents erect a wall of silence: don't ask, don't tell. Scary topics are off limits: "Don't tell me about your kid cutting herself and I won't tell you about the porn I found on my kid's computer." With older kids, we only mention things that are going well, not the things that are challenging: "Let's talk about soccer, and I won't ask about school and grades."

When I worked at a large private high school, the emphasis on admission into a four-year college dominated the students' senior year. Somehow, we had published statistics that 99% of our students were accepted at and attending a four-year college. I found this number difficult to believe, but the focus put an intense amount of pressure on the students. At the big year-end school assembly, seniors were asked to stand when the name of the college they would be attending was announced. Proudly, a few of the 100 seniors would stand when an elite college was mentioned. By the time local state colleges were announced, we saw the remainder of the students stand. Looking around the auditorium, I knew for a fact that many of those kids were not actually attending those colleges. We had placed them in the impossible situation of either choosing to lie in public or be shamed in public. As an educator, it was heartbreaking for me to see.

This so-called "celebration" of our seniors is emblematic of the way we have parented teens in America for many years. Students are constantly encouraged to succeed and are not encouraged to talk about their struggles or failures. They are not allowed to step off the path laid out before them or question the tenets of their education system. When teens come to adults with legitimate complaints, they are often dismissed with phrases like, "It's just part of growing up," or "Everyone has to get through it," or "You just have to change your attitude." How much suffering is swept under the rug in the name of compliance and conformity?

Parents, if your student feels this way, they are not alone. As parents, *you* are not alone. Together, we can create safe, proactive communities where we start vital conversations and share resources. We all want our children to be seen as whole people, so let's start talking. Let's start listening. When we start building connections with each other, we will find out that lots of families are hungry for a new way to educate their children.

Chapter Two

OUR RAINBOW OF OUTLIERS

Sometimes, being different feels a lot like being alone.
But with that being said, being true to that and being
true to my standards and my way of doing things in my
art and my music, everything that has made me feel
very different...in the end, it has made me the happiest.

—Lindsey Stirling

SO, WHAT KIND OF STUDENTS are in our colorful drawer of mismatched socks? Every kind! LEADPrep is not a school for a specific type of kid. It's a learning community where each teen and tween is known as an individual, and our differences are embraced and celebrated. We all have different strengths and weaknesses, and that's okay.

In this chapter, I'll describe nine kinds of educational "outliers." I use this in the sense of the statistical term. If you imagine a bunch of dots on a graph, and most of them are clustered in the center, the outliers would be the dots on the edge, a little bit set apart and unique. Human beings are complicated—we all have some qualities that would be considered normal, and some that make us different. We are all outliers in one way or another. These nine specific outliers are the type of learners who don't quite fit into one-size-fits-all education. I've personally known and taught students from all nine of these categories, and I've seen the difference a personalized, humanized education can make in their lives.

Some of these outlier types are commonly described as having a "disorder," and some are described as having a specific identity. Other outliers are grouped together using less technical terms regarding interests, history, or personality traits. Many of our students at LEADPrep fall into one, two, or five categories at once. As you read through this list, maybe you will recognize your own child, or recognize the children of friends, family members, or neighbors. Yes, we are all different, but we all have a lot in common. Separately, these outliers seem like an exception or minority of our students. Collectively, they actually become the majority of our students. Together, these students make up a beautiful rainbow of unique, precious human beings.

OUTLIER 1: STUDENTS WITH AUTISM

Autism is a general term used to describe a wide range of human experiences and behaviors. Everyone with autism is affected in different ways, and to a greater or lesser degree. This range is called the autism spectrum. If someone is on the autism spectrum, the most obvious outward sign is difficulty with social function and communication. A student with a milder form of autism may come across as socially awkward and unable to read subtle body language and facial cues. A student with a more severe form of autism may be unable to speak at all. Some students with autism have "weird" behaviors that distract other kids and adults. Others on the spectrum expend a lot of effort adapting their behavior to meet social norms, so their autism is less visible.

To an outside observer, signs of autism include repetitive behaviors, intense and perhaps narrow interests, and difficulty processing emotions. Autistic people, when advocating for themselves, describe their internal experience as living in a world where sights, sounds, smells, and textures can be incredibly overwhelming[18]. Managing sensory input is very important, so people with autism frequently use self-soothing visual, physical, or auditory stimulation. These repetitive "tics" or "stims" can be annoying to others in a classroom or social environment, but most people on the autism spectrum find them helpful for staying calm and focused[19]. From a perspective of heightened sensory sensitivity, the landscape of human interaction seems overly-complex and unintuitive. It's hard for someone on the autism spectrum to guess what someone else is experiencing because they're less able to process subtle social and environmental cues. People who are not on the autism spectrum process these social cues and respond to them intuitively, whereas people on the spectrum probably need things to be spelled out and explained more clearly. In other words, what is obvious to someone without autism is not always obvious to someone with autism. Kids and adults on the autism spectrum have a reputation for being "rigid," in part because they've had to come up with their own set of internal rules for living in a mysterious and chaotic world.

Students on the autism spectrum have received many labels over the years. In the past, if someone with autism displayed high verbal ability, they may have received a diagnosis of Asperger's syndrome. (Some autism advocates still identify as having Asperger's or use the nickname "Aspie.") If a student's sensory issues were more obvious than their social issues, they may have been diagnosed with Sensory Processing Disorder. Other students were diagnosed with Pervasive Developmental Disorder-Not Otherwise Specified. Today, all these diagnoses are folded together into the general category of Autism Spectrum Disorder (ASD). The umbrella of ASD includes all forms of autism, mild or intense. Keep in mind that ASD is a clinical diagnosis—a person who is on the spectrum may or may not have an official medical diagnosis. Social Pragmatic Communication Disorder is another new clinical diagnosis that relates to the autism spectrum.

This ever-changing patchwork of controversial labels describes a group of people whose brains seem to work a little bit (or a lot) differently than most people's brains. In the last decade, our awareness of autism and our ability to screen for it has greatly increased. This has led to a huge increase in the prevalence of autism diagnoses. In the 1970s and 1980s, about 1 in every 2,000 children was labeled as autistic. Today, the Center for Disease Control (CDC) estimates that about 1 in every 59 eight-year-olds is diagnosed with an autistic spectrum disorder[20]. With numbers this high, are we facing an "autism epidemic?" Or are we, as a society, becoming able to see the diversity of human brain function with greater precision?

At LEADPrep, we see a lot of kids on the autism spectrum, and often their parents confide that they, too, had similar difficulties with school and social interactions. Or perhaps a student has a "weird uncle" with quirky interests, who also struggled in school as a child. In fact, many older adults are receiving an autism diagnosis for the first time, and saying, "I'm so glad I have a name for it now. When I was a kid, no one knew how to help me."

The good news is, we can help kids with autism at micro-schools. The most important thing we remember is that every person with autism is *unique*. Autism is not a personality trait, or an ability level. Each student with autism is an individual human being with his/her/their own distinct characteristics, interests, and abilities. Some of our students with autism are extroverted and outgoing, and some are quiet and prefer to be alone. Some kids with autism have extremely high intelligence, and others have average or lower intelligence. Some are good with math, some are good with words, and some are kinesthetic learners. It's a myth that people with autism don't care about emotions; at LEADPrep, some of our most compassionate and empathetic kids are on the autism spectrum. These students may have difficulty reading the subtle signals of human emotion, but they care deeply for their fellow students and act generously. Some other LEADPrep kids with autism are going through the normal, age-appropriate, teen phase of grouchy self-centeredness. The variety among humans with autism is as wide-ranging as the variety among humans without autism.

At LEADPrep, kids on the autism spectrum can be seen and known for who they are, while still being supported in their challenges. Their strong interests keep us motivated and passionate, and their quirky insights give us fresh perspectives on life and learning.

Here are some specific ways a micro-school can help kids with autism thrive:

- Smaller class size to reduce sensory overload
- Multi-age classroom to let kids practice social skills at their own level
- Insistence on no bullying with adults available to coach other kids in kindness and understanding
- Adaptive and informed curriculum to meet a student's intense interests
- Encouragement for students to advocate for their sensory-processing needs and take breaks when they feel overwhelmed
- Specific support built in for concurrent learning disorders, such as ADHD, dyslexia, dyscalculia, or dyspraxia
- Advanced learning or enrichment provided for those who are gifted in a specific subject

OUTLIER 2: STUDENTS IDENTIFYING AS LGBTQIA+

Our society is experiencing a huge cultural shift around the issues of gender identity and expression. LGBT, LGBTQ, or LGBTQIA+? The evolving nature of this acronym reflects the ongoing conversation. These letters commonly stand for lesbian, gay, bisexual, transgender, queer (or questioning), intersex, and asexual. As parents and educators, we are playing catch up with this dramatic change in the definitions of gender and sexual attraction. Identities, vocabularies, and social norms are shifting rapidly, especially among younger generations of adults and teens.

The advocacy and resource group GenderSpectrum[21] shares these statistics from well-respected research organizations: A 2015 Fusion Millennial poll of adults ages 18-34 in the United States found that the majority sees gender as a spectrum rather than a male/female binary. In addition, a 2017 Harris Poll of millennials found that 12% identify as transgender or gender non-conforming, and research by J. Walter Thompson Intelligence (the research arm of the global marketing communications company) found that 56% of those aged 13-20 know someone who uses gender-neutral pronouns (such as they/them). According to the William's Institute[22] at UCLA, the younger you are, the more likely you are to identify as LGBT.

This generation gap can make it difficult for LGBTQIA+ teens to develop supportive relationships with adults. Perhaps that's the reason why 40% of gay and transgender teens have seriously considered suicide, and 40% of the homeless teens in our country are LGBTQIA+. Many teens have been ostracized, shamed, or kicked out of their homes by the adults who should be caring for them.

Although LGBT youth report greater acceptance from their peers than from adults, they are still twice as likely[23] to experience physical violence at school. With school overcrowding, and some administrators turning a blind eye to this kind of bullying, LGBTQIA+ students are at risk. Regardless of personal or religious convictions, we can hopefully agree that *all* students, *without exception,* should feel safe and supported at school.

We can't underestimate the power of connection with adults to shape teens' lives. The CDC reports[24] that for all children, feeling more connected to their schools and families during adolescence resulted in a dramatically lower risk of poor life outcomes in adulthood, including a 65% reduction in lifetime drug misuse and a 51% reduction in becoming the victim of physical violence. When we accept our vibrant and creative LGBTQIA+ kids, we set them on the path to a lifetime of health and well-being.

Within this protective community, students are free to explore identities and find out what fits. A new term, gender-creative[25], is being used[26] by parents and therapists to describe children who are exploring their gender expression. Gender-creative kids are doing important, personal work and broadening our social norms of how young people are allowed to express themselves. Children need the opportunity to play, question and evolve—how they decide to identify later in life is up to them. In a small group, our LEAD-Prep teens can choose labels without having to "come out" over and over again to a large group of people. Their peers and mentors get to know all their individual characteristics and interests, and that stability creates room to flex and learn and grow, without pressure or judgment.

Interestingly, a portion of our genderqueer students are also on the autism spectrum. New research[27] is coming out showing that people on the autism spectrum are more likely to be gender non-conforming, with higher rates of non-gendered self-concept, gender-dysphoria, asexuality, pansexuality, and greater dissatisfaction with culturally-dictated gender roles. Our school is always a safe place for young people with autism as they figure out their role in the greater cultural conversation around gender and sexuality.

At LEADPrep, our LGBTQIA+ and gender-creative kids are happy and vibrant. We celebrate them, respect their growth process, and encourage them to take ownership of their own identities. Their self-expression adds joy to our community and makes every kind of student feel more comfortable just being themselves.

Here are some specific features a micro-school can provide to help LGBTQIA+ kids thrive:

Over the past three years, one of our students, Andi, has changed his name twice and his gender identity once. The teens have an "of course" attitude and adapt instantly. The teachers do muddle a bit over being sure to use the right pronouns, but this is logistics only! Acceptance of Andi's identity exploration is 100%. And, of course, his classmates like to jump in and correct our old-person name/pronoun mistakes with laughter and good-natured exasperation. We're all doing our best to keep up!

- Easy access to all-gender restrooms

- Smaller class size where students are known personally, and their changing/emerging/chosen identities are respected

- Supportive relationships with adults (especially younger teachers who "get" them)

- A safe community with no bullying or violence—teachers and peers help create a welcoming community

- Less pressure for asexual and questioning students to date or "act normal"

- Opportunities for students of all identities to be leaders and make their voices heard

OUTLIER 3: STUDENTS WITH ANXIETY OR DEPRESSION

In the previous chapter, we discussed the anxiety epidemic sweeping our nation's teens and young adults. For many, anxiety is caused or greatly exacerbated by their school environment. Some people are genetically predisposed to anxiety and depression—that tendency is just part of who they are, as much as blue eyes or brown hair. But teens, in particular, are vulnerable to mental disorders. Neuroscientists have learned that the adolescent brain goes through drastic structural changes during puberty. This natural time of growth and plasticity makes our teens' brains very sensitive to stress. This is evidenced by the powerful memories we all forge in our teen years, and the reason why the teen years are usually the onset of serious psychological disorders. Symptoms of depression[28] and anxiety[29] in teens include emotional distress, loss of interest in activities, fixation on past failures or future fears, extreme irritation or new difficulties concentrating, self-harm, excessive sleeping, and insomnia. Combined with social isolation, excessive use of the internet and video games can be a way depressed and anxious teens self-soothe and retreat from their difficulties.

All people experience sadness and worry. New or challenging situations can be difficult. But teens with an anxiety disorder need more than assurances. They need support so the disorder does not shut them off from activities and life. There are many kinds of students identified as dealing with anxiety and depression. Some are feeling sad or worried because of learning disorders, autism, or ADHD. Some kids feel rejected for their gender identity and sexuality. Some kids are empathetic and feel the world very intensely. If your child is dealing with depression, please don't wait to address it. Extreme depression can lead a

Saoirse Kennedy, the granddaughter of Robert F Kennedy, battled severe depression that began in middle school. For high school, she attended the prestigious and affluent Deerfield Academy. In 2014, she wrote a heartfelt essay[30] for her school newspaper, saying "Many people are suffering, but because many people feel uncomfortable talking about it, no one is aware of the sufferers. This leaves people feeling even more alone. Since I spoke about this issue at a school meeting, I have had countless people approach me, telling me that they, too, are struggling and would love to be more open about it...we are all either struggling or know someone who is battling an illness; let's come together to make our community more inclusive and comfortable." Tragically, Saoirse died at 22, from a suspected drug overdose. In both rich and poor communities, our students' voices are crying out for help. We have an obligation to respond and take action.

child to think about or plan for suicide. For youth ages 10-24 years, according to the CDC, suicide is among the leading causes of death…[31]. If you're worried about your child and don't know where to start, the Association for Anxiety and Depression[32] is an excellent resource.

No matter the cause or the severity, teens with anxiety or depression can be helped by a close relationship within a holistic educational program. For these kids (and all kids!), school must address social, emotional, and physical needs as well as academic ones. Here are some statistics that explain why we need to create supportive communities for depressed or anxious kids. Clinical depression and/or bipolar disorder affects 14.3% of teens age 13-17; 15.9% of teen girls are suffering from depression, compared to 7.7% of teen boys. Scientists believe this gender gap is because of the way that different sex hormones affect the areas of the brain that trigger depression. If you have a daughter, she may or may not be dealing with depression, but she is almost certainly good friends with a girl who has depression. Our compassionate teens know when their friends are struggling. And with nearly one in three adolescents (31.9%) meeting the criteria for an anxiety disorder by the age of 18, our entire community is affected. Let's support these kids!

At LEADPrep, we use intentional morning check-ins with a custom Emotion Awareness Board that helps kids identify both positive and negative emotions. Social communication practice, student-centered work, expeditionary and service learning, and responsive teaching combine to get kids out of their heads and back into their lives. Using simple mindfulness and empowerment strategies, our teachers have intentionally created a caring community where absenteeism drops

Often, anxiety can be addressed just by changing the environment. We have had students in large schools who feel traumatized by the end of the day. The rush of getting from one side of campus to the other, with hundreds of other kids in the hallways, is grueling for them. Often, a smaller setting and more control over the environment can make a big difference. Anxiety goes down when there is less confusion, noise, and fewer social cues to juggle. At LEADPrep, which is a nonprofit school, one of our local public school districts asked if they could contract us as a non-public agency in order to serve some of their students with extreme anxiety. Although we only have a therapist/counselor come in for an hour each week, this district labeled us as having a "therapeutic milieu" because of our supportive teachers and staff. They hired us to serve Avery, a high-anxiety teen who had been in residential treatment to support this need. We are happy to work with the public school system and are pleased to report that Avery has found success and stability at our micro-school.

and teens are able to become healthy self-advocates.

Perhaps the most important part of caring for students with anxiety and depression is to let them know that they won't slip through the cracks. There will always be an adult available to help guide them through the dark times. As head of the school, I've coached many depressed and anxious kids out of bed over the phone, or out of their car in the parking lot. When students get out of isolation and back into the classroom with friends and meaningful learning opportunities, they rediscover their confidence and joy.

Here are some specific features a micro-school can use to help anxious and depressed teens recover and thrive:

- Smaller classrooms to provide more accountability and support
- Service learning and group work to reduce isolation
- Caring adults available to sit with kids during panic attacks and depressive episodes
- Curriculum that includes social/emotional coaching and CBT/mindfulness strategies
- Awareness of and support for root-cause anxiety triggers, such as ADHD, autism, and sensory processing difficulties
- Opportunities for students to discover the interests and passions that motivate them

OUTLIER 4: STUDENTS WITH ADHD

Attention Deficit Hyperactivity Disorder (ADHD) is the most common[33] of all these outlier types. About 9.4% of all teens and children in the United States have been diagnosed with ADHD. This can be ADHD with hyperactivity and impulsivity. It can also be inattentive ADHD (which was formerly called ADD). That means for every conventional classroom of 30 kids, there are two or three kids who have ADHD. Every public school teacher knows this is a fact! Walking into a classroom, they can immediately pick out "that kid" who is almost always disruptive, talkative, wiggly, and off-task. Kids like this are presenting with hyperactive-type ADHD. There's another child in the class who's a bit harder to spot; they're always daydreaming, spacing out, and living in a world of their own. Just like their disruptive classmate, this student is frequently off-task, but in a quiet way that doesn't distract others. Kids like this are presenting with inattentive-type ADHD. A kid who alternates between disruptive and checked-out is showing combined-type ADHD, with both hyperactive and inattentive symptoms.

What does it feel like to be one of those kids? Well, kids who can't stop moving and talking spend a lot of time feeling embarrassed and awkward. If you're a boy, maybe you compensate for this awkwardness by taking on the "class clown" persona. Maybe you're the girl who is so full of social energy that they can't stop whispering, passing notes, and bothering their friends. Maybe you're a kid who just HAS to talk to someone about what you're doing, so you follow the teacher around asking questions until she snaps at you. You are probably the kid who didn't hear all of the directions or can't stay on task during a project. All of these kids get in trouble a lot, and are punished, shamed, or rejected for not being able to control themselves. If you're the quiet kid struggling to pay attention in class, you might hide a book under your desk, or draw. When you miss explanations and assignments, it's embarrassing, and you don't know how to catch up.

Dr. Thomas E. Brown, a leading researcher of ADHD and clinical practitioner, says that ADHD is primarily a disorder of executive function. He divides executive function into six categories[34]:

1. Activation—organizing, prioritizing, and getting started
2. Focus—sustaining attention and shifting attention
3. Effort—alertness, persistence, and processing speed
4. Emotion—managing frustration and emotional response
5. Memory—short-term working memory and long-term recall
6. Action—monitoring and self-regulating movement and actions (a.k.a. keeping track of what you're doing!)

There are no hard boundaries among different kinds of executive function; they are overlapping and interactive. For example, a kid who is having trouble prioritizing is going to get frustrated, and a kid who is frustrated is going to have a hard time remembering things. Executive functioning tasks are also a challenge for people with autism, and ADHD is a frequently co-occurring diagnosis for students on the autism spectrum.

Russell Barkley, Ph.D.[35], describes executive function struggles in this way: "It is not that the individual does not know what to do. It is that somehow it does not get done." Watching a kid struggle with executive function is also frustrating for parents and teachers. Because adults are often impatient with them, students with ADHD absorb many negative messages about their abilities and intelligence. Bright, creative kids start believing that they are lazy or stupid. In reality, most of the time they are working double-time to compensate for their difficulties!

Ask any adult who grew up with ADHD and they'll tell you that middle and high school, with the constant barrage of assignments and expectations, was absolute torture. Boys are three times more likely[36] to get a diagnosis of ADHD than girls, with a third[37] of all diagnosed ADHD teens dropping out or having to repeat a grade. That's a lot of boys who are deciding that secondary school is not possible or just not worth the trouble. In contrast, many women who grew up with ADHD report that they were only able to pass their classes by becoming extremely vigilant and hyper-focused, leading to stress, health problems, and eating disorders. These anxious girls tend to get good grades, so they fly under the radar and are only diagnosed with ADHD in adulthood, if ever.

Students of all genders presenting with anxiety disorders are often found to have underlying ADHD issues that make life much more challenging for them. If their brains are having trouble keeping track of everything they have to do, anxiety is a natural (and reasonable) response. In addition, people with ADHD find it easier to work when they're in "crisis mode" because the adrenaline activates other neurotransmitters and make the ADHD brain work more effectively. If your kid always gets angry or worked up into a panic before doing their homework or waits until the last minute to do a big assignment, and then pulls a dramatic all-nighter, they might be relying on the stimulating effects of adrenaline to compensate for ADHD. Unfortunately, "crisis mode" is a vicious cycle because stress, poor nutrition, and inadequate sleep all lead to worse executive functioning.

The good news is that micro-schools are terrific places for students with both hyperactive and inattentive ADHD. Smaller class sizes are the first key to success, with fewer distractions and more adult attention. A standard intervention for kids with ADHD is to seat them in the front of the class. At LEADPrep, every seat is at the front of the class! Teachers are always close at hand to offer extra explanations, or small re-directs during an activity. At our school, we know that some kids need a little extra help getting started with something, even when they're smart and capable enough to do it. The other key to success is to reduce the executive function burdens on our kids. With a flipped model of learning, we only assign 5-15 minutes of video-based homework a day, and kids never have to carry or organize papers and books.

During the day, our lessons are active and project-based, which keeps kids stimulated and focused. And, in my opinion, ADHD kids are fun to work with; they're creative, humorous, and good at cheering people up. They're dreamers and thinkers who connect the dots in unique ways. When you spend time with ADHD kids, there's never a dull moment!

Here are some specific supports micro-schools can offer to help kids with ADHD thrive:

- Close relationships with teachers that increase self-esteem
- Small class size to receive more adult attention and assistance
- Group-work and close relationships with peers to keep kids motivated and included
- Empowerment for students to advocate for their own needs: fidget toys, breaks, extra time
- Less busy work and meaningless assignments
- Help for concurrent learning disorders, like dyslexia, dyscalculia, and memory problems
- Easy communication for kids on stimulant medication, with families and teachers collaborating about med changes, dose timing, and effectiveness

OUTLIER 5: KINESTHETIC LEARNERS

Most people have a preference for how they learn. It is how they best perceive, process, and retain new information. These are labeled "learning styles," and there are three broad categories: auditory, visual, and kinesthetic. Visual learners prefer whiteboards, slide-shows, diagrams, and textbooks. Auditory learners like to read out loud, watch videos, or hear people explain things to them. But there is another group that loves to roll up their sleeves and dive into hands-on projects. These are the kinesthetic learners and they understand best by doing. These are kids who complain of being bored in class, who squirm during lectures. Maybe they do okay in school, but they dash off their homework as quickly as possible so they can spend more time on sports, art, or robotics club.

Sadly, kinesthetic learners get the short end of the stick in conventional secondary schools. Classrooms are crowded, and kids are expected to stay in their seats. Physical activities are confined to P.E., and the "fun" learning

We accepted a new freshman girl at LEADPrep, named Claire. At first, Claire was withdrawn and didn't seem to like learning, or think of herself as a good student. When the science class was working on a circuitry project, something clicked. Claire became fully engaged in demonstrating the concept in her model house. She went above and beyond, even working on her house during breaks and lunch. That project made Claire see herself in a different way—as a curious, hard-working, capable, self-motivated "maker." She experienced success! Hands-on learning is good for all of us and it is essential for our kinesthetic learners.

activities of elementary school are left behind. Most schools are closing their traditional woodshops, auto body shops, and home economics labs, where kids used to do hands-on learning. More and more time is spent sitting in front of flat screens, at home and at school. But every once in a while, a few lucky teens will get a class with a teacher who has them up out of their seats, running and laughing and acting and using power tools and papier mâché. Many kinesthetic learners fall in love with lab science or visual art, but any subject can be taught kinesthetically. Robin Williams' masterful depiction of an eccentric English teacher in *Dead Poet's Society* is the perfect example of using motion to teach words.

Our LEADPrep teachers are brilliant at keeping kids moving, crafting, stretching, and making. Every year, we have two weeks of outdoor education in the forest, one in the fall and one in the spring. We do service projects and orienteering activities in our neighborhood. We have a 3-D printer and a STEM/design-thinking block class in addition to our lab science block class. Almost all our classes have some movement or creative component. There are no hard numbers as to how many of our students are kinesthetic learners, but I've never met a teen who doesn't benefit from more action!

Here are some specific ways a micro-school can help kinesthetic learners thrive:

- Hands-on, project-based learning!
- STEM design projects, maker-spaces, and creative presentations
- Experimental lesson plans bring the fun back into secondary school
- More freedom to get up and move around—students being allowed to work on the floor, under the desk, or while walking
- Field trips, service projects, and community exploration
- Did I mention hands-on, project-based learning?

OUTLIER 6: RELUCTANT LEARNERS

Some teens are really difficult to engage. Whether it is getting to school in the first place, or participating in learning activities once they arrive, there are extra barriers that must be overcome. At a micro-school, teachers can build learning around interests, give students choices, offer positive support, and spend time getting to know the student. Sometimes it is a specific subject that shuts a student down, and sometimes they're dealing with an adverse event outside of school. With a lower student-teacher ratio, teachers can work with students to find ways to get past the barriers.

Some of these reluctant teens are resentful, and rightfully so. They live in a world where everyone is bossing them around. School feels like an endless series of demands. When you're a teen, so many things are out of your control: parents getting a divorce, drama with friends, breaking up or being romantically rejected, making the team or getting cut. There are rules about driving, drinking, drugs, screen time, curfew, tardiness. Teens are almost young adults, and they crave freedom—it's no wonder some of them show up to school with a chip on their shoulder!

The best way to help this type of reluctant learner is to give them meaningful choices and a leadership role. Some of our grouchiest high schoolers come out of their shell when they get to be in charge of something! If a student has a motivating passion outside of school, then, with the support of one teacher and a little bit of "gaming the system," their personal interests can be turned into academic success through independent study or curriculum design. Kids who crave freedom love to feel like they're getting away with something sneaky, and building a close, trusting relationship with a favorite teacher can give them an ally for their explorations.

Often, a bad attitude can be a protective shell to defend a specific vulnerability, like dyslexia, dyscalculia, or ADHD. Kids are ashamed; they don't know how to get help. English might be fine, but math is a total roadblock. Doing a worksheet is okay, but planning a big project is intolerable. Some students who are defiant or lash out are actually dealing with anxiety or panic attacks. Again, building a close, trusting relationship with a teacher is so important. When a student knows that they are being seen as a whole person, and that their strengths are respected, they can slowly start to open up and show their secret needs. If the kids and adults around them are open and honest about their learning disorders and neurodiversity, these reluctant learners start to believe that it's not such a scary thing to share their own struggles, and it's not a big deal to get help when needed.

Sometimes, there is a reluctance to go to school at all. As a parent, if you're finding it more and more difficult to get your child out the door, and you're faced with endless mystery ailments like stomachaches and headaches, your kid might be having what experts call[38] "school refusal." This school refusal phenomenon can have many sources. Fear of bullying is a major source of school refusal, as well as specific phobias and anxiety about all the possible things that could go wrong during the day. Sensory integration issues, or depression, or chronic migraines can be the root of school refusal. Our kids know something is bothering them deeply, but they can't express what it is in words that make sense to us. It's important for school administrators to work with parents, pediatricians, and therapists to make sure that the underlying causes of school refusal are explored. The tragedy of school refusal is that it is a self-reinforcing cycle—the more time that's missed, the harder it is to get the student back on track.

As with many of our outlier challenges, relationships make all the difference. Teachers have time to notice and check in on missing kids, and classmates care a lot when their friends are gone. We are continually amazed at the way peers are able to engage each other. When a parent can't get a reluctant child out the door, it might be that one of our students can text the student with an encouraging message, and perhaps an invitation to lunch off-campus together. We foster this positive peer pressure to help students lead and make a difference. In a small community, we want all members to see the importance of their contributions. Sometimes, simply showing up can be a contribution, and give kids a sense of pride and purpose.

Here are some specific provisions micro-schools can offer to help reluctant learners engage and thrive:

- Offerings that promote a sense of agency (ability to act independently and make own choices) and control
- Curriculum adapted to students' interests
- Help for underlying issues such as learning disorders, ADHD, sensory processing, and anxiety/depression
- Acceptance to lessen embarrassment and shame around learning differences
- No-bullying culture where every child is seen and looked out for
- Social/emotional curriculum, such as cognitive behavioral therapy techniques for managing frustration
- Encouraging relationships with teachers and peers

OUTLIER 7: STUDENTS WITH MEDICAL CHALLENGES AND OTHER TRAUMA

We all know that the "stuff" in a student's life can get in the way of their well-being, and thus influence learning. Adverse or complex life events, such as experiencing cancer, being adopted or fostered, or being born to an opioid-addicted parent will impact a child's journey in a variety of ways.

Early childhood medical challenges are a common traumatic event that can alter cognitive abilities. Cancer survivors, especially survivors of leukemia and brain tumors, experience ADHD and school challenges at higher rates, as well as being at risk for anxiety, depression, and PTSD. According to the St. Baldrick's Foundation[39], there are over 420,000 survivors of childhood cancer in the United States (that's about 1 in 750 young adults). As treatments improve, that number is expected to exceed 500,000 by the year 2020. This growing community of cancer survivors is very vocal about their ongoing struggles with "chemo brain."[40] Another group, children with Type-1 Diabetes, frequently have learning difficulties[41] that present as inattentive-type ADHD. Diabetic students must also manage the stress and pressure of keeping track of diet, blood sugar, and insulin levels. These two groups of medically challenged kids may do very well in elementary school, and then run into difficulties in middle or high school, as their brains and bodies go through the structural and chemical changes of adolescence. A micro-school, where everyone can work at their own pace and find their own ability level, is a safe and supportive place for these kids, who have already gone through a lot of tough times.

Besides medical trauma, many children have been through troubling life circumstances that make it difficult for them to succeed in school. There is a movement in the education world to raise awareness of Adverse Childhood Experiences (ACEs). ACEs include

One of our students, Kyle, was diagnosed with acute lymphoblastic leukemia at age three. He went through three and a half years of chemotherapy, including monthly procedures where chemotherapy was injected into his spinal fluid to cross the blood/brain barrier. Kyle made a full recovery from cancer and is now a bright, insightful, outgoing middle-schooler with lots of energy. He does have an ADHD diagnosis and occasionally experiences something he calls "glitching out," where he randomly forgets something he just heard or said. This is a common working memory deficit for leukemia survivors. In a small classroom with group work and lots of teacher attention, it's easy for Kyle to ask for a repeat of the information he "glitched out on" without missing a beat.

physical or emotional abuse and/or neglect, as well as parental drug abuse and mental illness. Other ACEs are separation from parents due to divorce, foster care, or parental incarceration. Researchers are learning that early adversity has lasting impact. These adverse childhood experiences disrupt neurodevelopment[42], which can result in social, emotional, and cognitive impairment. CDC studies[43] show how experiencing one of the ACEs can impact chronic health conditions, school attendance, risky health behaviors, low life potential, and early death. As the number and severity of ACEs increase, so does the risk for these negative outcomes. The National Institute of Health[44] (NIH) has conducted research showing a significant association between ACE score and moderate-to-severe ADHD. They suggest that ADHD assessment could be improved with the addition of evaluating for and considering ACEs. Our response to troubled kids needs to be compassionate, trauma-informed, relationship-based care.

If we care about the children in this county, we have to discuss the opioid crisis. One of the advocates addressing this issue is Marian Edleman Wright, who is a personal heroine of mine. In the '90s I was privileged to listen to this relentless activist who founded The Children's Defense Fund in 1973 as part of the black civil rights movement. Her dedication to fierce child advocacy was one of my inspirations, and it should be a call to action for all of us. In 2017, Wright responded to the declaration of the opioid crisis as a US national health emergency. She identified parental substance abuse as one of the ACEs and outlined the emotional and physical abuse and family separation that can result. Here are some of her staggering statistics[45]: Among women who struggle with opioid abuse, 86 percent of pregnancies are unintended, compared with 56 percent of all pregnancies, and between 14 and 22 percent of women nationwide fill an opioid medication prescription during pregnancy. In 2012, an infant was born with Neonatal Abstinence Syndrome (NAS), a.k.a. infant opioid withdrawal, on average every 25 minutes in the United States. Across 28 states, the NAS rate increased by almost 300 percent between 1999 and 2013. Foster care systems in every state are flooded with the children of drug-addicted parents. In 2014, 40% of children fostered with relatives (grandparents, aunts, etc.) were there because of parental drug use.

The Children's Defense Fund's mission[46] is to ensure every child has "...a successful passage to adulthood with the help of caring families and communities." Community is key. All across the nation, relatives, teachers, foster parents, and adoptive parents are stepping up to deal with the crisis and help these precious children. Public and private schools, as well as churches and other community centers, must all play a role, and many more schools and programs are needed. Children with NAS have long-term developmental delays compared to other disadvantaged students, and for most students with NAS, the academic delays[47] follow them into middle school and high school. If your community is looking for solutions, I hope that you will find this book helpful. For those of us starting or running a micro-school, I hope we will all welcome and support adopted kids and those living with their extended families.

Several years ago, Jake, a sweet boy with undiagnosed NAS, asked to move to Washington and live with his dad for middle school. Jake's dad knew that the mom had been on painkillers while pregnant and that Jake had struggled through elementary school out-of-state. Dad also knew that Jake's older brother, Troy, abused painkillers as a middle school student, having helped Troy get off the drugs the last time he visited Washington. In middle school, Jake got involved in sports for the first time, and was able to qualify for special education. Even with special support, school had too many layers of homework and expectations, and Jake joined our micro-school for high school. Lots of caring teachers and various strategies helped him complete his first two years of high school. During a summer intern with a national forest program, his older brother Troy reconnected with Jake, and convinced him to run away and go back to live with him and his mother. The tragic ACEs trajectory caught up with Jake; he did not return to Washington, or to school, and his father has not heard from him in over a year. I wish we could have done more, but kids like Jake are navigating complex lives, and often make impulsive decisions that don't serve their best interests. Jake, I hope you're doing well. We love you.

Some of the most joyful and committed families at LEADPrep are our adoptive and blended families. Research shows[48] that adoption greatly benefits children from challenged backgrounds, but it is not a simple fix. In a 2016 study, the Institute for Family Studies[49] (IFS) addressed the concern that adopted children, while often in much better situations than that of their birth family, still struggle disproportionately in school. The majority of the adopted children in the survey enjoyed going to school and nearly half were doing well, but there were some disparities. Some 54% of adopted children had an ongoing cognitive, behavioral, or health condition. The most common diagnoses were ADHD (36%), specific learning disability (23%), speech impairment (16%), and developmental delay (15%). Compared to children from married biological parents, adopted students were twice as likely to have had their parents contacted in the last year due to schoolwork problems, and three times as likely to their parents being contacted in the last year due to classroom behavior problems. They were four times more likely to have repeated a grade, and three times more likely to have been suspended or expelled from school. When I hear statistics like this, it makes me wish all these kids could attend schools like LEADPrep and get compassionate, supportive, personalized education.

Although we tend to think of childhood trauma as being a socioeconomic issue, traumatic events can affect children from all walks of life. Mental illness, addiction, and abuse can occur in wealthy families as well as impoverished ones. Some teens suffer greatly from their parents' divorce. Children might experience the death or illness of a parent or sibling, or go through their own medical crisis. All of these events affect our student's school performance, and it's common for a child to have a complex mix of factors and accompanying diagnoses impacting learning. In a small school community, each student can be known and cared for. There is personal support and time to recover and grow.

I've experienced first-hand the way that strong relationships support the most challenged students. For a time, Kaplan (a for-profit business) offered free online education to about 300 students around Washington State. For the final year of this program, I was hired as the principal for KAWA (Kaplan Academy of Washington). Many of our online students were impacted by ACEs. As my brilliant team of teachers, many who had never met face to face, dove in, our metrics soared, becoming Kaplan's highest performing state in the US. Why? Because we first became a team with a common goal. Then we humanized the experience for these students in remote locations. We had regional cohorts with meet-ups for ice cream and skating. We had monthly pep assemblies with fun games and then regional meetings online. We added in online clubs. The teen mother club was run by a teacher with her own young child at home. I remember the uploaded photos of their babies in Halloween costumes and shared strategies for studying during baby nap times. Our disadvantaged students needed personal connection to succeed.

I'm encouraged that so many school systems are embracing the idea of trauma-informed education. Oregon's Gladstone School District is one of those systems. Superintendent Bob Stewart tells[50] that addressing ACEs necessitates "creating a school environment and culture that is calming and supportive of all kids." He goes on to recommend specific classroom strategies such as use of daily calming and self-regulation. He encourages teaching students about ACEs to increase self-understanding and help break the cycle of trauma. "A school culture that is safe and secure can do a lot to assist students;" Stewart continues, "the school can be the place where students feel like they belong."

Here are some specific offerings micro-schools can provide to help children who have experienced trauma recover and thrive:

- Multi-age classrooms to allow kids to work at their own pace, regardless of grade level

- Calming strategies and social/emotional learning that support all kids, especially those with with ACEs, PTSD, and medical trauma

- Help for cognitive challenges, especially ADHD and memory issues

- Community support for parents

- Close relationships with teachers to build trust and understanding

OUTLIER 8: STUDENTS WITH PERFECTIONIST/ OVERACHIEVER TENDENCIES

Perfectionistic students are often left out of the "learning outlier" conversation. Because they are meeting our expectations, their suffering is mostly invisible. These overachieving students, usually young women, are seen as "succeeding" in conventional private and public schools. Their grade point average is high, and they are constantly being commended and praised. To maintain this level of approval, this type of student pours every ounce of their being into academics and official extra-curricular activities, with little time for play or self-care.

Although they are very good students, perfectionistic kids are motivated by fear. They are highly sensitive to the judgments and emotional pressure coming from their teachers, parents, and coaches, and are terrified of disappointing them. They develop an incredibly harsh inner critic, and, in their minds, a B grade is just as much of a catastrophe as an F. Identity has become wrapped up in achievement and people-pleasing. This constant internalized pressure puts our beautiful, vulnerable teens at great risk for anxiety and eating disorders. How many nervous breakdowns and cases of anorexia or bulimia could be prevented if we stopped seeing good grades as an indicator of well-being?

Most people know that there is an established link[51] between perfectionistic tendencies and disordered eating. But new research[52] is coming out that anorexia and bulimia have genetic and metabolic tendencies as well. And most importantly for our teens, stress has been proven again and again to cause gastrointestinal distress, including the stomach aches and diarrhea that make our kids hate eating. Here's a quote from Harvard Health Publishing:[53]

> This "brain-gut axis" helps explain why researchers are interested in understanding how psychological or social stress might cause digestive problems. When a person becomes stressed enough to trigger the

fight-or-flight response, for example, digestion slows or even stops so that the body can divert all its internal energy to facing a perceived threat. In response to less severe stress, such as public speaking, the digestive process may slow or be temporarily disrupted, causing abdominal pain and other symptoms of functional gastrointestinal disorders. Of course, it can work the other way as well: persistent gastrointestinal problems can heighten anxiety and stress.

Unfortunately, it's quite rare for stressed-out overachievers to be placed in a micro-school, because these children are being held up as proof that the conventional school system works. The sad reality is that they are being damaged by school, year after year.

How much healthier would these young women be if they were in an environment that saw them as whole people, validating their own personal needs and desires? What if a sensitive, anxious student could find safety in deep, long-term relationships with teachers, instead of chasing after the shallow approval of good grades? What if all that energy were poured into innovation, curiosity, exploration, and leadership? What if mistakes were embraced instead of shamed? I know of one micro-school where students take turns standing up on their chairs to announce mistakes that they made, and the whole class claps and cheers. Being okay with mistakes and setbacks builds resilience for all kinds of students. At a micro-school, we can build a new kind of school culture, setting kids on a path to inner strength and confidence.

Here are some specific offerings micro-schools can provide to help students with perfectionistic and overachieving tendencies recover and thrive:

- More emphasis on relationships, less emphasis on grades
- Less busy work and meaningless assignments
- Acceptance, even celebration, of mistakes and students encouraged to "fail forward"
- Social/emotional curriculum to help students express their feelings in healthy ways
- Smaller, multi-age classrooms and project-based learning to reduce pressure to compete
- Encouragement for students to develop their own interests and leadership abilities
- More time to play, rest, and enjoy extracurricular activities

OUTLIER 9: FIERCE LEARNERS WHO DEMAND RELEVANCE

When I worked in a public at-risk school-within-a-school, I encountered many bright students who could not play the "high school game." Dayna was one of these students. Half-shaved head (not very common in the early '90s!), army boots, vintage shop clothing—she was refusing to conform to standards that didn't fit. Her grades weren't great because she couldn't make herself jump through hoops and do hours of homework when she saw no connection to her real life. In our micro-school, Connect, her intelligence was set free. She could blaze through an assignment with depth and quality work. For Dayna, having a relevant, fair curriculum model and a voice in her learning made the difference. Often, these brilliant and creative teens go on to non-traditional careers or to non-graded universities where they design their own degree. Although conventional schools can stifle their spirits, they do want to learn. They just need to be learning something they deem worthwhile.

Maybe you know a kid who has a passion. They've been composing, drawing, dancing, story-telling, programming, or engineering since before they could walk. These kids know what they want to accomplish in life, and they feel like school is just slowing them down. And you know what? Maybe they're right. A micro-school is a great place for highly motivated students who have a drive to succeed. They're able to bring their passions to school and tie them into their academic projects. And, with less homework or busy work, they have more time to pursue their talents and hone their abilities. We have a kid at LEADPrep who studies chess, microbiology, and economics in his spare time, and another kid who's seriously pursuing a soccer career.

Brilliant or talented kids sometimes feel incredibly bored at conventional schools and are held back by having to stay with their age cohort. At a small school, kids are able to work at their own pace, running ahead quickly in some subjects, and staying at grade level in others. In a multi-age classroom, a gifted junior high-aged kid gets a chance to work at a high school academic levels without being isolated from kids her own age. A tenth-grade boy who spent his whole life focused on academics but is way behind in social skills has a chance to practice making friends with a friendly seventh-grade boy who shares his interests. Students may take college classes off site and transfer the credit back to the micro-school, while also enjoying a "home base" with friends and teachers who care about them and see the whole person.

Micro-schools give kids a chance to let their voices and passions be heard. Curricula can be responsive, wrapping in students' interests. If students want to lobby for a change in policy, they know they have a seat at the negotiating table. And if a student is passionate about a cause, she has the chance to lead an activity or design a project from which the rest of the school can learn.

Here are some specific offerings micro-schools can provide to help fierce learners continue to thrive:

- Relevant, responsive, personalized curriculum
- Leadership opportunities
- Adults always available to answer questions and give the reasons behind rules
- Multi-age classrooms to let kids excel in some areas and catch up in others
- Less homework, meaning more time for individual interests
- Encouragement for students to explore and take ownership of their own education

As you can see, teenagers (like all humans) come in a wide array of abilities, neurotypes, personalities, preferences, and experiences. Even within these broad categories, each student is unique. If we treat each student as an individual, worthwhile person, wouldn't they learn more effectively? Most kids who are struggling in school benefit from the same kinds of intervention—smaller classes and stronger relationships, the chance to lead and self-advocate, and being treated like a whole person.

Taken in isolation, each group of outliers is a small section of our society. But if you add all the outliers together into one group, then you start to see that it's "normal" to be "not normal." By getting to know friends' and neighbors' kids, and talking about their educational experiences, parents can shift their perspective from a minority mindset to a majority-minority mindset. And while micro-schools can be the answer for kids with outlier qualities, it can also be a fantastic setting for non-outlier students who also benefit tremendously from being in a progressive, personalized educational setting with a diverse group of peers.

We all want the same things for our children—happiness, health, and meaningful, effective learning. There are enough of us to demand a change! Let's step back and see the whole rainbow together. Let's be inspired by these kids to create schools that will give them all a chance to be happy, quirky, well-loved humans.

Chapter Three

TRIBES THAT CREATE CHANGE

*A tribe is a group of people connected to one another,
connected to a leader, and connected to an idea. For
millions of years, human beings have been part of one
tribe or another. A group needs only two things to be
a tribe: a shared interest and a way to communicate.*

—Seth Godin

EVERY MICRO-SCHOOL BEGINS with a tribe of like-minded parents. The word "tribe" is just a simple way of referring to a small group of people who are all connected by a shared interest. If you're interested in providing your child with a more relevant, personalized education, the first step along the journey is to find your tribe.

Frustrated parents, you need to unite to make a difference. As we learned from our colorful rainbow of mismatched kids, the minority is the majority. There are other parents in your city or town who are raising "outlier" kids and are dreaming of finding a supportive community. The parents are the ones who see the need, and, together, parents have strength in numbers.

Kerry McDonald, the author of *Unschooled: Raising Curious, Well-Educated Children Outside the Conventional Classroom*[54] asks parents to challenge this default button of unthinkingly throwing our children into the school system our society blindly accepts:

> Better options than compulsory mass schooling do exist, and many more would be created if more parents challenged the default. We should be outraged that schooling has seized so much of childhood and adolescence, particularly when the results of all this schooling are lackluster at best and concerning at worst. We should be out-

raged that government schools increasingly look like prisons and that students are being schooled for jobs that no longer exist. We should question whether a system in which only one-quarter of high school seniors are proficient in math, and only a bit over one-third of them are proficient readers, should be given greater influence and authority over young people's lives. We should really wonder if it makes sense to place our children in this swelling system, whether they are toddlers or teens. Surely, we should consider alternative ways that the world could work.

What if you got to know one or two families who were also interested in personalized education? Start some conversations and see who's on the same page. It can be such a relief to talk to another parent who "gets it." Then, what if a few such families started to band together? When frustrated parents unite to create change, the possibilities are unlimited. Your tribe could start out as a support group for parents, suggesting and sharing resources. Once you gather some interest, you could branch out and look at local resources to provide customized learning. An after-school or weekend program? A co-op of sorts? A program within your local public school? Perhaps a private elementary school in your area would be interested in starting a small pilot program for older children. Once you gather your tribe and start exploring, fresh ideas and options will start to open. If you have a support group, don't be satisfied with sharing the same stories over and over. Turn your support group into an action group! The best kind of support is meaningful change.

Of course, not every potential parent is going to want to join you. You might know someone with a quirky kid that you think would be a great fit for your group, but when you bring it up, their family isn't interested, or they say they're too busy. That's okay; don't get discouraged—just move on and find other parents who are interested. When a tribe is just getting started, it's a discovery process. You'll find the people who are a natural fit. Raise your banner high, and the parents who want to work for new school options will be drawn to you. Then, as your tribe gains momentum, more and more families will be interested.

"That sounds great, but we're so busy!" This is a refrain I hear a lot nowadays when I invite people to participate in our tribe. The internet age, with its huge amounts of information and connections, makes forming local tribes both harder and easier. One of our moms in Seattle has a close friend in New York, a close friend in England, and a grandmother in California. These are the women she talks to every day via text, phone calls, and social media. But they can't cook dinner together, help each other's kids with homework, or start a carpool in the same town. The time we spend staying up-to-date on long-distance relationships uses up our bandwidth for creating and maintaining local relationships. Greater worker mobility and uneven housing markets drive people further away from friends, cousins, and grandparents. We're in touch with a lot more people in far away places, but our local support networks have degraded. That means a lot of people are feeling isolated and overburdened, and living more of their lives online.

On the other hand, the internet has brought us a wealth of convenient tools for creating our local communities. Facebook groups, Meetup.com, neighborhood and community center blogs, and even simple email groups are all ways we can use technology to bring parents together, face-to-face. If you are a member of an online support group for parenting, ask if anyone is in your local area, or if they know anyone else in your area who's searching for good school options. (Personally, I don't do much online connecting, but some of the other parents in our community do speak the language of social media and have a real knack for it. When we combine our skills within a tribe, we can accomplish so much more than we ever could alone.)

"Too busy" can also be the result of parents desperately trying to piece together solutions for a failing school situation. Various kinds of therapy, long tutoring sessions, and social skills groups are all trying to compensate for the conventional school models that are just not meeting our kids' needs. Even parents who are already paying for expensive private schools find themselves paying for additional tutoring. Parents who have children of different ages and ability levels have to manage multiple school and activity schedules. Families would be a LOT less busy if some of those tutoring needs could be met within a micro-school classroom, instead of crammed onto the end of an already exhausting school day. Even if you're not ready to launch a full micro-school, simply creating a group of like-minded parents who share classes, resources, and social needs can take some of the pressure off these over-scheduled moms and dads.

Parents aren't the only people who care about mismatched kids. Members of churches, synagogues, and mosques are invested in their communities and understand the needs of their youth. Maybe your own church or civic group has some retired empty-nesters who are still passionate about education. Maybe you can find a young education grad who's interested in alternative schools. Other people to invite into your tribe include YMCA directors, summer camp and outdoor education leaders, and local therapists. All of these people are great for networking; but, in my experience, the people who are the most motivated to create new education choices are fellow parents. The passion that comes from raising a unique child and wanting to see them succeed is very, very strong.

So you have the passion and the shared interest, now what? In order to shift the education paradigm away from business-as-usual and toward innovative learning, two qualities are required: **creativity** and **fierce tenacity**.

Creativity is what will allow the members of your tribe to find existing resources—an unused space, a passionate teacher between jobs, a population looking for the same type of learning—and bring them all together into the same place. Creativity means the ability to see connections and find solutions. Creativity also allows us to adapt to changing resources and needs.

As parents, we know a lot about dealing with change. Your kid starts out as an infant and progresses through all the phases to adulthood. As your child grows, you make changes to your parenting strategies along the way. You guide, and you release. You protect, and you let go. You make a boundary, and then you move a boundary. As a parent, if you find yourself always adjusting and flexing, then that means you're doing it right, because your child is growing up! This young person is developing new abilities, but they also have new needs and require new reassurances for their next phase of life. Figuring out how to adapt to, teach, and inspire your child is parental creativity at its best.

Growing a micro-school requires the same kind of creative mindset. The group starts out small. As it increases and matures, its needs change, and together you make adjustments as necessary. When your group encounters a setback, think of these challenges as puzzles to be solved with brainstorming and out-of-the-box thinking.

The great thing about working with a tribe is that there are more brains for brainstorming. There have been so many times on our micro-school journey when I feel like I've hit a brick wall, but then one of my fellow parents or educators has a brilliant, creative idea to solve the problem. Or maybe they have the ability to see the solution that was right under my nose the whole time. Or maybe someone with a whole different set of connections joins our group just in time. When you work together, different people hold different pieces of the puzzle. For example, one person knows of a park that needs work, another person knows some teens that need an activity on Friday, and another person has a big van. Voilà! Three people's ideas combine to create one community service project. The network is a source of creative energy.

Along with creativity, making innovative, humane education options requires tenacity—relentless tenacity. Creativity keeps us flexible and open-minded, while tenacity keeps us firmly on our path to the future.

Here are some of the things that fuel my tenacity: I believe that love of a parent for their child can be the most powerful force on earth. I believe that compassion, empathy, and fierce love can change the world. I believe in the abilities and good intentions of my fellow teachers and parents. I believe that our lives have a greater purpose. And the best fuel for my tenacity is this: when I meet one of our colorful, mismatched students, I fall in love with their uniqueness and I believe in their limitless potential.

I once knew a mom with four kids, all in different outlier categories, who had to drive her children to four different schools and various therapy sessions. When the oldest daughter, Holly, turned 16, her mom and dad set up an agreement: in exchange for a car and gas money, she would drive their youngest child, Mac, to school, psychotherapy, and language therapy. Mac (diagnosed with Asperger's syndrome) benefited from the extra attention, while Holly (an anxious ADHD overachiever) loved having important responsibilities and self-value outside of school and grades. As adult siblings, Holly and Mac are still very close. When we give students with varying abilities a chance to participate in the same tribe, it's amazing how often they help and inspire each other.

Fix your purpose in your mind and share that focus and determination with those around you. Remember that you're all doing this for kids who would otherwise fall through the cracks. You're doing this for all the kids who are bored, stressed out, or just in need of a caring community. You're doing this for the other parents out there who are desperate for their middle or high-schooler to find happiness. Students will have a new path to success because of your vision and hard work. Remember that tenacity doesn't mean never failing; *it means never giving up*. When your group inevitably hits an obstacle or two, or loses an important member, the rest of you will try again and find a new way.

No single person can be relentlessly focused 24 hours a day, 365 days of the year. We all need breaks sometimes, have an "off day," or get discouraged. That's when we really need our tribe. When a group of people all share the same vision, they can take turns being strong for each other. As the head of the school, I sometimes get bogged down with logistical complications, and that's when I rely on our Director of Learning or our school board president to encourage me. When I talk things out (or vent!) with my fellow tribe members, they remind me of the purpose behind the details—serving our kids.

Plus, we have the privilege of building friendships and sharing our tears and laughter along the way.

Let me tell you one last secret about tribes: they're never perfect. That's because people are never perfect. We all have our own idiosyncrasies and annoying qualities. We all have blind spots, and we all make mistakes. But within a caring relationship, family, or tribe, we work around each other's bad qualities and work with each other's good qualities, whatever they might be. So far in this book I've talked a lot about wanting our kids to be supported in their weaknesses and celebrated for their strengths. If that's what we want for our kids, we have to model that for each other as well. After all, our tweens and teenagers are paying closer attention to what we do than what we say. If we want our kids to be kind, flexible, and understanding, we have to show them how to do that in our adult relationships. In the same way, if we want our kids to be bold, brave, and confident, we have to give them an example to follow. So, let's be what we want for our kids! Don't wait around for the "perfect" people or the "ideal" space. Start making a difference in whatever place you can get, with whatever students you've got. These kids only have one chance at childhood, so let's get started!

In the overseas micro-schools I have directed, geography was the common denominator. Our schools were in very remote locations, on a mountain top in South America and in the jungles of Asia. Parents were happy to get involved and share their skills and energy. They wanted to be sure that their remote location did not limit the education that their children received. Scientists in both communities came in and did special projects with our students. (Who knew that our tap water in the Andes was purer than the local bottled water?!) With our strong community bond, the synergy was powerful.

Three Tasks to Do Now

1. Find a few other adults interested in exploring new learning options. You can be drawn together by shared geography, such as neighborhood, city, or school district. You could be drawn together by a common interest in a certain population of youth. Together, explore existing resources and allow yourselves to dream. You are now united and have "small tribe" status. Wonderful!

2. Determine your direction. Who is your audience? What is the geography? Age group? Service provided? Resources available? (Hint: Church spaces are often empty during the school week, and many non-religious schools have begun in this shared space.) Ideally, you draft a mission and give your vision an initial name: *We, the Pacific Academy, offer a middle school education in a creative, caring setting that supports this step of adolescent development with an emphasis on social and emotional growth. Learning is active and inclusive.* Or perhaps your drawer of colorful socks is younger: *The River Road Collective offers a curriculum to support third-fifth grade students in developing healthy social skills through games and social communication development.* Small collectives can fill a variety of educational niches, so follow the passion of your tribe. And if it seems bold to name your group and claim your mission before it even begins, just go for it! Now is the time to be audacious.

3. Find your greater tribe and begin to create the village. Stakeholders now have an idea of who you are. Getting critical mass is important to gaining momentum, so be willing to start your program with just a few students. My present micro-school began with six students. After six years, LEADPrep has over 30 students on two campuses, and each year we have grown and refined our model. If we hadn't begun small, "on a wing and a prayer," we most likely never would have begun at all. Some families need to see an existing school before they're willing to enroll their students. So, start small but start now! A core group of committed families is the tiny seed from which all micro-schools sprout.

Chapter Four

THE MICRO-SCHOOL VISION

*Theories and goals of education don't matter a whit
if you don't consider your students to be human beings.*

—Lou Ann Walker

SO, YOU HAVE YOUR TRIBE GATHERED. Together, you've seen a need in your community. You've gotten to know your unique kids, and you care about them deeply. You've heard their struggles and you want to give them the chance to attend an innovative school—a micro-school. You are ready to redesign secondary education one micro-school at a time.

Listening to the needs of children and prioritizing them is the heartbeat of student-centered, humane education. Just as a heartbeat pushes blood throughout the body, the drive for humane education pushes deep innovation throughout a micro-school. The point is not to duplicate failing conventional school systems in miniature, but rather to create a new kind of learning community.

A micro-school is a new paradigm, not a specific model. In science, when a concept no longer works with the new data presented, there is a need for a new paradigm. Our society sees the need for new learning, so we need to shift and transform the existing structure. In an ideal world, every micro-school would be unique, reflecting the values of the community that it serves. Your tribe will have its own set of goals, needs, and resources. In education, one size (or style) doesn't fit all. That's why some micro-schools are public, some are private, and some are co-ops. Some have access to outside funding, and some are funded entirely from within the community. Some micro-schools use a lot of online materials, and some don't. Some micro-schools have a permanent home base, and some are expeditionary schools with no classroom at all. We'll talk more about these differences later, but, in this chapter, we'll discuss what micro-schools have in common:

- Small size
- Adaptability and responsiveness
- Personalized learning
- Multi-age classrooms
- Teachers as guides, not lecturers
- Resources and technology that directly benefits students
- Innovative, holistic curriculum

SMALL SIZE

Here's the most obvious fact: "micro" simply means small. A micro-school can be as small as five or six students, or as big as 100-150 students. Every micro-school is different, but most micro-schools find their equilibrium with 30-60 students.

The size of a group is critical to human social functioning. When a group is too large, our limited human brains can't see all of the members as unique individuals. Anthropologists who study group behavior have discovered that a group of 150 individuals is the upper limit for maintaining casual acquaintances. If you want to know everyone well, that number[55] is 50 individuals max. Your group of close friends peaks at 15, and your most meaningful circle of confidantes is usually around five individuals.

Essentially, a micro-school is small enough for every member of the community of students and teachers to know each other. Personal, meaningful relationships are a natural result of this close community. Each student is valued as an individual, teachers know all the details of a student's learning style, and collaboration between teachers and staff happens naturally. And, most importantly, students benefit from face-to-face time with teachers. As we saw from our rainbow of outliers, our colorful, mismatched teens and tweens need trusting relationships with peers and adults to thrive.

When I first started LEADPrep, I couldn't picture a clear enrollment goal. As our school grew, we started to realize that the "right size" for our community was smaller. We decided to cap our enrollment at 60, with the goal of 30 students at our Seattle campus, and 30 students at our nearby Kirkland campus. In a classroom with 15-25 kids and two to three teachers, every student is known, befriended, and cared for. On Fridays, our two campuses come together for service projects, field trips, art classes, and physical education. For group size, this gives us the best of both worlds: students have a large enough social group to practice making friends and meeting new people, and a small enough working group to get personal attention in the classroom. At parent meetings, we usually have around 60 parents attending, which makes it easy for everyone to stay acquainted.

ADAPTABILITY AND RESPONSIVENESS

Besides creating meaningful relationships, a micro-school's size makes it nimble. A small school more easily adapts to the needs of its students. Relationships facilitate communication, and communication creates effective change.

If we want to teach kids how to be leaders and self-advocates, it's a two-way street. Why would students speak up if they knew no one was listening? And even if a school is listening to the concerns of students, parents, and teachers, listening will only make a difference if the organization has the power and ability to make meaningful adjustments.

Large schools are often locked in patterns that take them away from the deep mission of service they have intended to provide. Conventional public schools are almost always bogged down by bureaucracy and top-down policies. A student may have an idea to change something, and the teachers and principals may agree, but on many issues, they have to adhere to district-wide decisions, statewide policies, or even nationwide policies. These policies keep schools accountable, yes, but they also make changes happen slowly and push education toward the one-size-fits-all model.

At conventional private schools, administrators tend to make choices that prioritize compliance to school culture and the longevity of the organization, rather than prioritizing the needs of the students. When administrators and board members feel responsible for maintaining a large, traditional organization, they resist change because it can feel destabilizing and scary. And it's a lot easier to keep your academic and behavioral standards high when outlier students are not served or welcome. While it's true that not every school is the right fit for every child, at a micro-school there is more flexibility to accommodate both interesting students and progressive new ideas.

At a micro-school, it's effective to brainstorm new ideas with a small group of teachers. Everyone has a voice at the table, and each perspective gets airtime. Project-based learning allows us to design our projects, thinking through all of the steps and adjusting as needed. We value this process, which is called design thinking. So, at LEADPrep, when a young teacher comes to the group with a crazy, innovative idea, our first instinct is to say, "Yes, why not?" Sometimes we try a new plan for a set period of time, then have a school-wide discussion to get student feedback. As adults, we set an example for our kids that mistakes, evaluations, and corrections are part of the learning process, and we invite them to join the process. Because our school is small, it's simple to communicate the changes. This culture of design-thinking, with revisions and iterations, makes change low-risk. We try new things, and if they don't work, we try something else. The result is a truly progressive organization that's always adapting.

We encourage our students to communicate respectfully and love it when they self-advocate. One morning I was on the Seattle campus during math time. A few of the students were working on math in the hallway. As I walked by two students working in the stairwell, I noticed Sally had her novel tucked inside her math book. Ah ha! As a fellow book lover, I knew that trick for reading when I was supposed to be doing something else. I let her know that I would take her novel until math was over. And, with a smug smile, the book and I walked away. Two minutes later Sally came over to me. She explained that she reads as a reward after she has done eight problems. She elaborated that she is ahead of schedule on her math work and that this reading-as-a-reward system keeps her motivated. She stuck out her hand and I gave the book back to her. I told her I thought it was great that she had come up with the system, held me—the school principal—accountable, and had advocated for herself.

When students share a voice in how things are done, adults have to set aside their instincts to claim authority and instead practice collaboration skills. After explaining a task, one of our LEADPrep teachers is in the habit of asking the classroom, "Does that seem reasonable to you guys?" Then he listens and makes adjustments. Because this teacher shares his authority and is responsive, the students end up respecting his authority even more. It's not an authority that says "because-I-said-so;" it's an authority that grows naturally out of mutual respect and consideration. That's the kind of culture we want to encourage between teachers and students, and between teachers and administrators. We've discovered when students share the work of making rules and policies, they take those structures much more seriously and encourage each other to follow them.

PERSONALIZED LEARNING

If a school culture is responsive, personalized learning is the natural result. Students who are in close communication with adults are able to advocate for their own accommodations. Adults working in close communication are able to share which strategies work well for each student. Every student is seen as an individual.

Team members in micro-schools are continually identifying and tackling barriers to learning. For some students, these barriers might be executive functioning challenges, like task initiation. It might be content that is at the wrong level. Students might have a gap in their foundational learning that prevents them from adding new skills. Feedback among parents, teachers, students, and outside specialists allows us to see the big picture, and how things at home are affecting things at school, and vice versa. Within a small classroom, if a student is trying to succeed but keeps getting frustrated, we can break tasks down into smaller, more manageable steps. If a student is bored and coasting through, we can provide new, exciting challenges that help them find their own growth-edges. The pace at which a student works, and the particular skills they are working toward, can be adjusted based on the teacher's personal knowledge of the student's abilities and interests.

When Caleb joined mid-year, he was our youngest student. His previous private school had shut down suddenly and he hadn't been able to say goodbye to his beloved teacher. Caleb's mom explained that it took Caleb a long time to feel safe. Caleb didn't feel like he could trust us yet. Understanding that the problem was not with our model, we worked slowly to build trust and get him to start working independently (initiating) at work time, with limited success. His outside therapist came and observed. She assessed that his executive functioning limits required more support from us. This therapist explained that Caleb gave up before an assignment began because he couldn't navigate the starting routine of opening his Chromebook, pulling up and reading the assignment, and then joining his project team. Once this issue was on our radar, were able to take two steps to resolve this obstacle.

First, our English teacher sat down with Caleb to explain step-by-step how to open an assignment in Google Classroom, and they practiced the steps together. Second, I asked his favorite peer to assist when we had activities that required getting into Google Classroom. We reminded Caleb he could always ask for assistance. Once Caleb could keep up, he was much more willing to participate, and the learning process built up a trusting relationship with a teacher and a peer. Feedback from both Caleb's mom and therapist allowed us effectively to individualize his learning experience.

Best of all, micro-schools can help all types of kids thrive by encouraging them to design or adapt projects based on their own interests. For example, at LEADPrep, students design our clubs. They pick the topics and then vote on the top three at each campus: gaming, cooking, art, studying types of dogs, playing hacky sack...the choice is theirs. They also pick how they will demonstrate concepts within their projects. For example, as a final project exploring the themes of Romeo and Juliet, they chose to rewrite the ending and performed it for the parents. Our version had sword fights with many people dying (even more than the original!) plus a lot of cross-dressing, to honor the era and creative expression of our diverse kids. I don't know what Shakespeare would have thought, but the kids had a blast. No matter what their ability levels are, students working out of their own passions are unstoppable!

MULTI-AGE CLASSROOMS

For most micro-schools, the best way to provide personalized learning is in a multi-age classroom. Most humans have strengths and weaknesses—a set of skills that come easily and a set of skills that require longer to acquire. Grade-level refers to an average rate of competency across all students and all subjects, but hardly anyone develops every skill and ability at the same average rate. Students who are working below grade-level and those working above grade-level are following their own paths of development. It's also common for any given student to be advanced in one or two subject areas and to be average or delayed in others.

When you sort students by age cohort alone, that creates an artificial expectation for our kids. Outliers are often embarrassed, teased, and rejected for deviating from the average. They fake keeping up so they don't look stupid. Smart kids are sometimes encouraged to be competitive and stand out from the pack. Other times, they feel pressure to dumb it down and fit in. In contrast, when you combine ages and grade levels, it feels natural to have students working at various abilities and skill levels. The pressure to conform or compete is removed. If a student needs extra help, they can get it without being singled out. This is especially important for older kids with specific learning disabilities. At the same time, students who are working above their grade level aren't held back by the rest of the class because they can work with older students when they need to. Everyone works at the pace and level that's right for them.

Asher joined our school for his senior year. He was very bright, but also very shy and reluctant to engage socially. At the first school picnic in August, he sat alone the entire day, looking at the ground without speaking. When goal-setting with the school, Asher's parents asked to make a plan to improve his ability to make eye contact. In September, we took all our students on a week-long camping trip. Regardless of grade level, each student was allowed to choose between an easy hike and a challenging hike. Asher chose the challenging hike, along with a mixed group of high schoolers and 6th, 7th, and 8th graders. That was when the switch flipped—he came back from the hike talking and laughing!

Over the course of the year, Asher was able to get to know his 11th and 12th grade peers, but whenever the older group felt overwhelming, he could choose to play board games and practice socializing with the younger high school and junior high kids. By the end of his senior year, Asher was joking around and having fun with the rest of the 12th grade graduating class. We never saw the need to implement a specific eye contact plan for Asher, because he had discovered his own natural ways of connecting in a mixed-age group. He's now attending a four-year liberal arts college known for its small class size—a perfect fit for his personality.

What holds true for academic development also applies to social and emotional development. Students who are very academically gifted are allowed to pursue advanced learning while still socializing on an age-appropriate level. Older students who are still figuring out how to manage intense emotions can benefit from the same coaching as their younger classmates.

Student behavior is transformed in powerful and meaningful ways by a multi-age classroom. Younger students look up to older students as role models. They learn by watching and copying their mentors. They develop a vision for what their future selves could be. In turn, older students are motivated by the younger students. They enjoy being admired, and they want to prove to themselves how much they've matured. Older students often feel a sense of responsibility toward younger students and stand up for them if they're being teased or excluded. Older students are eager to take on leadership roles within the school as they grow in independence and creative vision. And trusted teachers are always on hand, finding opportunities to encourage leadership, social awareness, and positive peer pressure.

TEACHERS AS GUIDES, NOT LECTURERS

In order to provide this level of personal and differentiated learning, teachers at a micro-school can't just stand in front of the class delivering information while students passively absorb it. Teachers must be working side-by-side with the students, interacting with them. To achieve this goal, most micro-schools have a project-based curriculum, which creates motivation and gets kids into the drivers' seat of their own education. Some educators use a "flipped" classroom model, where a video mini-lecture is watched as homework, leaving time for hands-on learning during the school day. Teachers are in the trenches, coaching students on how to solve their own problems. The best teachers aren't giving the right answers; they're encouraging kids to ask the right questions.

When teachers are given the time and bandwidth to relate with kids, the classroom becomes intentionally inclusive. At LEADPrep, our educators co-teach and assist when they are not the primary instructor. This tag-team teaching allows for the same adults to be engaged with students throughout the day, creating continuity. Aides or paraeducators don't have to be hired and assigned to individual students with high needs. Instead, co-teachers walk around the class giving guidance and positive reinforcement wherever it's needed. They notice which daydreamer in the back row needs to be gently refocused. They have time to debate a point with a bright, impatient student. They can step in to coach a teen with autism in "reading the room" for social cues. They can give positive feedback to kids who are on task. In the meantime, all of the students see a myriad of interventions being modeled as a regular, everyday part of class. Getting help is normalized, and there is meaningful inclusion of various learning styles, abilities, and personalities.

RESOURCES AND TECHNOLOGY
DIRECTLY BENEFITING STUDENTS

Because micro-schools are small, resources are focused on the classroom—not facilities, upper management, generic professional development training, and unnecessary meetings. Time and finances are poured into the classroom, where the learning happens. We always focus and refocus on the most important question: How does this benefit our kids and their learning?

Without expensive infrastructure, students receive a greater portion of school operating funds. Teacher supply requests are handled without a lot of red tape. If a micro-school has a need for materials, they can put a message out to parents and community members. Often, a parent already owns the supplies, or is able to make a small donation, or knows someone else who has something that will work. The creative synergy of the tribe is engaged. Parents can see how their donations have an immediate impact in the classroom, and they feel welcomed as part of the collaborative community.

Effort is another kind of resource. Take field trips for example. Every Friday at LEADPrep, we have an experiential learning day. We can fit our students into two vans, and go to parks, museums, trails, beaches, libraries, and retirement homes. That's possible with 30 kids, but it would be a logistical nightmare with 300. Our teachers are able to organize and plan these trips because their effort is focused on a small number of students. In a micro-school, each teacher's efforts are more easily noticed and appreciated by the administration. Staying with individual kids for multiple years gives teachers and administrators the satisfaction of seeing growth and success. Parent effort is another important piece of the puzzle, as the community provides outreach to new and prospective families, extra instruction, fundraising, and all kinds of practical support behind the scenes.

When resources are concentrated in the classroom, it's easier to adopt new technologies. At LEADPrep, every student is given a Chromebook for school use. We received a grant to purchase a 3D printer, and, because our school is small, there's time for every student to print something. For programming and robotics, students can use hackable, inexpensive computer processors (Arduino and Raspberry Pi). Immediate and universal access to materials means technology isn't just a club or an elective, it's an integral part of the curriculum.

Every micro-school has a different relationship with technology, and it's a hot-button issue. Online schools are gaining popularity, but unlike a 100% online school, micro-schools have teachers working alongside students. Personal relationships provide face-to-face contact and teachers have the opportunity to assess the benefit of various online resources for individual students.

Technologically literate micro-schools take advantage of the vast array of information and learning tools available online. However, we must also teach students to practice focus and discernment. In a world with so much information and misinformation at our fingertips and access to everything from healthy to toxic points of view, students need guidance in learning to ask critical-thinking questions: Is this online math game too hard or too easy? Is this particular website a reliable source of information? Is this message board a positive community or a destructive one? Is this video based on pseudo-science or actual science? Is the internet distracting me from my goal, or helping me achieve my goal? Once again, close relationships are the key—kids will only have these conversations with an adult they trust and respect. Technology, like all other resources in a micro-school, must be continually adaptive and student-centered. As our society evolves, progressive micro-schools have a critical role to play in raising our internet-native kids.

Our parents enrich what we offer every year. They respond to specific requests for help. Like our students, they also enjoy working from strengths and interests. This past year, one Seattle mother asked if she could start a teacher appreciation committee. The result? Our monthly professional development days have great food provided by the parents and at the year-end, we all received lovely surprises. A Kirkland parent asked if she could team up with our student who plans out-of-school socials. Together, they have planned fun activities like ice skating, movies, and mini-golf outings. Parent effort enhances our community in many ways and keeps our tribe strong!

INNOVATIVE, HOLISTIC CURRICULUM

Personalized, student-centered curriculum sees kids as whole human beings. A micro-school can address the inner needs of our students, teaching social-emotional skills such as mindfulness, emotional awareness, self-regulation, etiquette, and empathy. A micro-school can look to the future of our students, teaching 21st-century skills such as collaboration, critical thinking, problem solving, and resilience.

Because micro-schools see the big picture, they can intentionally streamline to make classwork and homework relevant and manageable. Streamlining means looking at how resources (especially time) are used. It questions assumed worth and cuts back any extraneous traditions to get to the essentials. Assignments that are busy work with no relevance are eliminated. When students ask, "When will I ever use this?" there needs to be an answer. Because systems are simplified and streamlined, the teacher has more time and support to create intentional learning opportunities. Logistics flow easily when the whole school comes to an agreement on how classes are started, work is assigned, and work is turned in. Communication can be streamlined as well, with consistent visual and verbal cues. For students, school-wide systems reduce the mental strain of having seven "bosses" with differing styles and demands. Consistency and simplicity create cohesion. Cohesion prevents executive function overload and encourages interdisciplinary learning.

Content and systems aren't the only way micro-schools innovate. We can go even deeper, redesigning the way lessons are planned. Intentional learning is a backwards-design process we use at LEADPrep. First, the educator poses an "essential question" that will pique student's curiosity and drive the lesson. Then the teacher thinks about the skills students should master and weaves in ways to measure learning. Only after question, skills, and measurements have been chosen is a specific lesson planned. Many conventional schools never have the opportunity to practice this model, with traditional, district-adopted textbooks and state testing driving the learning.

Innovation is the lifeblood of the micro-school movement, and we can be the change we wish to see in the world. We are steering the conversation around educational options and showing what's possible. Ideally, each micro-school is a laboratory where new teaching strategies can be explored, refined, and proven. When innovations are adopted and shared, the micro-school movement is benefiting students across the nation.

Redesigning education takes studying these various features and looking at how other micro-schools operate. Don't reinvent every aspect of your school. As a micro-school founder, one of my favorite tongue-in-cheek mottos is our use of the CASE strategy: "We Copy And Steal Everything." If I talk to a micro-school administrator who has a part-time, shared counselor, I bring that counselor to LEADPrep, too. If a school has already created enrollment forms, I happily borrow their template to jump start the design of our forms. When another school is active in the WE Schools[56] service model, we join in and get great support on projects and our Nicaragua service trip. I love networking with other micro-school leaders. Their energy, creativity, and vision encourage our school to keep innovating. Other micro-schools are not our competition; they are our co-workers and collaborators. In community, we are stronger.

Micro-school energy is contagious! Have you caught the vision yet? Progressive, innovative, inclusive, flexible, and collaborative education is possible.

Our teens and tweens are not broken. The problem is our one-size-fits-all school system. Throughout human history, tribes of adults have educated small groups of young people in a way that made sense for their time and place. From the very first human tribes listening to songs and stories around the campfire, to village apprenticeships, to one-room frontier schoolhouses, to Sunday literacy schools for factory workers, parents and community elders have always adapted education to fit the needs of their culture. Today, we need to adapt our children's educational experience to fit a new era and a new culture. Our kids need us to transform school to make it relevant and meaningful. Time is of the essence, and change happens more quickly in a small group. Are you ready to find a tribe and transform frustration into action? Are you ready to acknowledge and honor our rainbow of outliers who are a collective majority? Are you ready to redesign education within your own micro-school?

If you're ready to get started, let's move onto Part Two and unveil the seven steps needed to launch your micro-school within a year!

Part Two

YOU CAN DO IT:

Seven Steps for Creating a New Micro-School

YOUR ACTION PLAN

The critical ingredient is getting off your butt and doing
something. It's as simple as that. A lot of people have
ideas, but there are few who decide to do something
about them now. Not tomorrow. Not next week. But
today. The true entrepreneur is a doer, not a dreamer.

—Nolan Bushnell

NOW IT'S TIME for the rubber to meet the road! These are the seven steps that will take your micro-school from a dream to reality.

The most important tool for starting a micro-school is a clearly written action plan. Appendix A has our Micro-School Action Plan outline for you to use to get started. As we discussed in Part One of this book, you already have a passionate tribe of parents and other adults with a vision for what the school should and could be. It's time to get specific and start committing this vision to writing. Although you may be full of excitement and ready to hit the ground running, do not rush through this action plan. To stay focused, you need to have a clear document that shows what you're trying to accomplish and how you plan to get there.

If the idea of writing a full action plan seems scary or intimidating, don't worry; the following chapters will bring clarity and focus. Each of the seven steps in this section of the book will help you create and refine your written plan. If you are jotting ideas on a laptop, also try keeping a handwritten journal of ideas. Writing out the words activates a different part of our brains. A journal is also a great place to sketch, ponder, and brain dump! Starting with the vision and working backward, step-by-step, you will lay out the path for your micro-school to open.

Guiding Questions

Step 1: Begin with the Mission
What is the vision and mission of our school? What does a graduate from our school look like? How do we deliver education?

Step 2: Recruit Energetic and Committed Trailblazers
Who will run our school? Who will teach our kids? How do we find these people?

Step 3: Engage Community Collaborators
How do we leverage the power of our tribe? What role do parents play? How do we fit into our neighborhood?

Step 4: Get the Word Out
What is the market for our school? How do we connect with our customers? What are the threats and opportunities we face? How will we get people interested?

Step 5: Choose What Makes Your School Special
How can we innovate with our educational model? What tools will we use to achieve our vision? How will we know if we are making an impact on learning?

Step 6: Get Creative with Funding
What will our operating costs be? How can we keep our operational costs to a minimum? How much tuition should we charge?

Step 7: Open Your Doors
What's the timeline for this project? What's holding us back? How can we make this plan a reality?

I can't stress enough how important it is to document your work formally in these seven steps. Set aside time to ask yourself the tough, practical questions. Get specific. I recommend making a draft of your Action Plan in Google Docs or some other online file-sharing workspace. That way, you can share your Action Plan easily with team members who need to read it, contribute to it, or make notes on it.

Here are some reasons to take time to create a thorough Micro-School Action Plan:

- Writing a clear mission statement will keep your team accountable to your original vision, since your vision is the source of your motivation.

- Collecting resources and research will prove to parents, donors, and collaborators that you are serious about starting your micro-school, and they will be more likely to join or help you.

- By working out your operational plans on paper, you will be able to see the gaps and fill in missing pieces before they become a problem.

- Starting a school requires a lot of different tasks. Having everything documented in one place will help you stay focused and on track once you implement the plan.

- When adding new members to your team, they will be able to see your school's priorities clearly and get on board from the beginning.

Keep in mind that your Action Plan won't be perfect right away. It's a living document to which you will always be referring, evaluating, and editing. You're giving it your best guess for now. With your tribe's creativity and fierce tenacity, your micro-school will adapt as new circumstances arise. But, in order to adapt a plan, you have to have a plan in the first place! As my great-grandfather liked to say, "You can't steer a boat unless it's moving."

Part Two is loaded with practical, how-to instructions. Stories and highlights are left out of this section so you can focus on your Action Plan. Instead, to remind you of the value of your planning, we're including short quotes from LEADPrep parents and students. As you're working, don't forget that you're creating a real school that will be transforming the lives of real kids!

Before we get started with our seven steps, I'd like you to look over this list of various school models, types, and affiliations. You can skim and notice which types of schools are a good match for your vision and which ones aren't a good match. Micro-schools are widely varied, and most fall into several different categories at once. As you continue to explore the world of education, these are some of the affiliations and models from which you will be choosing. Take notes about the pros, cons, and questions that arise as you read about the options.

Accredited. School accreditation is an external review by a nationally or regionally recognized neutral third-party organization that performs a comprehensive review of mission, stakeholder perspective, teaching, facilities, fiscal management, and governance. Accreditation is not mandatory, but rules may vary from state-to-state, and some colleges require additional information from students with a transcript from an unaccredited school. Although accreditation standards are a good thing to review up front, most agencies won't accredit a school until it has been operating at least two years.

Charter School. This type of public school is funded with tax dollars. It has a separate accrediting body from other public schools, while following state laws and state testing mandates. It is a popular option in more than 40 states. Common attributes include longer school years and days, school uniforms, and strict compliance. Unlike neighborhood public school boundaries, students may come from anywhere in the state and must apply for admission. Usually charter schools are not governed by the local school district.

Co-Op. A co-operative school relies on mandatory parent participation. Parents might teach, assist teachers, or do other administrative jobs. Most co-ops are elementary schools, and this model can be found in both public and private schools.

> "I've been able to form a close relationship with my peers and teachers."
> —PENN, 12TH GRADE

Culturally Responsive Teaching. This educational principle, also called culturally relevant teaching, is the idea that minority students should be allowed (and encouraged) to relate the course content to their own cultural context. This means teachers are trained to respect and value cultural diversity and to use cross-cultural education strategies. In the micro-school world, there is a growing movement of Black[57] and Native American[58] families establishing schools and co-ops that instruct students in the values and history of their community. These micro-schools provide better outcomes for students who might otherwise face prejudice and systemic racism in conventional school systems.

Democratic and Free Schools. This educational movement flourished in the 1960s and continues today. In a democratic school, student self-determination is a priority. This means students are free to choose their own classes and are encouraged to pursue their individual passions within a community of equals. The structure and rules of the school are deliberated at community meetings, and conflict resolution is usually a public process. Emphasized values include justice, respect, and trust.

Dual Enrollment. A student is officially enrolled in two educational institutions, with differing models. For example, a student might be attending both a public high school and a tutoring school; or a partially homeschooled student might be taking some classes at a private school. In Washington State, it is common for 11th and 12th grade students to be enrolled in both a public or private high school and community college. The state funds this program (called Running Start) and students are granted a year of high school credit plus a quarter of college credit for each five-credit class successfully completed. Earning Running Start credit has allowed some high school seniors to graduate with both a high school diploma and a college associate's degree (AA). Running Start is helpful for micro-schools who want to enrich their high school curriculum.

> "Many families find LEADPrep the answer for students who previously struggled in school, however my student just needed a middle school that would continue to be a developmentally appropriate educational setting for her once she outgrew her progressive elementary school."
> — JOYCE, GUARDIAN OF A HIGH SCHOOL DAUGHTER

Expeditionary Learning. The concept is based on the educational ideas of German educator Kurt Hahn, the founder of Outward Bound. Whether a full school or a component within a school, students learn by conducting "learning expeditions" rather than being taught in a classroom. By exposing students to a wide range of people and experiences, expeditionary learning develops empathy, resilience, and curiosity.

> "My favorite thing about school is the Friday activities."
> —EMBER, 7TH GRADE

For-Profit School. Although no school would describe itself up-front as being "for profit," this category includes any school with a for-profit business model. These schools are funded by investors who believe that a successful school business can bring a return on their investment. Although for-profit schools have access to investor funding, they are not allowed to use tax-deductible fundraising. Financial assistance for tuition is not a common offering at these schools.

Franchise. Sometimes referred to as "school in a box," an education franchise is an organization that provides comprehensive content and structure for others to follow in order to open their own local school. That individual school is then referred to as a "franchise school." Sometimes a franchise will provide financial assistance up-front in exchange for an amount of money in return once the school is established. There are for-profit and nonprofit school franchises, as well as franchises for charter schools and religiously-affiliated schools. A franchise school is generally required to adhere to the rules and teaching models of the original organization.

Homeschooling. As the name describes, this is a model where students learn at home, with parents taking the role of teacher. Different states have various requirements that parents need to meet in order to be allowed to homeschool their children. Homeschool families frequently collaborate formally or informally, often collaborating with a YMCA or other community resource. The line between a micro-school and a cooperative homeschooling community can be somewhat blurry, and many micro-schools got their start as a homeschooling cooperative.

Hybrid. Hybrid schooling is any system that combines two or more other models. For example, many homeschooled students are also enrolled in a co-op, or an online program in this hybrid fashion. Some private schools that don't have access to a full curriculum use extensive online resources. Hybrid online schools are also referred to as "flex" or "blended" schools.

International Baccalaureate (IB). This holistic program has an early years component (PYP), middle school component (MYP), and high school 11th-12th grade diploma program. The high school content is rigorous and includes service and Theory of Knowledge (philosophy and nature of learning). Year-end exams graded by an external agency determine if the student earns additional college credit for the course.

Middle College. This is an alternative high school program where students meet together at a community college campus and are allowed to attribute the college credits earned in middle college toward their future college career after they graduate. Most middle colleges are a collaboration between a community college and a local public school district.

"I think it's cool when my mom teaches art class but it's also kind of weird."
— KYLE, 7TH GRADE

Nonprofit School. Many private schools choose a nonprofit model with a board of directors governing. Compared to for-profit, this model typically offers more financial aid and does not have an owner or profit margins to consider. Fundraising and donations are a critical component of nonprofit organizations.

> "You can move ahead in math and that really helps me."
> — GAVIN, 6TH GRADE

Online Learning. Online schools allow students to receive lectures and assignments on the internet, and then complete the work at home. Projects, essays, and tests are then turned in online. Some online models include a teacher who is available to answer questions, as well as structured group lessons and due dates. Other programs let the student progress at their own pace. Online schools can be combined with other models to create a hybrid or dual-enrollment model and can be either public or private.

Private School. This model is funded through tuition and private sources, not public funding. Private schools include both for-profit and nonprofit schools, as well as religiously-affiliated schools, including Christian schools, Jewish day schools, and parochial or parish schools. However, many private schools are not religiously-affiliated.

Public School. In the United States, this is our prevalent model. It typically means students attend the school within their neighborhood boundary. The school district can grant waivers to allow students outside of these boundaries to attend. Our taxes pay for these schools and levy and bond initiatives support extra projects. Public school districts can start micro-schools as another educational option within their district. Those that do often select students by special qualification or lottery. It's important to note that students who do not attend public school still have a legal right to access sports, extracurricular programs, and other resources at their neighborhood public school.

Residential Therapeutic or Treatment Center. When a student needs intensive therapy, perhaps for anxiety, an eating disorder, or an addiction, these centers provide a boarding school with both academics and therapy. The model is often a year-long process, with the student learning new skills and patterns and then returning home.

Resource Center. This is a learning facility that provides educational support. A resource center is not a complete micro-school but could be a starting point or a component in a hybrid school model.

School-within-a-School Model. In a large school (often a high school) this refers to the creation of a smaller learning community that shares funding and resources with the larger school. Typically, a school-within-a-school meets in its own room for required classes, and students then take languages and electives on the main school campus. The goal is to provide alternative learning, increased personalization, and a sense of community within large schools.

Social-Emotional Learning. Social and emotional learning (SEL)[59] is the process through which students understand and manage emotions, set and achieve positive goals, feel and show empathy for others, establish and maintain positive relationships, and make responsible decisions. Schools with a social-emotional emphasis teach students skills such as mindfulness and restorative justice. SEL is also linked to the Whole Child[59] education movement, which includes physical, emotional, and community-supported well-being.

State-Approved. Private schools are monitored by the state as an important safeguard for children. State approval typically includes safety and fire inspections by public agencies, and often expects a minimum number of hours or days of instruction. I highly encourage every micro-school to complete the state approval process. Get this list of requirements and deadlines early in your micro-school planning process.

STEM School. This acronym stands for Science, Technology, Engineering, and Math. A STEM school teaches all subjects, but places specific emphasis on interdisciplinary learning among these four subjects. STEM schools teach students how to apply engineering principles, such as design thinking,

"LEADPrep's personalized approach to understanding and teaching my son has significantly lowered his frustration and anger toward school, while building his confidence, creativity and problem-solving ability."

—MARK AND MARGARET, PARENTS OF A HIGH SCHOOL SON

through various projects. Some educators expand the acronym to include additional subjects, such as the arts and reading.

Unschooling. This is a type of homeschooling. The major difference between unschooling and homeschooling is the learning approach. Rather than a parent-led model, unschooling operates from the premise that children are naturally curious and will follow their interests in their own way. When a student requests information, the parents can provide it, but unlike most educational models, the curriculum is entirely student-motivated.

———

Hopefully some of these school models are inspiring for you and are getting those creative juices flowing. Take some time to consider your notes. You will integrate what you learned as you move forward with creating a vision. Even the models you don't employ can help guide you toward the models you want to use. If you are energized and ready to start designing, turn the page to Step 1 and together we'll get specific on YOUR micro-school's vision.

STEP 1

BEGIN WITH THE MISSION

If you don't know where you're going,
you might not get there.

—Yogi Berra

GOAL

Starting with desired learning outcomes, design the vision
and mission statement of your micro-school.

CHALLENGE

YOU HAVE A TRIBE of interested and passionate adults with a strong desire to provide innovative education for students. You also have students with unique needs and their own desires for a new kind of school. The challenge in Step 1 is to articulate these desires into an inspiring, yet specific mission statement. You're not just creating the vague idea of a micro-school, you are striving toward real, achievable outcomes for graduates. Your school is preparing to step into the education landscape with a meaningful purpose. A good mission statement includes a vision and then describes that purpose and how you intend to achieve it.

SOLUTION

Brainstorm the basic outcomes and parameters of your model. Fill out the first step on your Action Plan outline (Appendix A), defining your mission-driven learning model.

Now it's time to answer some big questions. If you've read this far, I'm sure you already have some idea of the students you want to serve, as well as passions, core values, and community connections that are all jumbling together and sparking possibilities for your micro-school. Going through this questioning process will help you articulate these big ideas in a specific, practical way. Remember, student-centered learning means thinking about kids from the start. So, with your potential students in mind, here are the questions to answer:

What does the graduate of our school look like? *What holistic outcomes do we want for our grads? Do we want students who can step into STEM jobs? Start a business? Understand and pass on a cultural tradition? Do we want students who use 21st century communication, collaboration, and creativity skills? Students who know how to problem solve? Have a strong mind-body connection? Self-starting students? Self-aware students? Students who give back to the community, making a positive difference? Students who love and care for the earth?*

Include your deepest, most meaningful wishes for the children who will attend your learning community now and in the future. This vision of your graduates will be the guiding light for your micro-school.

Who will we serve? *Sixty elementary students? Fifteen middle school students? Students with a specific learning profile? Students who speak a certain language or belong to a certain cultural group? Alternative learners within a large public high school? Multi-age?* If you want to have a variety of grades, consider starting your school with one or two grades and building upward (i.e., have a 6th and 7th grade, and as your students progress up the grades, you will gradually add 8th, 9th, 10th, etc.).

Will we teach students who are working above grade level, and, if so, how far above grade level? Will we teach students below grade level, and, if so, how far below? What

"My son told me it's the best school year he's ever had, and that's great coming from an 8th grader!"

—ANN, MOTHER OF A MIDDLE SCHOOL SON

level of ability or disability will we be able to serve? Remember, your micro-school will not be able to solve every problem at once. If you try to be everything to everyone you will lose focus and do a disservice to your students. Determine your niche; it can evolve as your school grows. For now, start small and deliberately.

How will we serve them? Now is the time to think about the basic framework of how you deliver education to your students—where they go and how they spend their time. *Will we host students in a traditional school classroom with a full-day schedule? Will we use a hybrid (partially online) model with partial on-site attendance? Branch out from a homeschool cooperative? Use a dual enrollment model, where students take some classes at public schools or community colleges? Can we start as an extension of another school or institution? What makes our students excited to come to school? What would a school day or school week look like from our students' perspective? For what do our parents most hope? What big-picture education models will we be using? Will we focus on STEM, SEL, community connections, self-governance, or something else? If we had to tell someone the single most important thing about our school, what would it be?*

What affiliations do we want? *Will our school be public or private? For-profit or nonprofit? Will we be part of a franchise, or perhaps join an existing school network? When will we seek state approval or accreditation?* Each of these affiliations has financial ramifications and includes a commitment to certain expectations.

State-approval is a basic affiliation all micro-schools should seek because it ensures that schools are following basic student health and safety requirements. Legally, this is an important aspect of beginning any micro-school, so don't overlook it. Parents should be wary of sending their children to a school that does not meet state-approval requirements. Add "state-approved" to your Action Plan Step 1 under "Affiliations we choose are...." Check your state's education department website and ask this question: *What are the requirements for getting state-approved status, and what are the deadlines?*

Accreditation is the next level of affiliation. An accredited school has been evaluated by an approved third party, which gives its "official stamp of approval" to all aspects of how the school is run and what is taught. Knowing that a school is accredited gives confidence to prospective parents and college admissions boards. Generally, a school starts the accreditation process after being open for two years, but now is the time to ask: *What are the pros and cons of being an accredited school? How can we design our school to make accreditation easier in the future?*

As for financial affiliation, keep asking yourselves tough questions: *Do we want to work within the public school system and find a way to use existing public resources in new ways? Can we apply for charter-school status, and, if so, what are the rules for charter schools in our state and district? Do we want to be a private school, with freedom from state rules and testing but responsible for self-funding? If our school is private, will it be a non-profit with tuition, donations, and fund-raising, or a for-profit with tuition and possibly venture capital? What socioeconomic background will our students have, and how will that affect their ability to attend our micro-school?*

"My child is thriving in a micro-school because of the personalized learning environment. It has brought back his love of learning and saved him from certain academic failure."

—PHYLLIS, MOTHER OF A HIGH SCHOOL BOY

Micro-school franchises (which can also be nonprofit or for-profit) are organizations that provide start-up materials and some financial assistance for the first year. Some franchises work within a specific religious affiliation; so, if your tribe of parents is church-based, this might be an option to research. Some are designed for the charter-school market and some for the private micro-school market. Keep in mind that most micro-school franchises have a very specific curriculum that all subsidiary schools must use, as well as further financial obligations. Be sure to read all the fine print before choosing to join a franchise, and ask yourselves these questions: *Is our micro-school willing to go along with this organization's specific rules and restrictions? Who is promoting this franchise, and what is their agenda? Are the student learning outcomes we seek reflected in the priorities of this organization?*

As you answer these four big questions, you are constructing a clearer picture of your desired learning outcomes, population, and basic model. There are no right or wrong answers, there's only what's right for your community and your values. Stick with the big picture, and don't go too deeply into the details of structure and learning strategies. (These will be unpacked in Step 5.) If you find yourself getting bogged down in the details, come back again and again to your students: *Who are they? How will they grow? What will they learn? Which kind of learning community will make them happy, successful, whole human beings?*

Appendix B has a further list of guiding questions to help you gain clarity about your school's role and purpose. If you get stuck, it's always helpful to research other micro-schools around the country and see how they answer these big-picture questions. Find a micro-school you'd like to emulate and discover their affiliations and teaching models. Find out how large their class sizes are and what their teachers and students value. Remember, you're not alone—hundreds of schools around the country are doing the same work. Go to MicroSchoolCoalition.com for a list of schools and some encouragement and inspiration on your journey.

"Rather than stifle my son's individuality and squelch his inventive thoughts and dreams, the teachers appreciate my son's gifts and encourage him to study the subjects he enjoys in the way he learns best. LEADPrep is providing my son with exactly the tools he needs to thrive both academically and personally."

—MELANIE, MOTHER OF A HIGH SCHOOL STUDENT

If you're going through this brainstorming process with more than four people, consider inviting an outside facilitator to support your discussion. A facilitator can draw out varied perspectives and be a neutral party who looks for ways of blending ideas and creating synergy. Together, your tribe is finding the clarity needed to give your micro-school a consistent direction and message. This conversation will also help you select a name that reflects your micro-school's unique local identity.

Using material from these questions and conversations, you will then draft your mission statement. The mission statement shares the driving force behind your specific micro-school. You want your mission to take your long-term vision ("all students thriving") and excite others with descriptors of what your school provides. Have fun with this process and articulate the mission that fills your tribe with joy. You are pouring your heart into the vision of this school, so if you find a word or a phrase that makes you breathe in deeply and get a little teary-eyed, you're probably on the right track.

Go online and find five other schools who have a purpose similar to yours. Look at their mission statements. For a list of micro-schools go to MicroSchoolCoalition.com. Here are a few mission statements from real-life micro-schools:

> "At LEADPrep[61] we foster an educational community that cultivates *authentic voices* and strengths. We empower students to be *fearless* in their individuality and also *courageous* as local and global leaders." — Kirkland and Seattle, Washington

After a class discussion about our mission statement, we asked our students to finish this sentence—At LEADPrep I am...

Here are their answers:

At LEADPrep, I am accepted.

At LEADPrep, I am imaginative.

At LEADPrep, I am able to be myself.

At LEADPrep, I am a learner.

At LEADPrep, I am a community builder.

At LEADPrep, I am an artist.

At LEADPrep, I am funny.

At LEADPrep, I am curious.

At LEADPrep, I am optimistic.

At LEADPrep, I am active.

At LEADPrep, I am a great ambassador.

At LEADPrep, I am an amazing biological machine.

At LEADPrep, I am a basketball player.

At LEADPrep, I am a good student.

At LEADPrep, I am a friendly.

At LEADPrep, I am a helper.

At LEADPrep, I am awesome at many things including problem solving. Honestly, I don't even know most of them! What I do know is that I'm good
at linguistics...hence the speech....

Isn't this a beautiful picture of
what school can be for our happy, colorful kids?

"At Trackers[62] we are champions of land and village. We are navigators of an epic world that needs to exist. We are a community where we remember the celebration of hearth, family, respect for the land and a timeless human story." — Portland, Oregon

"Innovations Academy[63] was created to provide [high school] students a different pathway to completing their graduation requirements. Our goal is to create a community that meets the educational needs and unique learning styles of our students and re-engages students through a personalized approach to learning." — Fairbanks, Alaska

"At Peace Valley School[64] we encourage all learners to make education real. To do this, we learn by working together on real-world projects to solve universal problems. By practicing healthy communication to solve a common problem through inquiry, we can garner a sense of responsibility instead of entitlement. We can become perpetual learners with the courage and life-skills that entails. We can discover who we are and help each other grow. We can be the change we want to see in the world." — Dayton, Oregon

Congratulations! You've articulated your mission statement. You now have the destination set on your road map. This is the big-picture goal. From here, you can work backward and reverse-engineer the path that gets you to your destination. Chances are, as you look at your mission statement, names that describe your school have been bubbling up. You want to select a name that helps people understand your school or location. Take your time. Get input. Guided by this mission, you are naming and creating a real school with real students who will be getting the personalized education they so desperately need.

Work on the four brainstorming questions. Record your ideas in your Action Plan.

THREE TASKS TO DO NOW

1. Expand upon the brainstorming and formulate your own mission statement and name. Let your passion shine through! (See Appendix B.)

2. Take your newly formed mission and name and create your web presence. What URLs similar to your name are available? Will you link a Facebook page to your website? Instagram? How will you be searchable—and found—online? (See Appendix B.)

3. Ask at least five other trusted people (i.e., parents who will want to send their children) to look at Step 1 of your Action Plan. Ask them for their initial impressions, ideas, and if they think there is a market for this micro-school. Ask if they have any resource ideas such as a space to use, ideal teacher, etc. This feedback is the first step in your research process.

STEP 2

RECRUIT ENERGETIC AND COMMITTED TRAILBLAZERS

*If you think dealing with issues like worthiness and
authenticity and vulnerability are not worthwhile
because there are more pressing issues, like the bottom
line or attendance or standardized test scores, you
are sadly, sadly mistaken. It underpins everything.*

—Brené Brown

GOAL

Find the leader (or leaders) who will be the catalyst
for your micro-school's start-up phase.

CHALLENGE

EVERY MICRO-SCHOOL requires a strong leader to oversee both the administrative and educational aspects of the organization. Many tasks must be handled simultaneously in order to get a new school off the ground, and your school needs an official head to manage these tasks. The leader (or leaders) of a micro-school must be able to make connections with families, budget, schedule, priorities, and keep their eye on the school's big-picture educational goals. Most likely they will need to teach in the classroom as well. All of this requires energy and commitment. A micro-school leader must be action-oriented.

If you are starting your micro-school with an initial tribe of passionate parents, you may already have someone with a portion of these abilities. For example, you may have a motivated, organized leader who is committed to starting the micro-school as a small business, but has little or no teaching experience. Or perhaps you have an educational leader with a passion for classroom instruction, but who isn't comfortable with the business aspects of running a micro-school. The challenge will be to find another leader who brings the skills you need to the table, shares your commitment to the cause, and is able to work with your initial shoestring budget.

SOLUTION

Split up the leadership role into two jobs: a business leader and an educational leader. (See Appendix C for a sample micro-school job description.) Hire trailblazing people with the specific skill set you need, and who are committed to your vision, have a passion for kids, and are determined to see this micro-school get off the ground.

Dual leadership is a strategy where one person drives the business side of your school while another person leads the development of the educational model. This is ideal for a micro-school's start-up phase because a wide range of tasks are required, and you will be drawing on two areas of expertise instead of just one. These two positions need to be held by people you know will take action, work collaboratively, and move your school forward. If you can find a single determined educational leader who has been dreaming of starting their own school, that individual might be able to take on both business and education roles. But whether you hire one person or two, they must embody the creativity and fierce tenacity of your tribe. Starting a micro-school is a labor of love—a leader needs to bring the labor *and* the love. This isn't just a job, this is a deep-rooted personal quest to create a micro-school for the sake of our students.

Ideally, if someone is in a position to take on one of these leadership roles, they will have the time and personal resources to get the school through its first year before earning wages. (It's possible to create a contract that promises back-pay once the school is financially established.) While there may not be funding yet to pay these two leaders, you still need to interview candidates carefully and do full reference checks. These positions are serious jobs and need to be treated as such. If you're placing your tribe's children and finances into someone else's hands, you want to make sure that person is utterly trustworthy.

The business leader is the person in charge of the structure and finances of the school. Above all, they must be well organized and able to document their work thoroughly. Here are some tasks a micro-school business leader will accomplish:

- Establish the business entity and submit related paperwork for a nonprofit, charter, or for-profit organization
- Create and/or approve the school budget
- Open a business bank account and possibly apply for business credit card
- Oversee fundraising/investment efforts and manage operating costs
- Determine tuition and staff salaries
- Decide on name, purchase domain, create social media presence
- Track requirements for state approval or accreditation, and make a timeline to meet those requirements
- Find a facility with correct zoning and suitable location
- Sign a lease agreement and manage facilities, including furnishings and wi-fi
- Drive marketing/outreach efforts
- Communicate with parents about financial and legal requirements
- Form a school board and report to that board (or to investors, school district leadership, or franchise leadership, depending on your affiliation)

These tasks exist, even if your micro-school is very small, so even the tiniest school has to have someone officially managing administrative work. If you already have a brilliant educational leader, then having someone else manage finances and operations will free up the educational leader's time to focus on the kids. Don't underestimate the power of the business leadership role—without a budget and facilities, you won't have a school at all.

When hiring for this position, look for a person with a well-rounded business background that includes systems, finance, marketing, human relations, and the ability to navigate regulatory expectations. Look closely at a candidate's past portfolio. If they started businesses or schools before, how are those businesses doing now? Why did they leave? Avoid people who get excited about starting things and leave a trail of half-completed projects behind them. No matter what excuses these "entrepreneurs" have for abandoning their past ideas, chances are your school will be yet another momentary distraction that gets dropped when the going gets tough. Instead, look for someone who has been successful and faithful with their past responsibilities. For example, you could hire someone who successfully runs a home business, or someone who has experience managing the administrative office of a school, church, or other nonprofit organization. I know of an established micro-school that promoted its own secretary to be the business administrator because she had done such an excellent job running the school from behind the scenes. Superficial excitement is less important than a steady, abiding sense of responsibility and dedication.

On a deeper level, the micro-school mission is truly inspiring, so look for a businessperson who wants to accomplish something meaningful. You could look for a candidate among people who run fundraisers and other nonprofit efforts. Perhaps you could find a successful entrepreneur or manager who is retiring from the corporate world and wants to use their business acumen to give back to the community. If a business leader catches your tribe's vision and falls in love with the rainbow of outliers you serve, they will be joining you for the right reasons. A micro-school manager might deal with numbers and documents, but every part of the work has the direct purpose of helping, saving, and inspiring our kids. With strong energy and equally strong commitment, a business leader creates the structural integrity of the micro-school.

If a business leader is the one working ON the school, then the educational leader is the one working IN the school. The educational leader is in charge of the curriculum and classroom environment. They are generally the lead teacher, or perhaps the only teacher when the school first begins. Being the lead teacher in a micro-school is an exciting role! As we discussed in Chapter 4, personal relationships with students are the heartbeat of a micro-school, and innovation is the lifeblood. First and foremost, a micro-school education leader must love working with colorful, mismatched kids. Second, they must believe that education must be improved and transformed in vital ways. We'll talk more about school design in Step 5, but for now, here are some of the big-picture tasks a micro-school educational leader will accomplish:

- Serve as an ambassador for the evolving school culture and style
- Select and implement curriculum
- Develop a trusting relationship with each student
- Listen to students and respond to their questions, interests, and requests
- Set up the classroom environment
- Connect to educational groups and stay current on innovations and trends
- Design school-wide systems for sharing content and assignments
- Communicate with parents regarding their child's needs
- Manage behavior expectations and facilitate conflict management
- Coach other teachers and co-teachers

For an education leader, a well-rounded teaching background is the top priority. Micro-schools often have multi-age classrooms, with students working at various levels, so having experience with a wide range of ages is helpful.

Micro-schools are a place for students to be seen, heard, and valued. That means looking for a teacher who builds meaningful connections and supports the well-being of the entire student. Even if your micro-school is for older kids, I recommend looking for an education leader who has at least some experience in elementary schools. Most elementary school teachers expect to teach the whole child and pay attention to social, emotional, physical, and academic dimensions, as well as to vary the learning methodology. A micro-school takes this holistic model and applies it to middle school and high school as well. As we discussed in Part One, this relational, nurturing approach to education is exactly what our struggling teens and tweens are missing in conventional schools. Someone with a single-subject high school teaching background might be a good co-teacher at your school, but the education leader needs to have a big-picture, holistic approach.

When interviewing education leaders, expect to ask a lot of deep questions and give value to qualities beyond college degrees and years of experience. If you're looking for a dynamic, innovative education leader, long years of experience are not always a bonus. If a conventional educator comes into your school with 15 years of traditional teaching methods (along with 15 years of old handouts and lesson plans), then they probably won't be creating a progressive learning environment. If an educator is more interested in being "right" than being flexible, then you won't have a responsive learning environment. This isn't necessarily an age issue: there are some wonderfully innovative, flexible older teachers and quite a few rigid, stubborn younger teachers. Some teachers aren't comfortable with collaboration, and don't appreciate students having a voice, or parents volunteering in the classroom. If a teacher reacts to student debate by pulling rank or being authoritative, they aren't a good fit for the micro-school environment. No matter how much experience a teaching candidate has, look for responsiveness, compassion, creativity, high energy levels, and kindness.

In many states, private school teachers do not need a state teaching certificate. This opens up a whole new pool of education leaders from which to choose. At LEADPrep, some of our most successful teachers have been young people just starting their careers, who are passionate about working with kids. These new teachers want to reform education and bring youthful vitality and idealism to their work every day. Some of them are creating the schools they wish they could have attended. Some of them were raised in alternative education themselves and are passing on their experiences to the next generation. Talented homeschool moms are another wonderful source of teaching energy. The current director of learning at LEADPrep left public school teaching to become a homeschool mom for her son. She was designing in-depth science curricula for a homeschool co-op when we hired her to work at our micro-school. She's a treasure trove of wisdom and experience, especially when we are working with quirky ADHD kids and students on the autism spectrum. If you're starting an unconventional school, an unconventional leader might be a perfect fit.

Just as I mentioned about business leaders, be sure to look into the past portfolio of your potential education leader. If the candidate is an unemployed teacher, was there a professional problem that led to unemployment? That problem could (and most likely will) re-occur in your own school. Avoid people who are quick to complain or blame other people for their failures, because that probably means they won't be good teammates or collaborators. Instead, look for candidates who are cheerful and interested in many things. You might find a science teacher with a passion for literature, or an English teacher with a passion for outdoor education. You might find a math teacher who is also an artist. If an education leader likes to wear several hats, that's a sign of flexibility. A well-rounded, curious teacher is an excellent role model for students who are just starting to explore all the

"Every kid here is so nice and all the teachers are nice. I just like the way it feels." —DION, 6TH GRADE

amazing things life has to offer.

During this initial phase of your micro-school, it's important for both the business and education leaders to have a start-up mindset. People with a start-up mindset prioritize innovation over stability. They work with what they have instead of waiting around for what they wish they had. They work

"LEADPrep students are provided with the perfect balance of individualized attention and group interaction with teachers and students who are caring, kind, and respectful of each other. Indeed, the sense of community amongst the staff and students at LEADPrep is a delight to witness."
—MELANIE, MOTHER OF A HIGH SCHOOLER

quickly to get something off the ground, even if it's not perfect. The start-up mindset requires humility, because you have to learn as you go along, accept that there will be mistakes, collaborate with other team members, and work hard on whatever task needs to be done. Choosing to work for a start-up requires audacity as well, because upending the status quo isn't easy. So where can you find someone who is both humble and audacious? Creative and speedy and resourceful? Most people only find those qualities within themselves if they're working for something they love. The only way to start a micro-school is if you and your leaders believe in the work and are motivated by love for the students. If your leadership candidate really believes that kids are suffering in regular schools, wasting their potential, and falling through the cracks, then they will be able to access that internal motivation and strength of character. A trailblazer is someone who is trying to get to a new destination. Our destination is humane, innovative education.

As important as it is to find the right leader, I want to encourage you with the idea that you don't have to get it perfect right away. Sometimes the teacher or business leader who can start your school is not the one who will sustain it. Be okay with this possibility and evaluate the fit as you grow together. Keep an open mind and clear channels of communication. Remember that a good hire doesn't have to be a "forever hire." If you do find a qualified leader who's passionate about alternative education but has other life plans (retirement, moving, going back to school), perhaps they would be willing to donate one or two years to your school before hiring their own replacement. That would be the perfect opportunity to launch your micro-school with a bold, dynamic leader, and then pass it on to a different kind of leader who can work with something that's already established.

Thankfully, great leaders don't operate alone. A micro-school relies on the tribe of parent volunteers for support and vision. If you celebrate each other's creativity and fierce tenacity, you will create a culture of encouragement and positivity. The remainder of the tribe will work alongside their chosen leaders. Various members will become specialists, taking on specific tasks. Working together, the leaders and the tribe will set goals, move forward, and welcome students into a new micro-school.

Once you have hired these dynamic leaders, you will add their names to your official Action Plan.

THREE TASKS TO DO NOW

1. Create two job descriptions, one for the business leader and one for the school leader. Be sure that you have a comprehensive list of the expectations for each role. Commit to writing the specific qualifications you're seeking in Step 2 of your Action Plan. If you already have someone in your tribe who wants to take on one of these roles, make sure they meet the qualifications for the job.

2. Post the job descriptions on various platforms. By now you should have a website, Facebook presence, and possibly an Instagram account. Post on these and in at least six external sites that your prospective families might visit.

3. Talk to other business leaders and educators. Ask for names of potential candidates and ways to get the word out. This is also a good way to build interest and awareness of your new school.

STEP 3

ENGAGE COMMUNITY COLLABORATORS

*At the end of the day, the most overwhelming key to a
child's success is the positive involvement of parents.*

—Jane D. Hull

GOAL

Build your micro-school momentum with the power
of parent volunteers and real-life operational goals.

CHALLENGE

PARENTS HAVE BEEN the driving force in countless iterations of homeschools and co-ops around the country. They are passionate about being involved in their children's lives and ascertaining the quality of educational experiences. They are the first (and, frequently, the best) teachers of their children. A parent looks at their child and sees a whole human. They understand what schools can do and are incredibly invested. Yet, paradoxically, they are shut out of many school settings with no influence or ability to help. So how do we engage parents and maximize this valuable resource? This is your first challenge.

As we seek to engage parents and community members, we also need to be aware of the challenges faced when working with volunteers. The level of commitment and desire to have a strong voice is a different dynamic with volunteers than it is with employees. Volunteers often expect a return on their investment in lieu of the paycheck employees receive. They may also not be as dedicated as employees in honoring any commitments they make. Your second challenge is to work realistically within this volunteer framework.

SOLUTION

No one is more motivated to see a micro-school succeed than a parent who is worried about how their child is doing in a conventional school. Parents are unhappy and frustrated at the lack of power they have to influence their children's educational experience. They feel the pain of their children being underserved or overlooked. Parents of tweens and teens know the clock is ticking. Their child has only seven years of middle and high school before they are supposedly ready for college and independence, and every year time is wasted in a miserable school setting is agony. This powerful parental urgency is the jet fuel that will launch a micro-school like a rocket ship! There is no greater force on earth than a parent's love for their child, and a community-powered micro-school gives parents a positive, practical outlet for that love. That's why all parents should be engaged members of their child's school, in whatever way fits their time and abilities.

To proactively address the needs of volunteers to have a voice, use clear communication. Along with that parental love and energy comes a variety of parental expectations and personalities. Every individual in a group brings their own ideas and viewpoints. People have different styles of communication. Some parents in the community will find kindred spirits and become good friends with each other. Others might be more shy or aloof. Some parents might be brilliant collaborators who are cheerful and easy-going, while other parents might be more argumentative, scattered, or socially awkward (just like some of our kids!). Just remember that every family has a unique perspective, and every member of the group brings their own unique interests and skill sets. With clear communication, you can manage this varied and powerful resource our parents bring to support our micro-schools.

Ideally, you engage parents and the broader community in your micro-school. As your school makes the transition from concept to reality, begin to think of the immediate community, specifically potential community partnerships. Micro-schools benefit from networking with other schools, community centers, learning specialists, counselors, local businesses, and all kinds of nonprofit groups. Constantly ask parents to reach out to the community to increase the involvement in your tribe.

> "Although our stories may be different, there is a bond in witnessing the reclaiming of your child's educational spark. Seeing the love of learning presented in a way that engages each student is a beautiful thing."
> —BEA, PARENT OF A HIGH SCHOOL SON

As you begin to work with parent and community volunteers, ask about specific professional skills they can bring to the table. In my experience, parents who are professional graphic designers are usually eager to jump in on school logos, websites, and brochures (maybe because they hate seeing them done poorly). Other volunteers may have teaching or tutoring experience, or skills in art, cooking, gardening, programming, etc. In a project-based curriculum, any skill or interest can be turned into a classroom teaching opportunity. Parents who aren't interested in teaching can work behind the scenes painting, building shelves, and assembling supplies. When you're managing facilities, it's very handy to have at least one volunteer on your team who is a carpenter or contractor. If you have a parent who's a social media whiz, get them working on your Facebook account and website right away. There's no such thing as the perfect volunteer dream team. Every micro-school works with what they have and fills in the gaps however they can. You might be surprised at the interesting abilities and creative solutions your volunteers will generate.

When recruiting volunteers, don't just get a verbal agreement to help—write it down and make it official. You'll probably find that some volunteers are quick to jump in and offer services, while others are more reluctant to volunteer. Keeping tasks written down clearly helps both of these kinds of volunteers. Eager volunteers can keep track of the things to which they've already committed so they don't overcommit or forget something important. It's likely that a reluctant volunteer is perfectly willing to help, but just isn't sure how to get started. Try approaching them like this: "Max's mom Stella has already volunteered to set up the Facebook group, print brochures, and buy maker lab supplies. Would it be possible for you to take one of these things off her plate?" or, "I've made a Google spreadsheet with a list of things that need to be done in August. Can you take a look and see if any of these tasks are a good fit for your family?"

Here are samples of some of the many projects and responsibilities that can be distributed to volunteers:

- Marketing: graphic designing, creating a social media presence, serving as webmaster, making flyers, distributing yard signs

- Education assistance: supply shopping, lesson prep helping, classroom assisting, chaperoning field trips, tutoring

- Facilities: location scouting, painting, furniture hunting, shelf constructing, bathroom updating, gardening

- Community organizers: social event planning, attending parent meetings, coordinating volunteers

- Fundraising: auctions planning, finding corporate sponsorships, soliciting donations

- Administration: serving as school treasurer, managing state/city compliance, serving on interview team

As you can see, parents will be shouldering important pieces of your school operations. Assign specific areas of responsibility to specific parent volunteers. Keep an official list of which staff member or volunteer is responsible for each job. Fill out your action plan for operations. (See Appendix A, Part 3). Research and write down the legal requirements of your state, city, and/or school district. Keep your tribe focused and volunteer expectations high with a family-school-student commitment form. (See Appendix D.)

However, be mentally prepared for the inevitable moment when a volunteer promises to do something and then forgets or just doesn't follow through. You will have some days when you're scrambling to fill a gap, but that's okay. Model flexibility for your students. Other members of the tribe will step in with their own creativity and tenacity. When the going gets tough, you'll find out which parents are the resilient, flexible ones who love a good last-minute challenge. As we mentioned in our ADHD outlier section, some people thrive in an emergency situation!

Ask around at any micro-school, and they'll tell you which volunteers they treasure the most. Regardless of their skill set, these MVP volunteers share these two qualities: compassion for kids and a strong belief in the mission of the school. That belief fuels their energy and commitment. A good volunteer is generous, but also has boundaries. They know their own strengths and weaknesses, and they give what they have to offer. Their energy creates stability, not chaos. When you find this kind of trustworthy volunteer, hang on tight! Honor them and tell them how much you appreciate their contribution. Invite them into leadership roles and listen to their opinions.

On the other hand, if you find yourself dealing with a socially difficult parent, my best advice is to again focus on the students. Ultimately, your school exists to serve the child, not the parent. Every parent loves their child and wants them to succeed, so that's the common ground on which you have to build. As adults, we are capable of tolerating some minor social discomfort in order to build strong relationships with kids. If someone is rubbing you the wrong way, remind yourself of the good qualities they bring to your group, as well as the bad.

Let's talk about healthy conflict. During the intense start-up phase, you'll run into a few disagreements, miscommunications, and errors. It can be tricky to make sure everyone is heard and respected, while still maintaining a coherent group direction. In a micro-school, the parents are both volunteers and customers, which is a complicated set of roles to navigate. Your leaders will have to listen respectfully to a lot of parent input, while keeping everyone's expectations realistic at the same time. Not all ideas can be implemented in the first year, or even the second year. That doesn't mean they aren't terrific ideas! They just might need to be verbally affirmed and set aside in a "for later" file. As passionate and inspired as your tribe may be, keep in mind that you are starting a school, not a miracle factory. You are supporting kids and getting to know them for who they are, not transforming them into different people. When a parent's child is involved, there can be intense emotion to manage. Sometimes all the fear and anxiety we hold for our children's well-being comes out as anger (or at least as a loudly expressed opinion). That's acceptable, it's all part of the process. Honor the passion, but stay realistic. Stick to your mission statement and always bring it back to the students. How are we benefiting our kids? What student successes can we celebrate? If you've made a mistake, apologize and don't worry about saving face. Set an example you'd like your students to follow.

As a new group, a micro-school is collectively developing norms of communication. Keep your tribe in the loop. This could mean a weekly email update of successes and needs. It could mean a monthly evening meeting to share ideas and concerns. Spell out clearly defined roles, including who makes what decisions and how. Move quickly to address dissent or confusion, and answer questions as they arise. For example, what can and

"I like how close-knit the community is."

—LANDON, 10TH GRADE

can't be posted on the social media account? Can anyone propose a lesson? Is volunteering mandatory? Align your model with the mission and let it drive the method you use to engage parents. Take a look at Appendix D, the Sample Family-School-Student Commitment Form, and think about ways you can adapt it to your school community. The more clearly you outline specific roles and explain how your tribe can pull forward as one unit, the more effective you will be.

The best way to get everyone on the same page is to create a clear operations plan. (See Appendix A.) Assign responsibilities and make your start time and location official. This is the time to loop in the greater community influences, such as your state education department and your city regulations. Although legal requirements and insurance requirements aren't the most exciting part of opening a micro-school, they are important tools for keeping kids safe. The business checklist (Appendix F) includes more insurance specifications. If you are going through a charter school process, your district or education department will provide a list of requirements.

As another measure to keep kids safe, be sure to run a background check on anyone teaching or looking after students at school. Parent volunteers who work in the classroom alongside teachers in a group also require background checks. Your state board of education will have information on the level of background checks. For teachers, this often includes fingerprinting and looking at federal records. For volunteers, it may be a simple check with only name and birthdate required. As your school grows, consider adding official Safeguarding or Child Protection policies (classes and practices that are specifically designed to prevent abuse at schools, churches, and other institutions). Above all, pay attention to what your students tell you about any particular parent or volunteer. If they feel uncomfortable for any reason, follow up on it. At a micro-school, we should never ever sweep a child's concerns under the rug. The best protection for your community is listening to your students, trusting their observations, and keeping the lines of communication open at all times. Community-based group activities and lots of co-teaching helps keep everyone safe and accountable to each other. Familiarize yourself with state mandatory-reporting laws in case a student needs help with a situation outside of school.

Location is technically part of the operations plan. Some micro-schools, especially if they're founded within a church or a larger school, already have a location dialed in. For most micro-schools, physical location is a flexible issue that can be decided based on community resources. If you're still trying to determine the best neighborhood in which to locate the school, we'll talk about that in Step 4. If you're having trouble financing a space, we'll address that issue in Step 6. Once you've worked through those steps, you can circle back and finalize your location. For now, just commit to writing the proximity if you don't know the specific location.

"I like my school because the atmosphere is a comfortable place to study, learn and connect with my classmates. I also enjoy making new friends, taking part in fun activities and going on many school outings." —COLE, 10TH GRADE

Add approximately how much space you think you'll need, what the legal requirements will be, and what time of the day you'll be needing it. Send that information out to your tribe and see if anyone has a lead on a potential space.

As a general rule, getting the right families involved is more important than getting the right classroom. Your school can move around as you need to; but no matter where you go, the parents and students create the community, and the community creates the school. A core group of committed, helpful families is crucial, so invite them in and honor their work. Once you have your community engaged, this micro-school is on the path to success!

As a tribe, research and determine the components you will have in your operational plan. Record this in your Action Plan (Step 3).

THREE TASKS TO DO NOW

1. Determine your physical location. To maximize community involvement, you need to serve a specific town or neighborhood. Pin this down now to the best of your ability.

2. Create a commitment document for Year One families. Each family might contribute 60 hours of labor, fundraise, post flyers, recruit five potential families, etc. See Appendix D for a sample commitment form among parents, school, and students. Be sure to tap into parent strengths and interests. Ask parents what they would like to bring to the table to create a successful launch. Remind them that grandparents, close family friends, and other adults are very welcome to lend a hand.

3. Create opportunities for your core group to meet and connect. Consider having one volunteer dedicated to community relations from the start. Each opportunity for families and members of the community to interact creates a bond and provides a chance for creative synergy to elevate your school. Forging a sense of community begins immediately and should be considered at every step of the process.

STEP 4

GET THE WORD OUT

Excitement must lead to immediate action or you
will lose the power of momentum. More dreams die
because we fail to seize the moment. Do it now!

—Tony Robbins

GOAL

Connect with new families. Show them that your school exists,
invite them to learn more, and get their kids signed up
to come to your micro-school.

CHALLENGE

AT THIS POINT in the process, you're probably asking yourselves this big scary question: "How will we get enough families to come to our school?" It's a pretty good question! In the age of social media, one would think that getting the word out would be simple. But while there are many new digital platforms at our fingertips, there is also an influx of competing distractions. Getting—and maintaining—the interest of prospective families requires a concerted effort and some serious man-hours. Now is the time deliberately to market your school.

Your first marketing challenge is to have a specific customer base and a clear message. This will take research and reflection. Your second marketing challenge is to employ creative strategies to raise awareness. The third marketing challenge is to get your entire community involved in the effort.

SOLUTION

Know the landscape before you start this marketing campaign. It's time to do some more market research. You want start-up business data and information on your market to guide how you disseminate the information. Make a collection of useful information and fill out the SWOT (**s**trengths, **w**eaknesses, **o**pportunities, **t**hreats) analysis in the Action Plan. With this information in hand, you will then create a marketing plan, including an elevator speech (template in Appendix E) to guide your team to promote your micro-school.

Data Collection. While you are developing your marketing plan, be on the lookout for information that might be useful for overall planning of your school. Remember the CASE motto—Copy And Steal Everything! As you research the market of other micro-schools and small businesses, ask them what steps they took to determine their financial viability. Ask if they have a business plan or materials they would be willing to share. Reviewing other school's plans and financials can remind you of important elements. Compile materials related to school populations, operational funding projections, anticipated costs, tuition, etc. Take notes to use in the development of your Action Plan. This isn't the time to make big choices, it's only the time to look around and see how similar organizations do business.

Market Analysis. Knowing the landscape of the market means reflecting on your tribe and resources and knowing what is going on around you. A SWOT analysis guides how you market and to whom. This strategic tool is often used in business board retreats to help people look at the big picture. Let's walk through the parts of the SWOT analysis.

> "We are so happy that our son is thriving and learning rather than being put through the mill at a large school, set up for failure because he was falling through the cracks."
>
> —MARGARET, MOTHER OF A HIGH SCHOOL SON

Internal Strengths. What are the assets your school already has? For example, if you have an experienced alternative education leader on board, that's a core internal strength. Other strengths might be a connection with a church that will provide classroom space. If you've already established a parent support group, that tribe is a strength. Spell out the good resources and good people you already have in your corner. Sometimes it's easy to take the good things for granted, so take your time and count the blessings you already have. These are the resources that will make your school attractive to prospective students and parents.

Internal Weaknesses. What pieces are missing from your school? For example, you may not have someone in your tribe who's good at numbers and book-keeping, which is a definite weakness when you're running a small business. Other weaknesses for a micro-school might include a lack of technology resources, or a lack of connection to therapists and learning specialists. Tiny size can be a weakness—will new families want to join if they feel like there aren't enough students to make friends with their child? Don't be discouraged by this list of weaknesses. Use it as a checklist for acquiring help. Ask parents if they know a bookkeeper who wants to help. Make a plan to partner with another small school for social events. If you need a resource or a specialist, make a note to reach out to people in your community who provide those things. Be honest with yourselves! By acknowledging the gaps ahead of time, your school is making a practical plan for the future.

External opportunities. Looking at the neighborhood around you, what are the exciting outside factors that will contribute to your micro-school's success? For example, the Seattle metro area is having a population boom. That means more families moving into the area, and therefore more potential students. It also means overcrowded conventional schools and greater parent dissatisfaction, which means more people will be seeking alternatives. If your public high school just hired a new principal, maybe that's an opportunity to pitch a school-within-a-school option. Or, if you're starting a private middle school, is there an opportunity to collaborate with a local private elementary school? An underserved market is always an opportunity. Which outlier parents are looking for a new school, and what kind of school are they seeking? Researching opportunities will help you get excited about your micro-school's potential and teach you how to adapt your school to the needs of the greater community.

External Threats. What are the things outside of your organization that might cause a problem for your school? These are factors that are out of your sphere of control. You can't stop them, but you can still take them into consideration and plan around them. For example, maybe there's a freeway construction project planned that will increase traffic delays and disrupt access to your location. Perhaps the greatest threat to any small business is market over-saturation. Are there already one or two alternative micro-schools in your neighborhood? If so, would it be possible to move your school to an area that's underserved? Economic factors can also be a serious issue. If parents can't afford tuition to your private school, you'll need to look into other funding models or find ways to save on costs. (We will talk about his more in Step 6.) Being aware of external threats isn't paranoid, it's pragmatic. It's helpful to know where you fit into the marketplace of educational options.

Everything in the SWOT analysis helps you plan, organize, and run your school, and it also helps you pitch your school to prospective parents. You know there's a need for your school, now get out there and find those under-served parents who need to hear your message. Complete this assessment in your Action Plan. Then fill out an elevator pitch template (Appendix E). Set aside money and man-hours for a multi-pronged marketing campaign with digital, print, and face-to-face marketing strategies. Have your parent volunteers commit to spreading the word in a way that's compatible with their background and skill set.

Now that you know the SWOT landscape, the primary prerequisite in any marketing campaign is becoming clear on your target audience. You need to know with whom you are trying to communicate and why they will be interested. The *why* part is actually the most important of your marketing efforts. As Simon Sinek[65] (of TED Talk fame) explains: "People don't buy WHAT you do; they buy WHY you do it." To go along with this principle, Simon uses a simple graphic of three concentric circles. The outermost circle is *what* you do, the middle circle is *how* you do it, and the core—the golden circle—is *why*. That inner circle, where the *why* of your story lives, is where you will get the buy-in from people you meet.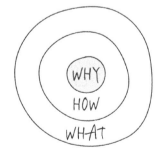

The good news is that you already know why you're starting a micro-school. In fact, you and your tribe are incredibly passionate about your why. You care about kids who are struggling, you've gathered together a tribe, and you've written a whole mission statement about it! You've done a ton of market research already, without even realizing it. Your tribe is your first market and your first set of customers. If you have a small group of parents with a certain set of fears, desires, hopes, and plans, you know there have to be other people out there who are feeling the same way. You just have to let them know that you're here and ready to go.

If you're starting a micro-school for altruistic or idealistic reasons, it is easy to feel uncomfortable "selling" your school, as if it were a product. Many schools fail at this step by sliding into an "if we build it, they will come" attitude. This is a terrible idea! Getting known is the most important step in opening your school. You can have the best plans in the world, but with no students, it just won't work. Momentum is needed to encourage other families to join. Now is not the time to be shy.

To overcome this potential pitfall, reframe your communication intent. You are not selling a product for purchase; you are offering a way out of despair. You are providing a solution to families' pain. You are committing to see, hear, value, and educate a student who may be self-doubting, and turned off to the joy of learning. Go back to Part One and remind yourself of the many students who are suffering, and the beautiful rainbow of outliers just waiting to be encouraged and celebrated. There are parents out there desperately wanting a learning community where their children can be successful. Let people know you exist and that you have room for their unique kid. Let them know that you want to help them see their child's learning needs happily met.

For this phase of your micro-school, be sure that each team member and parent volunteer has a shared set of talking points and a 30-second "elevator speech" (that is, how you would describe your school to a prospective parent as the two of you take an elevator up to the tenth floor). Your elevator speech needs to address the "why" and then who you are. Explain how your school can benefit a family. This clear, brief message is like a tiny commercial for your micro-school. All good elevator speeches conclude with a call to action. You have to put the ball in the listener's court and give them a specific action to take as the next step. (Imagine the "call now!" part of an infomercial.) At LEADPrep, I try to make sure each parent has my contact information in their phone, so they can share it with other prospective parents as conversations happen. An elevator speech template is included in Appendix E.

Decide on a numerical goal of how many families you want to enroll. If you're trying to start a micro-school with thirty students, make a concrete goal of getting at least ten before you open. If your goal is to build a tiny micro-school of twelve, and you already have four kids who are interested, go get two more. Within your tribe, you've had a ton of practice "selling" the idea of your school to each other and

"I can work at my own level not just at my grade level. There are a lot less people than my other school and that makes it a lot easier. I don't feel stressed while I walk into school each morning." —JASON, 10TH GRADE

getting excited about it. Now it's time to invite other people into the tribe. Keep your momentum, and your enthusiasm will be contagious. Continue the work you started in Part One, with word-of-mouth approaches. On top of that, add in more focused efforts with digital, print, and face-to-face marketing strategies.

Armed with a common pitch and talking points, distribute marketing jobs to your staff and parents. It's not enough to think about doing something, you must actually do it. Make sure everyone commits to helping with at least one of these marketing tasks:

- Make sure your website is fully functional and has all your contact information, and a phrase like, "Now accepting applications for 2020 (insert current school year)!"

- Post weekly on Facebook, Instagram, and/or Twitter.

- Write about your school on neighborhood blogs and parent-support message boards.

- Make yard signs to put in strategic locations. Signsonthecheap.com has good prices.

- Print flyers with tear-off telephone numbers and post them in local coffee shops, grocery stores, and community centers. Or, even telephone poles next to the lost dog flyers!

- Try using a direct mailing postcard. The post office has something called "Every Door Direct Mail" that will deliver to zip codes of your choice.

- Attend various local parent groups to share information about your school.

- Set up an information booth at a parent resource fair, or your local farmer's market.

- Schedule a Q&A or an open house at your city's public library.

- Have each family commit to contacting a certain number of other prospective families.

You don't have to do every single one of these tasks, but make sure you're getting your message out on the internet, media, and face-to-face connections. Just like in the elevator speech, end every pitch with a call to action that transforms interest into further connection. Throw everything at the wall and see what sticks! Ask your parents what ideas they have to get the word out.

One strategy we've found helpful is networking with other private schools. If you are starting a middle school, talk to local elementary schools and ask if you can present at a parent meeting, or just leave a stack of brochures. The graduates of these schools will be looking for a place to continue their education. If you have a parent whose child attended this local school, they're already a part of the community and can network easily with other parents. Don't be afraid to also contact larger private middle and high schools. Chances are, they have students who might do better in a smaller classroom. For example, LEADPrep teaches STEM as one of our core classes. There is a large STEM school in Seattle, and one of our more outgoing parents offered to create a relationship with the staff of the larger school. They tactfully made sure that all of the key stakeholders knew about our micro-school model. That way, if any students feel like a big school is not the right fit or if they are not accepted, the school can refer them to LEADPrep. This creative "business-to-business" strategy is one of several cool marketing plans spearheaded by the parents of our school.

When designing marketing materials, please don't get caught up in the minutiae of logos, website design, etc. These are necessary backdrops, but they don't have to be perfect. Design work can be done quickly and prepared simul-

"I enjoy helping with school projects, because I get to combine two passions: my kids' education and my creative work."
—JOELLE, MOTHER OF A MIDDLE SCHOOL SON

taneously with getting the word out. Don't let the wrapping of the package become a bigger focus than the actual gift inside.

When meeting prospective parents, be the change you want to see in the world. People join micro-schools because they are looking for a personalized, supportive learning community. Therefore, give them a personalized, supportive experience right from the start. As the head of a micro-school, when a prospective parent calls or wants to meet, I drop everything else to make it happen immediately. I'm demonstrating with my actions that our school is responsive and flexible. When parents are feeling isolated and concerned, just listening to them is a great first step. Ask them what their hopes and dreams are for their child's school. In that first phone call, let them know that their outlier student is valued and cherished. That's why we started the school in the first place, right? We are inviting people into our tribe and showing them that we want to get to know their kid as an individual, not a faceless number.

Finally, the best advice I can give you for marketing is ASK! Ask everyone in your community and neighborhood for help and recommendations on everything. You're creating this school for our kids' sake, so swallow your dignity and put yourself out there. While you are asking people about local parent group meetings or potential school sites, be sure to explain enough about your vision so that you are getting the word out while you network. I guarantee that every adult you meet knows at least one colorful, mismatched kid who would benefit from your micro-school. You never know where you will make a connection or find a valuable ally. Asking for help and ideas generates more word-of-mouth marketing and more support. And, best of all, many kind people along the way will respond to your asking with "yes!"

Take a moment now to update your Action Plan (in Step 4) with your market research and commitment to getting the word out.

THREE TASKS TO DO NOW

1. Have ten families with eligible students signed up in two months' time. Let this target drive you. Start marketing, while you're still recruiting teachers, finding a site, and designing the instructional model. Getting the word out needs to be your number one activity. No kids? No funding. No school.

2. Make it easy for people to join your efforts. Have signs and flyers available to be distributed. Prepare talking points and social media blurbs. Get testimonials from founding families about their excitement at this new opportunity.

3. Ask six different community members (therapists, pastors, rabbis, librarians, other school leaders) for ideas and help.

STEP 5

CHOOSE WHAT MAKES
YOUR SCHOOL SPECIAL

---

*The beauty of the universe consists not only of
unity in variety, but also of variety in unity.*

—Umberto Eco

GOAL

Based on the needs of your student population and your mission statement, determine the features of your overall school structure and specific teaching strategies that will help your students thrive.

CHALLENGE

HOW WILL YOU set up your overarching model? What specific teaching strategies will you employ? In this step, you'll dive into both the structure of the school and classroom strategies. Remember, a micro-school should be innovating education, not simply replicating broken systems in miniature. Micro-schools succeed by choosing specific goals and creating school structure and strategies to meet them. Now is the time to select some cool new ideas about how your school will deliver learning and what learning it will emphasize.

This section will list some of the real-life education choices that are effectively making a difference in non-traditional schools around the country. Some schools use several of these tools at once, and some use different tools that aren't listed here. If you love alternative education like I do, this is the most exciting step of the process, and it's easy to geek out on all the choices. The list of options is long, and we so deeply desire ALL the good things for our students. But don't try to juggle too many balls at once. For now, focus on just a few ideas so you can execute them well. Your challenge is to find your own micro-school's unique "sweet spots" that will deliver innovative learning to your group of individual students.

SOLUTION

Go back to your school's mission statement and remind yourself of your school's fundamental goals. Starting with the ideas in this section, research alternative structures and plan how they will impact your set of unique students. Think of the following pages as a collection of options from which to pick and choose. Select and prioritize a few of these strategies and write them down in the learning section in your Action Plan. Stay focused by remembering that these are the features you will use to start. You will adjust or add more later as your school grows and adapts to its students' needs.

Choosing the Structure of Your School Model

Let's begin with structure. When you're shopping for a car, you start by deciding on the basic design—are you looking for an SUV or a sedan? In the same way, deciding on the structural elements of your school will determine the overall model of your school. These big-picture choices reflect your priorities. What will you do, as an institution, to bring your school's mission into focus? Below are some of the structural options a micro-school has available.

Proactively Foster and Demand Inclusion. A micro-school that's committed to this standard will admit a wide range of outliers and diverse learners. If it's your school's priority to be a humane option where students are kind to one another, then you need to enroll the students who will most benefit from kindness. Large conventional middle and high schools do not have the ability to create welcoming and caring communities for all, so bullying and exclusion are the frequent result. Some private schools maintain the illusion of peace by not enrolling outliers, or asking them to find a different school. Before you open your micro-school, determine which ability levels you are capable of serving. Within that ability level, enroll as wide a variety of students as you can. Then make sure every enrolled student is purposefully included to create a caring learning space. Set a high bar for student behavior and encourage inclusion, kindness, and conflict resolution. Reward leadership and generosity. Students of all types will benefit from this strategy.

Put the Adults Where the Learning Happens. If you have the vision of strong relationships between adults and students, then your staffing and resource decisions need to reflect this priority. Maximize the student-teacher ratio. A traditional school or district has to fund many non-teaching positions. At a micro-school, the funding can shift from paying non-educators to paying more teachers to be working directly with our students. Your micro-school could have a 10:1 student-teacher ratio or less. You could also have parent volunteers adding additional support. A school with this priority will focus on getting adults in the classroom to support individual students with their learning.

> "The kids are like a family and get along really well, considering the age ranges and the totally different personalities. They are so welcoming to other kids."
> —LACEY, MOTHER OF A HIGH SCHOOL DAUGHTER

> "The teacher to student ratio is helpful when you want to get help on your work." — AIDAN, 12TH GRADE

Increase Student Agency and Participation. Agency means empowerment. A micro-school that believes in its students will prioritize giving them the power to act. Student voices gets lost in big systems, but in micro-schools you can raise the bar on listening to your students and encourage them to participate fully. This empowerment needs to happen repeatedly in small, daily ways. One resource for giving students voice and leadership opportunities is Alfred Adler's class meeting model. Adlerian psychology is the foundation of Jane Nelsen's *Positive Discipline in the Classroom*[66]. She suggests a shift away from teacher-generated meetings and toward student-generated meetings with a focus on solutions. Her website and books lay out a process for creating a community where students feel capable, understand that they belong and have significance, and are motivated to follow the solutions they help design. If this is a priority in your school, always ask yourself, "Where can students take the lead? Run the class? Make meaningful decisions?" Socratic methodology can be combined with design thinking to help students plan their own learning. Teaching habits of success can help students guide their own behavior. Once they are empowered, there is no stopping our youth!

Eliminate Unrealistic Executive Functioning Demands. If your school wants high student investment and deep engagement, don't weigh them down with a multitude of varied expectations. The epidemic of anxiety and executive functioning failures could be greatly reduced with a clear, coherent education model. Many students do better when we don't ask their adolescent brains to deal with six or seven different bosses each day. Instead, set up one classroom management model for all teachers to use. Write class goals clearly, with visual aids. Homework can be assigned intentionally and collaboratively so that students don't get dumped on by all their teachers in one day. Better yet, homework could be interdisciplinary and not assigned in every separate subject. If executive functioning demands are a priority for your school, look into using assignment streamlining software like Google Classroom.

Get Flexible with Grades, Credits, and Age Groupings. Micro-schools don't have to grade students for being on time or homework completion. They don't even have to grade with tests. They can measure for mastery of competencies instead. Do you even want the pressure of grades at all? The pass-fail system can work just as well. Try a report card based on narrative comments instead of letter grades. Micro-schools don't have to keep a class in lockstep pace, with everyone being held to the same standard. Our K-12 system is the only time in life where learning is segregated by the age of the student. Try mixing ages and doing self-paced learning,

"This school is not easier, but it helps me get more work done and most of the time I can stay focused more than my other school. The teachers don't follow herd mentality, they work for the individual instead of just the whole school. They don't stress about working in only one way and say there is no other option, instead they work with us and make sure we know our stuff before we move forward. And it's more fun in this school in general."—TOBY, 9TH GRADE with all students demonstrating mastery before moving on to the next level. If your micro-school is serving high school students, then dual enrollment might be a good priority to have, allowing your students to earn high school and college credits simultaneously.

Choosing Specific Learning Strategies

Now that you've determined your school's structural priorities, it's time to decide which teaching and learning strategies you will include in your micro-school. Going back to our car metaphor, the structure is the basic metal frame, and the strategies are the things that go inside the frame—the seats, the engine, and the power steering. Your learning strategies are what you use within your teaching structure.

Being able to choose these learning strategies is the most delightful aspect of creating a micro-school. It's like going to the ice cream parlor and drooling over all 32 flavors! You get to decide what is important for your micro-school and what flavors of education you will scoop onto the sundae. For your startup, it is ideal for your tribe to agree on and begin with two or three basic instructional components. That's enough to create a vision and have a common story to tell. Let the problems you are seeking to solve guide this decision-making process.

Have fun with this process and spend time daydreaming about components you will implement. Think of what you loved as a child. If you're a parent, what models or components were successful for your child? What do you absolutely want to avoid? What is the school of the future? Use your imagination to put yourself into your micro-school. Look around. What is happening and how? Jot down what you envision. Here are four ideas to jump-start your thinking process.

Flip the Classroom. One of the many benefits of running a micro-school is the opportunity to try brilliant new learning strategies. The flipped classroom is perhaps the best educational idea education in the last 20 years. Flipped learning is a model where the lecture happens at home and the work happens at school. This means that students watch a mini-lecture (often called a "flip") the night before school. Then they come to class prepared to apply the content and take ownership of their learning. Flipped learning frees the teacher from lecturing. The teacher becomes a guide in the classroom, referring to the content of the flip as shared background knowledge. Research has found that when teachers lecture students, retention and focus is low[67]. In a flipped model, where students are engaged in the learning and have the support of the teacher, more information is retained, critical thinking is engaged, and student satisfaction is much higher[68]. Knowing this research, we need teachers to shift from being the experts who dispenses knowledge to facilitators who shares highlights and guide students in the discovery of knowledge.

Make Learning Project-Based. Project-based or problem-based learning works well in the flipped classroom model. When students are expected to apply knowledge to a real-life situation or project, the learning goes deep. Information becomes practical and contextualized. Project management and design thinking skills are developed. Project-based learning prepares our students for our 21st century world that is constantly changing. Education is no longer about memorizing information because students today have access to an infinite amount of information online. We need to teach them how to apply information to real-world situations. With a voice in the projects they undertake, they have ownership and buy-in. Project-based learning does all of this. The Buck Institute[69] is the leader in project-based learning. They have many resources and trainings to help educators make this monumental shift to engaged learning.

One very cool way to do project-based learning is to get out of the classroom. Or, to put it another way, treat the whole world as your classroom. At LEADPrep, we have two sessions per year of "Week Without Walls," where students camp and hike in the forest, or work with the outdoor education group at Mountain to Sound Greenway[70]. Students at a micro-school can take on big volunteering projects for local needs. They can learn about culture from museums, galleries, theater, music, and dance performances. They can start construction projects. They can do a history project by making friends with elders and recording their stories. If this is something that interests you, be sure to check out the Expeditionary School model pioneered by educator Kurt Hahn[71]. Perhaps the best way to prepare your students for the real world is to take them out into the real world.

> "What do I like about this school? More engaged classwork and the flipped system. Homework is terrible so it's nice to not have it." —ASHER, 12TH GRADE

Implement Personalized Learning Plans for All Learners. Although teens think about themselves a lot, they tend to lack self-awareness and objectivity. Teens are almost always harshly self-critical. Social media and online forums encourage false bravado. What if we, as educators, could guide students toward compassionate, accurate self-assessment strategies? When students are able to acknowledge their strengths and weaknesses in an accurate way, and see how others are different, personalized learning becomes possible. A trusted teacher (perhaps with parent input), can work with the student on setting achievable, personal goals for their own individual growth edges.

"We like that our son is taught at the level he's at. He's a unique individual and LEADPrep has been a good match."
—RICHARD AND SHELLY, PARENTS OF A HIGH SCHOOL SON

A learning style profile is a tool that helps students identify how they best learn and helps them self-advocate for a plan that matches their learning style. Here are some possibilities for helping students create their own learning profile:

- Have students self-assess strengths and challenges with a formal rubric. There are many options available, such as habits of success[72], learning styles[73], and personality indicators[74]. There are many ways to create baselines. Let your students know a goal in your class is to promote self-advocacy. Explain that this rubric will help give words and concepts to areas students can ask for (or offer) help. Make sure your lessons provide differentiation options for student preference.

- Have students affirm one personal strength. Provide students with a list of strengths[75], and ask them to circle the strengths they possess. Then ask them to describe a time they used one of their strengths to make a positive difference. Help students identify one emerging strength that they want to cultivate during the coming year. This isn't a weakness, it's a new strength that is just starting to grow. Have students think of this emerging quality as a little sapling that can be watered and cared for until it grows into a tree.

- Have students write one goal. Ask this question: "If you could gain one new ability or improve one habit to be a better learner, what would it be?" Then have students frame the question in an "I can" affirmation as if the goal had already been met. Brainstorm specific external and internal influences that could help transform the future vision into achievable reality. Ask questions like, "What are some things that stop a statement from being true?" and "What are some times when this statement does feel true?" Although teachers may have presupposed ideas, be sure to let students decide their own goals and discover their own answers. Their insights will surprise you.

Any of these tools can be the foundation for a student-centered, personalized learning plan. Whatever system you use, make sure the whole school is using it at the same time. This will help adults and kids develop a shared vocabulary and move in the same direction. It works best to stick with one model for a whole semester or a whole year so that students have the chance to look back and reflect on what they learned. (Later you can try new models to keep things fresh.) Individual goals add purpose to education and create intentional behaviors, and individual reflection allows the student to build self-awareness and take ownership of their own choices.

Depending on the ability level of your students, your micro-school may have children who require a more in-depth, adult-guided learning plan. If it's within the scope of the school model, micro-schools can provide developmental tools for students with more intense ADHD and autism, or students who are further behind in their social/emotional development. For example, a student might be dealing with inappropriate outbursts when frustrated. Instead of punishing the student for outbursts or rewarding them for staying calm, look at the reason behind the outburst and the reason behind the frustration. Then provide a "tool kit" that the student can access when they are frustrated. If the student is frustrated because they're getting stuck on schoolwork, coach them ahead of time on how they can ask teachers for help, or create a buddy system where another student agrees to be available to give assistance. This ties back into the principle of inclusion and gives the other students the chance to practice both compassion and leadership.

As we work with various kinds of students, our LEADPrep teaching team has slowly discovered that developmental approaches are the most effective and humane way to deal with many learning and behavior issues. We are becoming more versed in looking at the "why" behind a behavior (students do

"I like how diverse the learning is."
—SHANE, 9TH GRADE

many different things to make sense of their worlds and reduce anxiety!) and consult with occupational therapists, behaviorists, counselors, and speech therapists. As your micro-school responds to student needs, your team will collect their own set of tools for dealing with a diverse student population.

Foster 21st Century Skills. How can we equip students for life in the future? What skills will they need to learn in order to find success in college and the workforce? To answer these questions, educators and researchers have been proposing various lists of 21st Century Skills[76], including things like collaboration, communication, creativity, and caring. Some lists include things like flexibility, initiative, and grit. Others include cultural literacy and media literacy. These 21st century skills include the soft skills needed to interact with colleagues and the out-of-box skills needed to design new solutions. They do not fall within a single subject area, so all teachers must be intentional about infusing the development of 21st century skills into their classroom. Many employers are now insisting on these skills, and students need to practice them in high school to be able to transfer them to university projects and on-the-job expectations. If you choose to teach 21st Century Skills at your micro-school, come up with your own list based on your mission statement and the desired educational outcomes. Fortunately, personalized learning and project-based learning are a great context for coaching students in these new ways of thinking.

> "I like that it is really personalized. I get the attention that I need."
> —KYLE, 7TH GRADE

These are just a few of the many educational strategies you can use in your micro-school. You won't get an exact combination of structure and strategies the first time around, and that's okay. Micro-schools have flexibility. A nimble design process allows for new ideas and speedy adjustments. However, as you open your micro-school, be sure to stick with your original set of ideas for at least the first semester. You'll want to give yourself at least half a year to settle in before you start tweaking things. Once your student body stabilizes and new resources come your way, you can adapt your model and strategies to better serve your students. As your school and students grow, you'll start finding the "sweet spots" that make your school unique and special.

Families want relief. They want to see their children learning and thriving. Always bring the focus back to the students and show how each tool you select will benefit and instruct them. Keeping

> "Thank you from the bottom of my heart for helping my son rediscover how bright and capable he is. Even more important than grades on paper, our son is extremely proud of himself. The entire LEADPrep staff has brought the twinkle back to our boy's eyes. Thank you."
> —MELANIE AND DAVE, PARENTS OF A HIGH SCHOOL SON

student impact in mind, transform your general mission into specific goals. As you are filling out the education section in your Action Plan, list one or two structural ideas on which you will focus, and then three or four learning strategies you will use. List the impact you plan to make and how you choose to measure success.

Here's an example of how this plays out in our own school. Civics is a mandatory class in all high schools. At conventional schools, civics may mean passively absorbing information about far-off government structures. Because our mission statement includes the phrase "*courageous* as local and global leaders," our civics class is about guiding and equipping students actively to make a difference in their own society. Together we develop mindful observation skills, empathy, goal setting, and problem solving—building the leadership skills that are we prioritized in our LEADPrep mission.

After goal setting at the personal level for the first three quarters of the year, our civics students were challenged to identify a need relating to a passion of theirs and create a positive impact in the community.

Sixth-grade Ciara created a campaign to save Greyhound dogs. Her question was, "How might I, as a pet owner in Kirkland, improve other animals' lives to give them the best life possible?" From that question she created a project that brought awareness to shelters and created beautiful hand-drawn posters. Her action steps were to make and place posters in high traffic areas to encourage families to take in Greyhound dogs as rescue pets. Eleventh-grade Xander articulated his own driving question: "How might I, an 18-year-old 'kid,' contact a government official, so that we can help spread the word of positive change to youth in today's world in order to lead to more acceptance to stop bullying?" Working from this personal idea, he crafted a well-designed project proposal and a letter campaign to a government official.

"It's great to have the freedom to choose a lot of your own activities."

—ARLIE, 9TH GRADE

Reflecting, setting goals, and taking action had started at the beginning of the year when students were asked to review a list of ten habits of success. As the class conversation unpacked concepts such as optimism and purpose, students began to engage. The teacher frequently checked-in on the students' progress, framing questions through the lens of social/emotional learning: "How could grit help your group right now?" "How can we use social intelligence to address this concern?" Words like grit and social intelligence can seem overly abstract when taken out of context, but when they are applied to real-life situations, students are able to discover their true meaning.

Over the course of the year, students selected two goals and noted their progress. As the civics teacher noted, "It's amazing how much clarity students are gaining as they take ownership for their goals." Reflection, referencing an innovative rubric, and goal setting all contributed to student agency. Leadership bubbled up naturally out of kids' interests. And students courageously effected a real impact within the local community, thus fulfilling the mission statement of LEADPrep.

THREE TASKS TO DO NOW

1. Working backward from the mission statement, have a team discussion about the focal points of your micro-school. Pick two or three options from the structure and strategies list above or create your own components. Consider the idea of weaving them into a revised version of your mission statement.

2. Add these varied parts of your particular model into your marketing and blogs. Be determined to make these components foundational in your micro-school. Let prospective parents know all the things that make your school unique and special.

3. Recruit one or more of your tribe members to become an expert on each of these components. Have them research existing schools that are using these strategies. Sharing the labor is vital because research, marketing, and getting ready to open should all be happening simultaneously. Divide and conquer!

STEP 6

GET CLEAR AND CREATIVE
ON RESOURCES

*It's not about money or connections. It's the willingness
to outwork and outlearn everyone when it comes
to your business. And if it fails, you learn from
what happened and do a better job next time.*

—Mark Cuban

GOAL

Figure out what funding your micro-school requires
to operate and find creative ways to meet or reduce those costs.

CHALLENGE

THE FIRST CHALLENGE of every micro-school is self-sufficiency. In the past
three years, I've coached several other groups that wanted to start a school,
and I've also spoken with educational innovators around the United States.
I've talked to a lot of potential school founders who had great ideas for a
school but couldn't turn their dream into a reality. Why? Because they were

waiting for money to magically appear. Their plan relied on an outside funding source. I've seen educators put off their dream and waste years courting the money. Then, after all that, the funding didn't pan out, or there was a conflict or misunderstanding over how much or how it would come, or the funding didn't last, or there were too many strings attached. In all likelihood, looking outside of your school for funding is a pipe dream. Don't wait around for a fairy godmother to wave the magic wand of donated funds.

The second challenge is to stay within your budget. Just like we help young adults learn to look at their earnings and only purchase what they can afford, we need to get creative and possibly downsize our initial vision of our micro-school to meet the reality of the funds we have.

SOLUTION

Work out your financial plan (Appendix G). Crunch the numbers. Look at how much money you need coming in versus how much money will be going out (your revenues and expenses). If all the numbers start freaking you out, find someone with a solid accountant-type personality to help with this work. Next, it's time to get thrifty! Brainstorm ideas creatively to reduce those expenses and do things on the cheap.

Crunching Numbers. Your goal here is to find the space, students, teachers, and funding to make the school a reality. Pull out Appendix G, our Expense and Revenue Template. Your costs will determine what tuition you charge. Let's begin with taking a comprehensive look at your expenses.

Start-up Costs. Advertising is required to get the word out. You can get a lot of mileage out of social media, but you'll definitely need a website for your online presence. Look at the costs to purchase your domain and build your website. You will also need print media, even if it is just signs hung in coffee shops. Are you borrowing money? If so, at what cost or interest rate? Does the school facility include furniture? Even if it does, chances are you will need computers, whiteboards, and other school-specific furniture. Supplies will be needed before you open, so figure out the costs of textbooks, software, and other classroom materials.

There are also costs for the intangibles. Find out if you will need to make a deposit on the space. Look into insurance for your school. Be sure to factor in all the affiliation costs for incorporation, licenses, memberships, and permits.

Monthly Operational Costs. The largest expense, up to half of your budget, will be directed toward salaries. Not only do you need to pay your employees, you will also need to plan for a number of related state and federal payroll costs. Monthly rent is the other big expense to take into account. On a smaller scale,

> "Thank you, Maureen, for all the great work and effort you and the rest of the teachers provided to our son. It made a huge difference, and for the first time, he really enjoyed going to school."
>
> —AHMED, FATHER OF A HIGH SCHOOL SON

you may have utility fees and technology expenses such as wi-fi costs, computer support and maintenance, and website hosting to keep in mind.

Note these expenses in Appendix G. Now you're ready to polish up your overall financial plan. Don't skip this critical step! Writing a financial plan will make sure your micro-school funding needs are covered. You just determined your expenses. Now what funding do you need to start up and then stay operational? Be realistic. If you need $30,000 to open your doors and $10,000 a month for the ten months of your school year, you need to generate $130,000 with a cushion. So round up to $150,000 needed. Divide this by your number of students. For ten students, tuition would need to be $15,000. Your basic financial plan is now drafted.

For nonprofit schools, knowing (and keeping excellent records of) the financial details of your micro-school is incredibly important. The IRS and public demand transparency about where donations are going. Get outside help, if needed, to create a thorough, accurate financial plan. Hire a bookkeeper or find one who will donate time or work at a discounted rate for a good cause. Find out if one of your parents has accounting or bookkeeping experience and get them on board right from the start. Maybe someone has an aunt or an uncle or a parent who does everyone's taxes and loves to talk about 401Ks. If you don't already have a number cruncher in your tribe, find one now. Have them sit down with you and show you how to make your plan as clear and comprehensive as possible.

Now it's time to get creative. Don't count on a handout! Instead, look at resources through the lens of possibility. Depending on your school's basic affiliation, you'll be able to get creative in different ways.

For a public charter or school-within-a-school model (SWAS), you often need to collaborate at the school or district level. Public funds exist, but sometimes it takes ingenuity to access them. When I opened a school-within-a-school, this meant collaborating with an equally determined and innovative teacher at the other high school in the district. Together we wrote and received a federal grant to create an innovative option for high school students at risk of dropping out. I then worked closely with my school administrator to maximize school resources. By adding a business class into our SWAS, we were able to get extra vocational funding and lower class-size requirements. When we added a federal reading support component into the SWAS, we received even more funding, a special teacher, and a teaching assistant. By thinking outside of the box, we accessed the money we needed with the added bonus of having a more meaningful, in-depth curriculum.

For a private school, there are other affiliations and partnerships that can lead to more funding options. One possibility is working with a larger nonprofit organization, like a synagogue, mosque, church, or community center. There are communities all around the country that are concerned about at-risk kids in their neighborhood. People want to help, but they don't know how. If your parent tribe originally started within a specific religious community, or if your town has a large church that's looking to make a difference in the world, be sure to check in with the leadership to see if a financial partnership is an option. Even a small donation would be helpful, or assistance with fundraising to cover start-up costs. Synagogues, mosques, and churches may also have classroom space that they might be willing to donate. Another partnership idea is working with an alternative elementary school that wants to add a middle school or high school option. Remember, if you have a clear action plan already set in place, with well-written financial details, other organizations will be far more likely to take you seriously.

Reducing Costs. Now let's brainstorm a few hacks for saving money. What will our operating costs be? How can we keep our operational costs to a minimum? Here in Seattle, we like to say we're crunchy (like crunchy granola). We may not be glamorous, but we find resources within our community and we find ways to reduce, reuse, and recycle. One micro-school in Seattle has students make artwork and sculptures out of random cardboard and trash items people bring in. Not only is this creative, it lowers the cost of school supplies. The school calls it "scrounge art." Crunchy, right? And the kids absolutely love it. For the first year, you can cut costs and your whole micro-school can be a form of "scrounge art."

If you need computers, talk to your local e-waste recyclers. They have a ton of old laptops and computer parts and they can help you put together cheap web browsing computers for online learning. (Many e-waste recycling companies are nonprofits, so they're also a great place for your techy kids to volunteer.) For copy costs, check out services like Ricoh, which charge a fraction of what the local copy centers charge, or perhaps a parent can do printing at their workplace. Want to get thrifty on rental space? I know of one micro-school that roved around the neighborhood for its entire first year. With a community-centered focus, this school met at a YMCA teen space a few days a week and then met in a public library, filling in other days with field trips and service outings. I know of schools that have started in theater lobbies, masonic lodges, and even people's dining rooms. Are you looking for discounts on furniture? Get on the mailing list for your local school district's bi-annual surplus sales. Colleges also have furniture surplus sales. Yes, at LEADPrep this has meant standing in a parking lot using a screwdriver to take the legs off of multiple $5.00 tables in order to squeeze them in our SUV, but we are not complaining! Office supplies? Our local community college business office gave us a variety of materials from their spring cleaning. Books for a school library? Our local Half-Price Books boxes up teen books to sell in bulk, and just $10 buys over 20 books. Craigslist, Facebook Marketplace, yard sales, and thrift stores are also our friends as we cut costs.

"When my kid was at public school, I wasted so much time and energy advocating for him and dealing with his stress levels. Now that school is easier, I have more time to volunteer—and volunteering is more fun."
—KESTER, MOTHER OF A MIDDLE SCHOOL SON

One of the tricky things about starting a new school is that you find yourself stuck in a circular pattern of needs and results. The logic goes like this: We need students to sign up so we can get tuition. We need tuition so we can pay for teachers and space. We need teachers and space before we can get students to sign up. You need what you don't yet have in order to get what you need.

So, how do we keep from getting stuck? Well, let's think about how the human body walks forward. Walking is actually a series of controlled falls. When you walk, you tip your body forward and then put a foot out to catch yourself. You have to lean forward and trust that your weight will be held up by the next step, and the next. Of course, that motion seems intuitive now, but everyone has to learn how to walk. When you watch a toddler who's just taking their first steps, you realize how challenging it is at the beginning. Your micro-school is just learning how to walk forward, and it feels like a huge leap of faith.

Therefore, find people who get it. Find parents and volunteers who are willing to hold the toddler's hand while it starts to stumble forward. As I've mentioned a few times in this book, look for retirees who want to give back to the community, or college students and new grads who are willing to work for experience with a lower salary and grow with your school. A few committed, energetic stay-at-home parents (or parents with flexible schedules) can provide critical man-hours for keeping expenses down. At LEADPrep, one of our most committed volunteers likes to say, "Helping at school is a lot of work, but it's still way easier than homeschooling would be!" Some parents will see the school as something they are passively *buying* for their child, and some parents will see the school as something they are actively *creating* for their child. The creators are the ones who will help your school move forward. Some schools have an official co-op model, where costs are reduced by every parent officially chipping in and taking on an important job. Even if your micro-school is not technically a co-op, it should definitely function like one in the first two or three years.

When you tap into your tribe of passionate collaborators, you'll start to see funding in a broader sense; it's about accessing community resources. For example, say you are searching for a location, perhaps underutilized during school hours, that could be borrowed or rented inexpensively. If you ask 20 adults to help you search, and each adult follows up on three leads, that's 60 different possibilities! And some of them will be weird ones you had never thought of before, like the guy who knows another guy who runs a small business and has a conference room he'd be happy to share with you. When you throw things out to the community, problems begin to have many possible solutions. Sometimes networking is far more valuable than actual cash.

"We have been thrilled with our decision. The things we were concerned about (a smaller school, missing out on dances, etc.) turned out to be non-issues. She now has time for extracurricular activities, and the homework battle is gone. It's been a great experience and I cannot express enough what an impact the school has had on our family."

—KIM, MOTHER OF A HIGH SCHOOL DAUGHTER

We have a grand tradition of barn raising and community support in the United States. Historically, neighbors would get together to help build a barn, harvest a crop, or sew a quilt. In modern times, there are many 5K runs or "X-a-thons" to support a myriad of causes. Ordinary people love to help, you just have to ask. Let a bunch of small generosities add up to a patchwork quilt of funding. Of course, if you do get a big donor to support your school, that would be very welcome, but don't lose track of your dream by waiting around for easy money. I want your micro-school to have a plan that doesn't rely on outside funding, so you can open your doors as fast as possible and start serving the kids who really need your help.

THREE TASKS TO DO RIGHT NOW

1. Talk to other micro-schools (there is a list at MicroSchoolCoalition. com) and small business owners. What costs did they have as a start-up and for the first year? What words of wisdom can they offer? Resources they can share?

2. Crunch the numbers—expenses and revenues. While it may seem daunting, having this bottom line of finances adds clarity and frees you up to align your vision with financial reality. Put your numbers into your Action Plan (Appendix A, Part 6).

3. Ask for what you need. When you put out the intention to open your micro-school, be bold. Ask for folks to help you find the right space, teachers, and students. Ask for discounts. Ask for partnerships. Ask for trades. Every time you ask, you are expanding your network and your potential tribe. If someone says no, you haven't lost anything. If someone says yes, you're that much closer to helping your amazing students.

STEP 7

OPEN YOUR DOORS

Excellence is the result of caring more than others
think is wise, risking more than others think is safe,
dreaming more than others think is practical, and
expecting more than others think is possible.

—Howard Schultz

GOAL

Open a micro-school in a year or less!
The sooner your micro-school opens, the sooner you will
provide relief to the students who are struggling today.

CHALLENGE

ALTHOUGH MANY PEOPLE are frustrated, very few are stepping forward with the resources and willpower to make micro-schools happen. Four mental blocks stand in the way: hesitancy, discouragement, fear of failure, and distraction. Your challenge is to face these mental blocks and overcome them. In order to overcome them, you must bring your school out of the mental, theoretical realm and firmly into the physical dimensions of time and space. We have to make this school a reality!

SOLUTION

Confront the four mental blocks directly. Analyze your excuses and get the support you need to succeed. Working backwards from your opening date, fill out a month-by-month timeline for opening your micro-school in your Action Plan. Finally, finish your plan by writing an Executive Summary (Appendix I).

So, what's stopping you from opening a micro-school? Let's imagine that you already have the urge and the vision to create a new educational option. You see the need, you care about kids, and you believe deeply in alternative education. And, yet, something is still standing in your way. What? Chances are, you're experiencing a mental block—a worry or an excuse that hasn't yet been confronted and resolved. I've spoken with a lot of micro-school founders, as well as many people who wanted to start micro-schools but got stuck. In my experience, they all experienced one of the following four blocks:

Hesitancy. To put it simply, hesitancy means not feeling ready to start. With most great ventures, it's common not to feel completely ready before launching. Take parenting, for example. Is any first-time mom or dad ever truly "ready" to be a parent? No matter how many books you've read or classes you've taken or nieces and nephews you've held, nothing can prepare you for that moment when you are entirely responsible for your own child's well-being. When it comes to parenting, everyone has to figure it out as they go along. In fact, most new skills can only be learned by doing. Whether it's parenting, driving a car, throwing a clay pot on a wheel, or creating a micro-school, you'll never learn how until you jump in and give it a try.

Many people who dream of starting a micro-school may feel like they are not fully equipped. They're worried that they don't have the right skill set, background, or temperament. Well, guess what? Nobody has everything they need to start a micro-school. Everyone has to rely on their partners, team members, community, and tribe to provide the pieces they are missing. Humans aren't meant to be self-sufficient loners; we're meant to be in supportive relationships. Knowing your flaws and weaknesses is a good thing because it means you can humbly seek help and deeply appreciate your fellow workers.

If you're hesitant about your abilities, find co-workers with complementary skills. As I mentioned before, if you're a dreamer and a visionary, find your practical, level-headed counterpart. Just because they don't articulate themselves quite as poetically doesn't mean they don't care just as deeply. Or, maybe you're a practical, grounded person, but you're having a hard time selling your ideas. In that case look for your extroverted, passionate counterpart. You provide the solutions and structure; they provide the personal connections and marketing. If you're an educator, find your business person. If you're a business person, find your educator. If you've got both of those qualities covered, look for cheerful, flexible parents who can help check things off your to-do list. Whatever your strengths and weaknesses are, this is not a solo flight. Hesitancy may just signify that you need to strengthen your team.

Regardless of how equipped or supported you are, here is the plain truth: every new venture requires a leap of faith. You do as much market research as you can, but there will never be a moment when you are 100% certain. Fear of the unknown is a powerful motivator. Yet certainty is always an illusion, because no one can perfectly predict the future. There will always be surprises or complications that come up, and that's part of the growth process. At the end of the day, you're creating this school for your students and your students only. Those kids need you. Keep your eyes fixed on that purpose and take a step into the unknown.

> "I used to come home crying every day and now I come home happy and proud of my success. I feel motivated, confident, and empowered because at LEADPrep I have the support and care to succeed."
> —AUDREY, 9TH GRADE

Discouragement. Real talk: creating a micro-school is hard. It's difficult to put all the pieces together. There will be days when it feels really, really challenging. You will have some days or weeks when you think, "This might be too hard for me!" It's totally okay to feel this way! Let me repeat: feeling challenged is okay. You can do hard things.

Starting a micro-school is difficult, but it's worthwhile; and anything worthwhile is difficult at times. Unfortunately, big businesses have made trillions of dollars by racing to bring us things quickly and more easily: one-click ordering, single-day shipping, ready-made food, instant entertainment. Being coddled by a culture of "quick and easy" means we don't get a chance to practice patience and grit. Our grandparents and great-grandparents had to pump their own water out of a well and wait for a letter in the mail to hear from loved ones. They had to work hard and play the long game. Generations before us had to fight for religious freedom, workers' rights, civil rights, and children's rights. Do we want to live in a world where people just accept whatever big business and big government decide to give us? Or are we going to organize at the grassroots level and demand change? If we want a new future for our students, it's going to require some old-fashioned grit and perseverance.

When you're feeling discouraged, reframe that feeling. In your mind, let it be a signal that you're actually doing something worthwhile. Doing something challenging means you are living your life with purpose and direction. It means you've found your own growth edges, and you're learning and stretching yourself, practicing resilience. At LEADPrep, we teach project-based learning because we've found that kids learn best when they are faced with real problems that require curiosity and innovative thinking. When a student gets stuck, we encourage them to ask new questions. So, if you're stuck on something hard, ask yourself these questions: *How can I break this large task down into smaller steps? What's my biggest priority right now? Is there another path I could take to achieve the same goal? Are there other tools or resources I haven't tried yet? Am I seeing only the bad things and not the good things? Who is available to help me?* Rely on your tribe to brainstorm solutions. As we've already discussed, working within a team and a community creates a much wider range of creative possibilities. Always ask boldly for suggestions and assistance.

> "I used to not like school, and now I do like it. I feel like I'm successful, because at LEADPrep I'm hard at work."
>
> —BRIAN, 9TH GRADE

Some steps along your journey are going to be genuinely disappointing. People mean well but sometimes let you down. Plans fall through and have to be remade. Mistakes are inevitable. In the face of these challenges, discouragement does not deserve any of your attention. Put on your Teflon-coated superhero cape and push past the hard times with your eye on the prize.

One of the best ways to stay encouraged is to practice celebration. Be intentional about celebrating milestones with your tribe. Did you get your first family enrolled? Wonderful! Pop some bubbly and have a happy-dance moment with your team. Find a good location? Post the success on social media. See your micro-school the same way you want to see your students, full of hope and possibilities. Encourage each other and let abundance and positivity lead you forward into the future.

Fear of Failing. It's often stated that 50% of small businesses fail in the first two years. That is definitely an intimidating statistic, but let's break it down a little bit. The term "small business" is referring to for-profit businesses. That includes notoriously unstable start-ups like restaurants, construction companies, and boutique storefronts. If you look only at nonprofit businesses, the survival rate is much, much higher: about 84%[77] of nonprofits will survive their first five years. According to the Urban Institute's National Center for Charitable Statistics, financial donations to nonprofit organizations (including private schools) increased 11.5 percent from 2007-2017, adjusting for inflation. Over 25% of Americans regularly volunteer for nonprofit organizations, and volunteers donate an average of 2.86 hours a day. Wow! Isn't that encouraging? People want to give, and they want to help.

Still worried? Just keep confronting the fear head-on. The Small Business Association[78] lists these top five reasons why a small business might fail: no market need, lack of capital, not the right team, competition, and pricing. Let's address each of these concerns now:

Market Need. There is a huge market need for innovative, personalized education, as we parents of colorful mismatched kids very well know. For micro-schools, the problem isn't market need so much as market visibility. Engaging parents and getting the word out (Steps 4 and 5) are key steps to success in this area.

Lack of Capital. This is probably the most specific challenge for micro-schools. Your tribe will have to pool resources and make sacrifices to fund the initial phase of the school. Tuition will become your primary revenue stream. Again, marketing to get students and resources is critical. This process is much easier when you start with a tribe of committed parents who are all interested in signing up their child.

Not the Right Team. With limited funding, this is a tricky one, as mentioned in Step 3. You have to find an innovative educator, who is flexible and hardworking, and with hope won't need the benefits package of a larger company. This must be someone with a proven track record of stability and determination, and someone who willingly steps into the role of trailblazer for your start-up phase.

Steve Hogan is the founder of Tech-Rx, a consulting firm that coaches stumbling tech start-ups. According to Hogan, the biggest red flag for failure is when a founder tries to do it alone. Businesses that begin with a partnership are much more likely to succeed[79]. I know I've been repeating this again and again, but the best way to start a micro-school is with a strong tribe and a dual leadership model. Find someone with a complementary skill set and work together. Modern rugged individualism is silly and ineffective compared to the strength found in teamwork. Almost every ancient culture around the world has a proverb about how "sticks in a bundle are not easily broken."

Competition. What a lack of options we have for our wonderful kids! The market is wide open with limited competition. The real problem is that we are competing with old ideas that have become entrenched beliefs. One of our prospective parents said they loved LEADPrep and they knew their child would thrive in the caring, hands-on setting. But they couldn't let go of the idea that their quiet, introverted child needed to have football games, dances, and pep rallies. The parent had loved these things as a teen. So, they were going to continue with high school and outside tutoring and therapy to help make high school work for their child. It can be hard for some parents to acknowledge that their child will have an entirely different set of experiences than their own teen years. It's also important to remember that schools are NOT in competition with each other. Students who are attending private schools and home schools are still allowed to participate in public school clubs, electives, and sports. Every educator wants to see a child succeed. The more options there are, the more likely it is that a student will find the right school for their learning style.

Pricing. With a little local market research, you can see what other private schools charge and get a sense of the pricing that is feasible. Start on the low side, since families are taking a risk on something untried. Perhaps a 50% tuition discount for folks joining the first year? A discount for siblings? Talk to Rotary clubs and religious groups to see if they would be willing to sponsor a student. If you're worried about economic diversity, plan next year's budget with scholarships in mind. Check your state's rules about vouchers and education savings accounts. Go back to Step 6 and get qualified financial advice if necessary.

If you're still afraid of failing, ask yourself this final question: *How do we define success and failure?* If you run a school for one year only, is that a waste of time? I am here to tell you that for students who are depressed, anxious, bullied, or developing a negative self-image, even one single year can make a difference. These kids need a supportive environment with adults who are caring and really trying to understand them. Our precious tweens and teens are tender and impressionable. They will carry their memories of junior high and high school for the rest of their lives. A single year of support, care, and understanding can redirect a student's trajectory forever. So yes, one year of running a micro-school can be infinitely valuable to our kids and is already a success to be celebrated.

Suppose your micro-school stays open for seven years. That's enough time to see a whole classroom full of kids grow up from age 11 to age 18. What a triumph! If your micro-school taught an average of 15 kids each year, for seven years that would be over 105 student-years of growth and improved well-being. That's an entire lifetime's worth of meaningful change accomplished in less than a decade. Even if your school closes after that, it has been a success for those specific students. If you're afraid of failing, remember that we are measuring success with a different yardstick. A true learning community does not measure its worth in money or prestige. Instead, we find our worth from helping individual children during the years they need us most.

> "Thank you for your unwavering support of our son at LEADPrep through his many ups and downs—never giving up on him and leading him to his high school diploma!"
>
> —DAVE AND DENISE, PARENTS OF A HIGH SCHOOL SON

Distraction. Also known as lack of follow-through, distraction is a mental block I see all the time in potential school founders. Although we love our sparkly, artistic, creative-idea folks, they aren't necessarily the ones who will do the heavy lifting needed during the first few years. We do need creativity, but we also need fierce tenacity. Of course, everyone has a different style of getting things done—some leaders are extroverted, and some are quiet. Some work with huge bursts of energy and some work at a steady pace. It doesn't matter what your working style is as long as you keep coming back to the job again and again. Make it as much a part of your life as eating and sleeping. Wake up every day and take a few steps to move your micro-school forward.

Distraction can also take the form of life getting in the way. Just like every job, starting a micro-school must be balanced with family obligations. When you begin creating your micro-school, make sure you have the support of your family before you start. During your start-up year, just like in every year, there will be a normal share of health crises, emergency calls, and holidays. But if your family believes in you, you'll have the support you need to return to the job. Family support can take the form of a spouse who can shoulder the income for a year while staying supportive of the hours you spend working on the micro-school. Maybe you have a parent or adult sibling who takes on some of your household or childcare duties. My adult daughter helps me as my trusted administrative assistant (or as we like to call it, the "everything else" coordinator). Perhaps you have a relative who is willing to lend or donate start-up money. Or maybe Grandma and Grandpa can take on Christmas planning and gift shopping this year to give you another month of steady focus. Don't be afraid to ask.

If you're worried about getting distracted, find accountability partners and moral support within your tribe and family. Let your children know about your latest project and ask them to cheer you on. The more people who know your vision, the better your chances are for success. You can create momentum and accountability. Tell everyone what you are doing and ask for their support and positive energy.

Another form of distraction is getting bogged down in the details. Keep your eye on the big picture and choose your battles wisely. If a small planning detail is giving you a ton of trouble, just remember that things won't be perfect right out of the gate. Maybe your location isn't right, or maybe your teaching systems aren't really settled. That's okay for now. Once you get off the ground, you'll have more bandwidth to analyze and edit your school model, and more perspective on what's actually needed. It's so much easier to tweak things after you get momentum. In this first year, you're giving everything your best guess, so don't get hung up on the small things.

I know of a talented, dynamic educator who started a micro-school with lots of momentum and big ideas. He hired two young, innovative teachers. In the school's first full year, this director had a difference of opinion with one of the teachers about the method she was using to teach arithmetic. This small issue ended up turning into an irreconcilable difference. Both teachers quit, and the school closed down. I can't help but think that if the director had been more flexible and not so determined to fight over a small detail, the school might have succeeded. Perhaps it would have been better for the director to move ahead with an imperfect math curriculum or teaching style, and plan on hiring a different teacher in a year or two. Instead, the disagreement became a distraction that derailed the whole school.

Don't turn a minor issue into a deal-breaker. If you're getting distracted by details or strong emotions, take a step back and look at the big picture. Talk to a trusted accountability partner who can give you perspective. Finally, think of the students—would they be better off if the school closed down? If it never opened in the first place? Even if your micro-school is imperfect or needs future adjustments, it will still be a place where our beautiful, mismatched outliers can find understanding and meaningful relationships.

All four of these mental blocks—hesitancy, discouragement, fear of failure, and distraction—can create excuses in our minds. Everyone has excuses (although we usually call them "reasons") for why they aren't pursuing their dreams. When you're talking out loud to other people, listen to your own excuses and see how they might flow from each kind of mental block. If your excuse is *I'm just not sure I'm up to the task*, then you're experiencing hesitancy. If you're thinking *I brought it up and someone told me it was a stupid idea*, then you're experiencing discouragement. If your brain keeps popping up thoughts like *oh gosh, no one's going to sign up and we're going to run out of money*, that's a sign that you're afraid of failure. If your excuse is *I would have done it except this, that, and the other thing happened*, then you're letting yourself get distracted.

Everyone experiences these mental blocks sometimes, but they don't have to stop you. Hesitation, discouragement, fear, and distraction can all be alleviated by building a strong community. Just like our kids, we need meaningful, trusting relationships to support us. Talk honestly about the things that are weighing you down and understand what is causing the blocks. Get the support you need. Don't let discomfort stop you—our children are waiting and the clock is ticking. Kids are falling through the cracks while we worry and don't join in creating a solution. It's time to commit.

Here is one of my favorite quotes about starting a great endeavor. Although it is often attributed to Goethe, it was actually written by the Scottish mountain climber and WWII POW veteran, William. H. Murray. He was a trailblazer who knew a thing or two about grit and determination. In speaking of his expedition to the Himalayas, he writes[80]:

> We had definitely committed ourselves and were halfway out of our ruts. We had put down our passage money—booked a sailing to Bombay. This may sound too simple, but is great in consequence. Until one is committed, there is hesitancy, the chance to draw back, always ineffectiveness...The moment one definitely commits oneself, then Providence moves, too. A whole stream of events issues from the decision, raising in one's favor all manner of unforeseen incidents, meetings, and material assistance, which no man could have dreamt would have come his way...Whatever you can do or dream you can, begin it. Boldness has genius, power and magic in it!

I have often felt that same power of Providence when I am working for the good of my students. Once you have determined your course, you will encounter all the people, resources, and serendipitous meetings that you need

"I used to be depressed and now I'm fine. I feel happy at school because at school it's fine. At school I get to have fun and that feels good."
—MOHAMMED, 9TH GRADE

to make your micro-school happen. It may not turn out exactly how you planned. In fact, it will probably turn out better than you even hoped.

Change will happen one micro-school at a time. It's going to happen when the homeschool co-op becomes a micro-school. It's going to happen when the large public high school adds a school-within-a-school. This is hard work that takes visionaries and action-oriented people, but together your tribe can accomplish this change. For our final step, turn to the timeline in your Action Plan. This timeline will consolidate information from the first six steps of your Action Plan. List each of your goals. For each goal, note the person responsible, intended outcomes, and desired date of completion. Spread out the tasks over a year, working backwards from when you plan to open your doors. This completed Action Plan is your roadmap to opening the doors of your micro-school within one year.

Why should you take a year? Well, it is possible to do it in slightly less time. If it is January and you want to open your doors in September, maybe you would be able to do it in eight months. If you have momentum, I have no doubt that you can push through challenges, but I do want to make sure you have access to the best resource of all: enough time. The seven steps listed in this book take time to complete. There will be various delays in the process. Maybe you will need extra time to find the right location, or to get through your state's private-approval steps. Maybe you will need a few months to research your teaching strategies, or to make the right hires. Yes, creating a micro-school takes hard work, but it also takes patience over time.

Without clear steps or enough time set aside, many enthusiastic educational innovators do not reverse engineer their plan. They miss out on the vital business development process and may be blindsided by unexpected complications. But, if you follow the seven steps carefully, you will have created your learning model, completed your market research, and drafted your Action Plan. This will put you in an excellent position for success. (If you want more information, Donorbox[81] has a succinct blog that further explains the steps of writing a business plan from a nonprofit perspective.)

There's no set formula for laying out your timeline. Depending on the resources available, it's going to look different for every micro-school. As I'm writing this book, I'm advising two micro-school founders who are working in completely different ways. One is a career educator who is opening a micro-school on a compressed schedule. Although his team missed their deadlines for state approval, they decided to open in the fall anyway because they had enough funding available. Their timeline this year involves finding a location and planning for next year's state deadlines. The other founder I'm coaching is a homeschool mom who already has a church space and a student population. She's a bit more cautious and has scheduled a timeline that is more than a year long. Both of these founders are doing a great job working with the resources they have available. There's no right or wrong way to make your timeline—you'll have to figure out what works best for you and your community.

"I used to hate Mondays for school,

And now they aren't as bad

I feel comfortably assisted

Because at LEADPrep I get more of what I need

At LEADPrep I get to work on my personalized classes and extracurriculars,

It's like killing two potatoes with one stone.

(I didn't want to use birds because that would be too violent.) Thank you!"

—DAKOTA, 11TH GRADE

Wrap-Up. You now have your mission-driven model, market research, and a comprehensive action plan. You are ready for one last step to turn your Action Plan into a professional business plan. It's time to write an executive summary and attach any needed appendices.

Executive Summary. While you need the detailed business plan, you'll also want to create a summary that introduces and sells your micro-school (use the outline provided in Appendix H). Be clear and concise. You are writing a single page, not a novel! Start with your mission and purpose. Then summarize your market analysis that proves an identifiable need and explain how your nonprofit will meet that need. The Executive Summary is written last, but would be placed at the start of your business plan. (See Appendix I for an example of my own Executive Summary for the Micro-School Coalition.)

Appendices. The last part of your business plan is to include an appendix of any extra document that is relevant: budget, list of board members, IRS status letter, balance sheets, and so forth. These are practical details that prove that you are reverse engineering your school and treating your vision like the real business it is.

Caring, innovative, and hardworking adults can form tribes of support; these tribes can collaborate to design a micro-school. The new micro-school can open within a year. If you're the parent of a tween or teen, I want you to know that it IS possible to create an educational option while your own children are still young enough to benefit directly from it. Do it for your kids. Do it for all of our kids.

Tom Vander Ark poses this possibility in Forbes[82], "What if you could start a school in six weeks instead of six years? What if you could launch a school for $50,000 rather than $50 million? What if you could test an innovation with 20 kids rather than 2,000?" This is the realm of possibility that exists for nimble, personalized micro-schools. Whether publicly or privately funded, micro-schools are needed by all communities as a ready option for their outlier students—the majority minority. Students of all kinds could have a myriad of choices, finding innovative schools that resonate with how they learn and what ignites their passions. There are so many colorful, mismatched, beloved children who need our help. Get clear on your Action Plan to make this possibility a reality.

Firmly **commit** to building your micro-school with **creativity** and **fierce tenacity**. Make it a goal to open your micro-school within a year, serving at least ten students.

THREE TASKS TO DO NOW

1. Set your goal. Envision your micro-school open within the next year.
2. Activate your tribe. Bring as many people on board as you can.
3. Start marketing your school. Write your executive summary and share it, and use your elevator speech whenever you can. Turn to the Micro-School Coalition if step-by-step support and being a part of a cohort is helpful. Make your plan public. When we speak our plans out loud and share them with others, they much more readily come to life.

What? You want more specifics? You want to know how our tribe followed these steps to fund, open, and run our micro-school, Leadership Preparatory Academy, now in operation for over six years? If you are bravely taking on this micro-school challenge, you deserve the personal story. Turn the page and read my True Confessions of a Micro-School Founder!

Part Three

HOW WE DID IT:

Opening LEADPrep's Doors to Serve Happy Colorful Mismatched Kids

OUR LEADPREP STORY

You may not always have a comfortable life and you will not always be able to solve all of the world's problems at once but don't ever underestimate the importance you can have because history has shown us that courage can be contagious and hope can take on a life of its own.

—Michelle Obama

IN 2009, I was a single-mom leading a 1,000-student private high school when my girls' educational worlds fell apart. A year earlier, after many years overseas, my daughters and I moved to Seattle. I had hoped it would offer some of the international feel with which my girls had grown up. Also, my family was spread throughout Eastern Washington, so Seattle seemed like a good fit. Instead, I ended up frustrated, alarmed, and overwhelmed. The international school model had worked for my girls for over a decade, yet it took eight models of high school to get my girls through their final four years. High school was so painful that I ended up helping one daughter graduate early just to be done.

During this tumultuous school journey, I began to get mad. Appalled by the struggles I faced finding high schools where my girls could thrive, I began to research. In Washington State, I discovered high dropout rates, rigid refusal to support varied options, like charter schools, and mandatory state testing that parents boycotted as pointless. I thought Seattle was supposed to be progressive Silicon Valley 2.0! *Where was the school that could have personalized just a little bit for each of my girls? What about the other kids who didn't have a parent/educator determined to get them across the finish line?* I ranted. At my church, my fellow prayer chaplains held space for this unfolding story. Gently, they posed the thought that maybe I, Maureen, was the person to rewrite the story and transform how a high school could look. Conflicted, I cried. The idea resonated deeply as a calling, but I knew it would be incredibly hard work. *Who was I to take on making a whole school?* I'd opened micro-schools twice before, but using someone else's funding and marketing. What did I know about the business of starting a business?

In January 2013, I had just returned from an interim principal position in Central America. One daughter, Jadrian, had recently graduated, and the other, Giana, was vehemently "done" with high school and resigned to finish her last year and a half in a dual-enrollment college program. I was tired of dreaming about my wish for my girls: a school small enough for each student to be seen, heard, and valued; a school where the focus is on the whole human and a community is created to support this holistic development; a school where teachers and parents create a tribe to support varied learning styles and overcome challenges together. Plenty of parents were angsting over the same problem. I didn't want to wallow. I wanted to fix this glaring injustice. It was time to channel my anger and hopes for our youth. In September 2013, Leadership Preparatory Academy (LEADPrep) opened its doors.

As a school leader and parent, I work hard to "walk my talk." Here I am walking the talk with you. I am that despairing parent we talked about in Part One. With fierce determination, I took the seven steps in Part Two and created LEADPrep, with no outside funding. Let me help you in your process of creating a micro-school by sharing how LEADPrep took the seven steps. For each step, I will share:

- The LEADPrep Approach
- Our Biggest Success
- Challenges We Faced
- What We Learned
- LEADPrep Action Plan Responses

My hope is that our LEADPrep journey will be a catalyst for you also to walk your talk and turn frustration into action. You may want to add reflections in your journal and notes in your Action Plan as you read our story and clarify your own vision. The Micro-School Coalition and I want to support you in opening *your* micro-school within the next year.

STEP 1

BEGIN WITH THE MISSION

These are difficult times for educators who believe that learning is worth pursuing for its own sake and that the chief purpose of school is the nurturing of students as whole human beings.

—Thomas Armstrong

TO TRANSFORM the high school experience, I started planning my microschool by reverse engineering. What end results and vision for learners did I have? What outcomes did I want to achieve? I wanted to be sure I was redesigning high school with learning in mind, and I definitely knew we didn't need more traditional schools. For Step 1, I will show you how LEADPrep turned its vision into a mission. Next, I'll address how I determined our learning model. It was fortunate that I had worked in various models around the globe. I was ready to steal from the best! I also wanted to avoid the nonsensical features that only seemed to cause pain and extinguish a child's love of learning and self-worth. LEADPrep would be a learning haven.

Before I talk about LEADPrep's journey, let me share two notes:

1. I have included some LEADPrep information here that is a reflection of our first few years, not just our planning phase.

2. Our school began as L & E Academy—Leadership and Entrepreneurship Academy. It is still the name of our nonprofit foundation but was too much of a mouthful. In Year Two, our students helped us redesign the name. So our school name is now L & E Academy Foundation, dba (doing business as) Leadership Preparatory Academy.

THE LEADPREP APPROACH TO MISSION

Guided by the vision of a relevant and kind high school experience with the latest innovations, I fleshed out my initial mission statement: "L & E Academy prepares students for academic excellence and success in their personal goals. L & E Academy strives to harnesses the power of a flexible learning environment and modern educational technology to serve students who seek an educational experience that is more than or different from a traditional high school."

Four considerations drove my planning. The first consideration was how I would blend the goal of a strong sense of caring community between students (as in my daughters' wonderful church youth group) with the flexibility I saw in online learning. I had recently run a public online school and loved the flexibility online learning provided. The second was my goal of offering maximum service-learning opportunities out in the community. Third was

---

Our Spanish teacher, Ale, marveled at our strong sense of kindness and community: "I have this great memory of visiting Marina Park in downtown Kirkland with all the kids and being by the lake with John (11th grade) and David (8th grade). It was a beautiful day in spring with the sun reflecting on the water.

We were all amazed by John's ability at skipping stones. David was trying and trying and the rocks would just hit the water and sink, no skipping at all. So John took on the job of teaching David, from selecting the stones, to how to throw them, the movement of the arm, the speed, and the 'hand tossing' in John's words.

By the end of it, David was able to do a triple skip! It was so powerful watching John putting effort into teaching his skills and the excitement of everybody with David's achievement."

---

supporting teens as leaders, creators, and entrepreneurs. Finally, I wanted student strengths to be celebrated, with interests and personal goals driving a personalized version of high school learning.

In Part Two, I asked you to answer four questions to shape your mission statement, so now I'll share the LEADPrep answers. These questions and answers guided my hopes of creating a new opportunity for our students. As I share our LEADPrep responses, I will be weaving the evolution of our school into the responses. If you have a similar vision for your school, I hope that seeing our process will allow you to streamline some of the earlier phases of your own design process. Here are the ways we answered the four guiding questions from Step 1.

What does the graduate of our school look like? Over the first few years, our board worked diligently to refine our student profile. What qualities did our profile list? As we were opening our doors, our profile included having students who were kind, actively engaged in learning, comfortable with learning through group projects, and willing to give back to their community to make a positive difference. Since micro-schools get to be nimble and responsive, our graduate profile continues to be refined.

Who will we serve? LEADPrep began as a high school. High school was where I had personally felt the pain as a mom. While raising my daughters, I had desperately sought a humane and innovative high school option. Our board and I were determined that our school be kind and intentionally inclusive. We were driven NOT to be another square-peg-round-hole mismatch for the students we enrolled. Although it was difficult to explain in a marketing pitch, we didn't want a simple label to pigeonhole us. Folks asked, "Are you a school for gifted?" "For autism?" They wanted to have a one-word descriptor for us. We saw that limiting, labeling focus as a major problem in the traditional education model. Who says the assembly-line approach with one slot for one group of kids, i.e., "This is the class for 15-year-olds to take their freshman English," is a valid way of grouping learners? We wanted to welcome individual learners, knowing we could group them in a more authentic way. So we determined that our school would be a microcosm of the population, rich with neurodiversity in learning needs and styles. We also wanted diversity of age, gender, socioeconomics, and race.

To create this safe learning community, we determined that we would not be able to support students who were non-compliant or had oppositional

---

A parent came to us at the end of our second year. She asked, "Will you help me? My daughter has a homeless friend named Claire who keeps being moved around. Claire wants stability and support for her senior year. We have her mother's permission for her to live with us. Can she come to LEAD-Prep?" Claire was a bright girl who had all her high school credits and was a hard worker. I looked at the situation through the lens of our mission. As a nonprofit, and not at capacity, it aligned for us to add Claire to our school. In my years of international service work, I learned from wise service organizations that we want people to be empowered and invested. We give a hand up, not a hand out. So I offered Claire tuition-free admission based on her completing 30 minutes of service back to the school daily. Claire agreed, and was a stellar student, holding down a job and attending school at the same time. Claire was a wonderful role model for our other students and received her diploma as one of our three graduates of LEADPrep in Year Three.

---

challenges. Twice we had students who were learning well for a few months but then became angrier and less compliant. In one case, the parents found a great school that had more structure for addressing defiant learners. The second time, with the student close to graduation, we provided a combination of direct instruction in the basement office of the church we were renting and tutoring from the local public library. Keeping a sense of sanctuary has been non-negotiable for our model. LEADPrep students learn by collaborating and building relationships. We were also clear that we could not take students with significant learning needs that required a highly specialized approach. During the admissions process, it can be hard to turn down a parent who is searching for the right fit for their unique child, but our micro-school can only provide the education for students who are able to work in small, project-based peer groups.

Per parent requests, our school added seventh and eighth grade half way through our first year and sixth grade the following year. Over time, we decided to be a two-campus micro-school at the request of our families struggling with Seattle's congested traffic. To know the total population of students well, this meant capping our enrollment at no more than 30 students on each campus. We still wanted to be one community, so we share teachers between campuses and have Friday service and expedition days as one larger group. This two-campus model has turned out to be a wonderful way to give students more scope to make friends and socialize.

How will we serve them? Because LEADPrep was small and not cookie-cutter, we knew we would be a multi-age school. Online flexibility was appealing and I had just served as the Kaplan online high school principal for 300+ students in Washington. But, to foster community and collaboration, and combat the growing isolation the digital world was breeding, we wanted to have all of our students present every day, talking to real people and building relationships. (We kept online flexibility with our high school math program.) As another part of our effort to build community and get to know students well, we eliminated the option of having part-time students who come and go during the week. However, we do make an exception to this rule for 11th and 12th grade students, so that we can offer them variety of community options to follow their interests and prepare for post-high school life. When answering the question of how we structure our school, our guiding light has always been a deep desire to meet and value students exactly where they are.

Another part of reverse engineering the learning model was to align LEAD-Prep's daily expectations with our overall vision. How do we want to serve students on a daily basis? We wanted to be welcoming and participatory. We also wanted mistakes to be an accepted part of the design and learning process. We celebrate and learn from mistakes, errors, and failed attempts. Academic mistakes are not punished or shamed; they get "re-dos." Students complete math test corrections for credit and to fill in learning gaps. They rework airplane designs when the plane doesn't fly. Our teachers model the important paradigm of making mistakes and then using the reworking process. In terms of behavioral mistakes, we use restorative justice. When a student does something that doesn't honor the community or its norms, the goal is to restore the sense of community, not punish the student. Again, mistakes are learning opportunities. Our model is set up for students to make amends and move on. No "Breakfast Club" detention punishments for us! Because we are a welcoming and caring community,

As part of our community-building strategy, our third week of every school year is a camping trip. I had known our brilliant and quirky new sixth grader, Cameron, for two weeks prior to this trip. Since students are screen-free for the week and Cameron was homesick, I loaned him my phone to talk to his mom. He talked to his mom and then went off with friends. Cameron's mom, Diana, then texts: "Check your email sent box." Much to my surprise I see a just-sent email to Diana: Dear Diana, This is Moreen. Cameron needs to go home. Please come get him." My super-smart new student had just hacked into my email! Diana and I laughed and agreed Cameron was definitely staying on the camping trip for the full week. Nice try, Cameron!

Having two campuses, 20 minutes apart, allows for deliberate placement of a student on a specific campus. When our Seattle campus was opening, we had a brilliant middle school boy, Scott, enrolled. He was a tech genius and so funny. I was quickly enamored by his irascible, can-do personality. His parents were involved volunteers and wonderful community members. However, we couldn't get Scott to focus and comply with our lesson plans. On our smaller Seattle campus, this created too much of a distraction for other kids. Both of our campuses use the same model and share many teachers, so we moved Scott to Kirkland, where the population had older students and a larger space. We hoped the larger space would give Scott more options for where to learn and how to manage noise levels.

Even with this change, we couldn't create an environment where Scott could settle in. We worked with great outside support and learned that Scott's sensory processing needs were not met by our collaborative model. Running out of options to support Scott, we sadly asked his family to find another school and recommended some 1:1 school options. As much as we want to, we don't get to be the right fit for each student.

However, this story had a happy ending. The specialist petitioned Scott's local school district to fund his 1:1 learning. We were able to join in the petition and provide information about the strategies Scott needed. The district is now funding Scott's special education program. A few months after the move to this school, Scott met with my favorite teacher and me for pizza and to hear about Scott's life after LEADPrep. The supportive relationship was still important to Scott and to us. We weren't the right educational fit, but we were happy to be a friendly stepping stone for this brilliant boy and his family.

---

most students look forward to their day at LEADPrep.

Screen time was the other daily operation question we carefully addressed. It is hard to feel seen and valued if other people are glued to screens. This screen fixation also hinders active participation. We became intentional about when students' Chromebooks would be available for use. For phones, we tried the honor system, but the temptation was just too great. We had to get tougher. Kids now deposit their phones in our "phone jail" (a hanging shoe holder with a labeled pocket for each student) at the start of class and the phones are locked in the office during class time. Also, phones don't come out until ten minutes into lunch. This policy is to encourage something that is becoming obsolete: small talk and face-to-face interaction at meal time. For some of our students this requires intentional adult modeling, so we sit down and interact with them at lunch time. We even have small talk question cards to help the flow of lunchtime conversations! Compared with previous generations, our screen-dependent society doesn't encourage body movement. Although some of our students love to play basketball or hacky sack, other students would be perfectly happy to gather around a screen for their breaks. We always make sure our movement-resistant kids are getting outside and walking around during at least one break during the day.

For LEADPrep to be successful, our desired outcomes must drive what and how we teach. Prospective parents needed to know the intended learning results and, as a school, we needed to be sure we were heading in this stated direction. Impact we were able to demonstrate included:

- Improved student attitude and willingness to learn through more school participation and less homework
- Introduction to (and increased skills in) real-world learning such as STEM and public speaking
- Engagement with the community through service and field trips
- Increased chance of graduation, with personalized learning plans, flexible pacing, and lots of adult coaching

What affiliations do we want? We chose four affiliations. When a school is small, new, and doesn't look like the traditional model, having affiliations can help sell the concept and create credibility. The first step for us was to become an approved private school in Washington State. We went to the Washington State Department of Education website[83] and completed the steps necessary to be on its public list of approved schools. This affiliation should be a priority in all micro-schools. State approval includes safety inspections by local health and fire departments. It addresses graduation requirements and hours of instruction. It forces schools to create a handbook and clarify their parameters. We completed this process for the May 1 deadline the spring before we opened our school. Parents look for affiliations and legitimacy when they are exploring school options. Published on the state website for approved private schools, LEADPrep had its first affiliation and a stamp of legitimacy.

The second affiliation for LEADPrep was registering to become a nonprofit organization. We submitted our articles of incorporation and bylaws to the IRS. Even though the IRS approval process can take over a year, having the application submitted and in process meant that we could declare ourselves a nonprofit, take advantage of any donations, and be able to provide the donor a nonprofit tax donation receipt.

Charlie came to us after having a bad experience in an all-boys' school early in his ninth grade year. After his difficulties, he suffered from school refusal and depression; he was unable to attend school for the rest of the year. He joined LEADPrep to try ninth grade again, and quickly made friends. However, school attendance was still a challenge. After long weekends and holidays, getting Charlie back into school was an uphill battle. One day at school, he started crying. He couldn't explain why. Two of his friends asked to take him upstairs for privacy. They stayed with him for the rest of the day. As adults, of course we were worried, but we chose to respect our students' ability to handle the situation. Later his friends explained that he had just had his heart broken by a girl. We were grateful that our school was a safe place for his feelings. When a fellow student is in distress, our community values kids showing kindness much more than kids sitting in class.

During our third semester of operation, LEADPrep hosted the regional AdvancEd accreditation team. By the end of our second school year, we were accredited by this agency, which is the same one that accredits many other private and public high schools in our community. This compliance with external standards and being evaluated by an accreditation team increased LEADPrep's credibility and made it easier for our credits to transfer to other secondary and post-secondary institutions. This was a major stamp of legitimacy because many prospective parents ask if we are accredited.

The final affiliation sought was to become a part of our regional independent school association, Northwest Association of Independent Schools (NWAIS). Independent schools can be a variety of sizes and models, but this affiliation tends to be the gold standard. Collegiality and professional development opportunities are additional benefits. That spring we became a subscriber school in NWAIS.

The final component of reverse engineering our learning model was to bring in the special resources to which we had access. A unique community creates a unique school. (More on this in Step 5.) Personally, I had experience being a member of a Toastmasters International public speaking club. I believe that leaders need to be able to express themselves verbally with confidence, so we added weekly Toastmaster meetings as a component of LEADPrep's curriculum. In our early days, we offered this at the end of Wednesdays (our neighborhood school district's early release day). Local students from other schools were welcome to join in. Of course, every community has access to different resources, so this process will look different for each school. Are you located next to a forest? Do you have a parent with experience helping students volunteer at the zoo? Don't miss out on adding in the special ingredients unique to your tribe. LEADPrep is still engaged in the ongoing process of weaving in parent and student interests.

OUR BIGGEST MISSION SUCCESS

Remaining true to a few core components has been LEADPrep's greatest strength as a micro-school. We created four pillars and have continued to build around them. The four pillars are Flip, STEM, Lead, and Bridge.

- **Flip:** Our classes are flipped to let students learn at school and eliminate unnecessary homework.
- **STEM:** Design thinking is an integral part of our curriculum, with hands-on projects based around science, technology, engineering, and mathematics.
- **Lead:** Leadership opportunities are given within project activities, among students, and in service to the community.
- **Bridge:** At LEADPrep, bridge means we smooth the transitions into and from our micro-school, aligning our strategies with each student's goals.

I want to elaborate on the bridge concept. When a prospective family expresses interest in LEADPrep, I send an introduction email to a few of our families with students who have a similar profile. Our parents are quick to pay forward the kindness they received when looking at LEADPrep. They offer to phone chat or meet for coffee to answer LEADPrep and other parenting questions. There's no gatekeeping, there's only gate-welcoming. We want a smooth and friendly transition into our school.

On the other end of the bridge, we help our students with their post-secondary plans. We take our high school students on various college visits. When some upperclassmen expressed interest in Western Washington University (a few hours north of us), one of our team (a recent Western grad) loaded them into the van and took them up for a tour. They had lunch with a friend of hers who ran a campus club. That same team member helps students test into, sign up for, and take an online English 101 class to experience the pace and rigor of college with our support during their 11th or 12th grade year. When

Here is my initial business card with highlights of the learning model of our fledgling micro-school. We used the image of a gear to denote our inclusion of STEM and wove in our blue and gold school colors. Welcoming and personalized were always top priorities of our school.

we provide this bridge to college and give assistance in dual-enrollment, students are encouraged to aim high. One of our seniors planned to attend beauty school, but working on English 101 at LEADPrep was a game changer. With new-found confidence, her trajectory was changed. She set her sights on a degree at a nearby community college.

At LEADPrep, we became clear on the *what* and *why* that defined our school. Our biggest success has been remaining true to that foundation: Flip, STEM, Lead, Bridge. These were pillars in 2008 and remain the same today.

CHALLENGES WE FACED WITH MISSION

One of the challenges we faced at LEADPrep was focusing our goals. At the beginning, the doors were wide open with possibility. I believe we found success by not having too many initial goals. We started with a narrow age group and added grades as demand rose. The structure of our different affiliations (state approved, nonprofit, AdvanceEd accredited, NWAIS member) helped us avoid the challenges of drifting in a sea of endless choices. Each affiliation came with certain requirements, which brought focus and created very specific to-do lists.

Another challenge we experienced in maintaining mission-driven focus was "too many cooks in the kitchen." When I was first starting a micro-school, it felt like everybody had a different idea of how I should run it. Some parents, peers, and community members had strong opinions about the work they thought I should do. Sadly, these suggestions were not usually accompanied by an offer actually to help with the work or funding. It was a constant challenge to filter the focused ideas from the distracting ideas. Throughout this process, I've learned to distinguish the offers of practical help from the offers of "free critique." From writing grants (which, by the way, is not an easy nor reliable funding source) to using favorite teaching strategies, these unfocused ideas can become quicksand. I'm glad I stuck with my original action plan without getting bogged down. Over the course of six years, LEADPrep has naturally made many adjustments, but they have been based on actual student needs and our experiences as educators on the ground. Fundamentally, we stuck to our basic, original ideas and teaching strategies, and that focus has created stability for our students.

Our students lead through service and form a deep connection to our local community through that service. Our Seattle campus is on Phinney Avenue. The Phinney Neighborhood Association reporter, Rylan Bauermeister, wrote about our students' leadership through service in *Helping Them Help*[84]:

There are two quotes we love to throw at our young folk like fish in Pike Place Market. The first is the old Gandhi quote: "Be the change you wish to see in the world." The second quote is "Kids are our future." We toss these lines at our puberty riddled, financially dependent, transportation limited kids. In a single phrase, we leverage an exceptional weight of responsibility combined with an insurmountably massive task and drop it directly on top of them. But what happens when instead of burdening them with philosophy, we give them an outlet? What happens if we give our youth the resources to get involved?

Maureen O'Shaughnessy is the founding executive director of Leadership Preparatory Academy, a grades 6-12 micro-school operating out of PNA's brick building. She had an answer for the question. "We see them gaining an awareness that they can make a difference to others at a developmental phase where it is normally all about them," she said, enthusiasm plain. "They look at others and know they can contribute. This knowledge is a central tenet of Leadership Prep, where Fridays are dedicated to 'experiential learning,' a concept that commonly includes community service or civic projects. Students are encouraged to engage with the world.

"It decreases anxiety," Maureen commented. "It makes them happier, gives them a purpose."

WHAT WE LEARNED ABOUT MISSION

To design a realistic mission statement, it is crucial to learn from decision makers who bring real-life experience to the design of your school. As I reflect on my decision to start LEADPrep, I realize I brought almost 30 years of educational background, graduate studies in alternative education and systems, and parenting two neurodiverse daughters. This real-life research informed many of my decisions. Because I worked with two international micro-schools, I knew how vital and fun it was to engage parents deeply in the school. My doctoral studies taught me the organic nature of systems theory and my research exposed me to the stories of many other educational innovators. Most importantly, as a mom, I knew what I had desperately wanted for both of my girls—for them to be seen, heard, and valued—to have their strengths mirrored back to them and for learning to be relevant and make sense. I wanted each of my girls to use that support as a springboard to being a positive force in the world. My real-life experience was vital. Taking that experience into my community, I then benefited from the help of many other wonderful parents and teachers. Our tribe created the synergy to hone and implement our school design. Together, we opened LEADPrep, and we are still keeping it open according to the original mission.

LEADPREP ACTION PLAN RESPONSES TO STEP 1

What is the vision and mission of our school? Our vision is to redesign the face of secondary education. Our present mission is: *At LEADPrep we foster an educational community that cultivates authentic voices and strengths. We empower students to be fearless in their individuality and also courageous as local and global leaders.*

What does a graduate from our school look like? LEADPrep graduates operate from their strengths. They are kind, mindful, and making a positive difference in the world. Their excellent interpersonal skills and ability to project manage is combined with an understanding of the interdisciplinary nature of learning. They are welcoming and inclusive.

How do we deliver education? We are an intentional community that delivers education in a face-to-face model. Lessons are flipped and project-based. Teachers are guides.

What is our learning impact? LEADPrep students become more comfortable with group work and conflict management. They learn self-awareness, self-regulation skills, and how to ask vital questions about the subjects they study. They are encouraged to bring their personal interests into their academic projects. A LEADPrep student is given opportunities to practice leadership within the school and community, helping them prepare for college, the workforce, and life.

What affiliations do we choose? LEADPrep is state-approved, nonprofit, AdvancEd accredited, and affiliated with the Northwest Association of Independent Schools.

Chances are our story has brought up questions or ideas. Take a moment to update your Action Plan or jot some thoughts in your journal. With the multitude of moving parts in the adventure of opening your micro-school, you will want to have a good system for keeping track of ideas and tasks.

STEP 2

RECRUIT ENERGETIC AND COMMITTED TRAILBLAZERS

The secret of change is to focus all of your energy,
not on fighting the old, but on building the new.

—Socrates

IN MY EXPERIENCE starting LEADPrep, the trickiest part was finding leaders who were willing to go along with our initial shoestring budget. Fortunately, I had the savings to be able to set aside my salary and donate my work for the first year. I can be an intense driving force when I have to be. I'm a high energy person—my daughter jokingly says I drink jet fuel for breakfast! I had been a school head, principal, and president. I knew a lot about education and school administration, but very little about managing a nonprofit small business.

Remember our note in Part Two encouraging a dual-leadership model to increase the chance of success? During our start-up phase, I was definitely seeking that business partnership. I had serious gaps to fill and was learning on the fly. I was willing to do the work but had a lot to learn and little time to learn it. Here's how LEADPrep found the business coaching we needed to get off the ground.

LEADPREP APPROACH TO BUSINESS LEADERSHIP

To begin, I crammed as many business-learning opportunities as possible into my eight months of planning. I reached out to the Small Business Association (SBA), which offered free classes and business mentors. I took advantage of both. The SBA provided me with a helpful business owner on the East Coast as a mentor; he and I had weekly video calls while I was crafting LEADPrep. I peppered many business owners and specialists with questions to aid my learning. Asking for help has always been one of my specialties.

I joined three local networking associations and watched how others were running and marketing their businesses. These groups also gave me a place to get the word out about my micro-school. Finally, the breakthrough came that I so desperately needed: one of my networking associates suggested that her husband, René, should be on our start-up board. Thankfully, he agreed! Having grown up in the Netherlands, René brought a progressive educational view to our team, along with a great deal of business experience from his leadership position at Microsoft. Another kind entrepreneur, Paul, agreed to be my inaugural board treasurer. The business savvy of René and Paul helped me get clear on the business of running a school. I am grateful for their generous help and shared belief in the value of innovative micro-schools.

A few months into planning this micro-school, I recruited a friend of mine who was the technology director from another Seattle private school. She worked on developing the STEM aspects of LEADPrep. I then recruited a mom who was active in robotics and homeschooling. The three of us became a collaborative tribe of educators, each teaching one-third of the classes. Together we stepped into the unknown. After five weeks, both of my collaborators resigned. Since we weren't paid the first year, the demands outweighed the benefits for the two of them. I didn't realize they both had seen this job as a career step and wanted the recognition for a new role. They hadn't understood how much work these new roles would actually require. To be honest, their resignation was a dark moment for me. Unfortunately, having people quit in the hard work start-up phase is not uncommon. Although it was difficult, the mishap added to my learning experience and also had a silver lining. Collaborating with these two other educators had given me a much-needed boost of confidence as I embarked on this daunting odyssey. It also made me realize how much I deeply desired a collaborative tribe of support for our learners, and it inspired me to seek out more of those relationships as I moved forward.

LEADPREP APPROACH TO EDUCATIONAL LEADERSHIP

For the first year, I was the main teacher. I want to emphasize the point that I had budgeted the school with the assumption that I would work this year without receiving a salary. It was rare for me to find teachers who could volunteer their time as I was doing. I paid all the teachers who joined later, except for our first innovative STEM teacher, James. His children had been able to attend a personalized school and he believed in our vision. He graciously donated two years of instruction, making sure the STEM pillar of LEADPrep was hands-on and creative. I believe that you will find one or two of these generous resource people once you step boldly down your path. Being brave, talking about my vision to everyone, and asking for help made the difference on my journey.

The second year, I posted the lead teacher position. A young English teacher substituting in a nearby school applied. I observed him teach in a large public high school. He was engaging and energetic. Then he came and taught a lesson for our students. He gamified the concepts, creating an interactive activity out of the lesson. The students and I really enjoyed his teaching style. He became my first full-time hire and our Year Two lead teacher. The remainder of the team were part-time specialists.

Our first STEM teacher, James, was a volunteer from my church. James is a creative, kind-hearted renaissance guy who had retired from a nearby tech megacompany. Being adaptable is an important trait for micro-school teachers, as James relates, "I got up early one day and downloaded an update to the robot software we were using. It broke all our programs! While I reported the bug to the vendor, I needed to come up with a new lesson plan in a couple of hours before school. I found my video game lesson was ready for prime time, and the kids enjoyed it so much we moved away from robots and programmed video games exclusively for months! The kids ended up working together on a game that went on an online marketplace, though it didn't make anyone rich. So my misfortune of breaking the robots by downloading an update at the last minute turned into good fortune for everyone who became 'professional' video game developers."

In this hiring process, we discovered a trend. Teachers with experience tended to lean on traditional top-down discipline, and to use conventional lecture and discussions as their primary teaching strategies. This was NOT redesigning learning; it was just applying the same ideas that had frustrated our learning outliers in conventional schools. We had far more success implementing our model when we hired newer teachers, who were still flexible and had not yet locked in on a teaching style. We needed teachers who would embrace our flipped classroom model and create projects for active student learning. We also needed a lead teacher who could "wear lots of hats," manage the daily operations, and be a welcoming, enthusiastic presence. Because we support the whole student, a LEADPrep teacher needs a holistic view of students, as is common in elementary schools or middle school advisory classes. We've learned how to recruit these ideal teachers and have provided them with lots of support and bandwidth for experimenting with their own innovative ideas. In our quest to create the school of the future, newer teachers have become our go-to teaching population.

Retention is another important aspect in maintaining an excellent teaching staff. If you have a great teacher, how can you hang on to them? At LEADPrep, we've done our best to address the salary and benefits package as well as the non-tangible support needs that keep teachers on our team. Over the first few years, we slowly moved from many part-time specialists to full-time hires. Then we increased our salary to match the state teacher's salary base pay. We added retirement and medical benefits in our fourth through seventh years of operation. Growing from that one full-time teacher in Years Two and Three, we are pleased to have eleven full-time teachers now, with several additional part-time teachers and consultants! The synergy of our educational team members is critical to our ongoing effort to innovate and hone our learning model.

Emotional support is more important than the salary and benefits. It can be lonely, hard work being an educational innovator. My doctoral dissertation included qualitative research (research based on histories and personal interviews) conducted with educational innovators in two cutting edge learning models: 21st Century Schools and the Foxfire Initiative. I researched the internal dilemmas that make innovation difficult to sustain. These wonderful educators, mostly in public schools, found educational innovation to be an isolating experience. Not only did other teachers and administrators not share their passion, there was often hostility from those with a more traditional perspective. Change threatens the status quo, and most people have a hardwired instinct to protect themselves from the new and the unknown. Colleagues were not always able to support innovation by their peers. This pushback, sometimes passive and other times aggressive, made some innovators step back. The innovators who found ways to get regular support persevered. They deliberately employed strategies to keep themselves encouraged: taking regular walks around Green Lake (a popular Seattle meeting place) with an innovation partner and sharing successes. Check-ins with other educators trying the same innovations also supported them. These social tools kept the stumbling blocks of loneliness and challenges at bay. As I planned LEADPrep, I created a Mastermind accountability group with two other church members designing small businesses. It was great to have weekly check-ins, prayers, and moral support. In my experience, an innovator has to be ready for some pushback. My supportive tribe members sometimes laugh about needing to spray ourselves with Teflon to let any naysayer comments roll off our backs. So far, it's working!

In my first assistant high school principal position in the mid-'90s, I had a wise mentoring principal, Steve. As he participated in union negotiations, he taught me a lesson that has stuck for over twenty years: "It's the dignity issues that matter." He explained that a pay increase isn't enough. If humans don't feel heard and valued on the daily "little" issues, a nice paycheck won't make everything fine. I embraced Steve's perspective while I served as planning principal for a new high school. Practicing this priority at LEADPrep helped me operate with deep respect for and attention to the dignity issues of our faculty and staff (and students, of course!).

Twenty-five years after my first conversation with Steve, I am still very intentional about respecting and supporting my existing team. I'm not a perfect manager, but I always try to ask myself these questions:

- Am I planning professional development days, aligned with their needs, in a thoughtful manner that builds inclusion?

- Am I creating regular team building activities to be sure we are a team and not a group of isolated individuals?

- Am I providing aides or support to allow teachers to focus on teaching?

- Am I serving as a buffer for external (sometimes parental) concerns, so that my teachers can focus on teaching?

- Am I responding promptly to teacher queries, texts, and resource requests?

- Am I protecting their out-of-school time? (This is tricky. I tend to have "great ideas" at weird hours. Often, I draft emails to send later. My team knows that sometimes they are copied on stuff in off hours but no replies are expected outside of school hours.)

- Am I listening to and acting on teacher ideas and concerns in a prompt and responsive manner?

- Am I feeding and "caffeinating" our teachers on planning days?

I know our team at LEADPrep goes above and beyond the call of duty in a multitude of ways. It's a priority for me to be intentional in showing my gratitude and respect, and to remember those dignity issues that make our school a fulfilling workplace for our staff members.

OUR BIGGEST HIRING SUCCESS

The quality of our team of teachers makes all of the difference. Over the past six years, there have been a wide variety of caring adults who have taught and mentored our LEADPrep students. The generosity from which they led—whether volunteering or earning less than other teaching jobs in the early days, or giving extra attention to a student in need—has set the tone of our school. I love the fact that we now have over ten teachers. Our team members have peers with whom to collaborate, celebrate, and commiserate. Having inspired teachers aligned with our mission and empowering our students in ever-unfolding wonderful ways is our biggest success story. They are building the trust, relationships, and care that lead to student success in a micro-school, and our entire LEADPrep community is deeply grateful.

HIRING CHALLENGES WE FACED

Setting the bar high on teacher qualifications while on a strict budget created a double challenge when launching our micro-school. In the beginning, I sometimes felt like there was a need to "settle" on someone willing to take on this challenge. If the fit didn't seem ideal, we would look to see what adjustments might make the match work. Or we decided to wait for a better option. We found that some teachers were a good enough fit for a one-year contract, and came to a mutual decision to part ways the following year.

Another challenge was finding teaching candidates with the pioneering, design-thinking mindset that start-ups need. Unlike larger schools, there is not an established program. Teachers don't rely on their peers to borrow content and lesson plans. For the first few years, our teachers needed to create curricula and refine systems while the school was still defining itself. Unless you thrive on the unexpected, this process can be intimidating. At LEADPrep, we ask our students to use the design process in their projects, and yet our new teachers haven't been trained in design thinking. Combine this steep learning curve with our project-based design model of teaching, and the result is a rigorous, authentic teaching challenge. We ask a great deal more of teachers than following a district-adopted curriculum. Our teachers need extra training to guide this student-led learning. There are no "right answers" in the back of some teacher guide book. But this challenge can also be an exhilarating adventure. If teachers love watching kids explore, then the process can be incredibly rewarding.

We consistently ask teachers to look through a student-led project lens and not to fall back on traditional lecturing. LEADPrep students are creating and the teachers are responding to this creative process with encouragement and assistance. Some teachers can't stretch in this way. Over the years, the LEADPrep hiring team has become more adept at describing this expectation, screening candidates, and training and supporting our new teachers so that they can create and manage student-led, inclusive learning.

Jacob, our English teacher, shares, "Whenever I find myself stressing out about the minutiae of lesson planning, or getting annoyed that things aren't happening the way I want them to, I remember that time we were having a faculty meeting and a parent came in and told us, through tears, how thankful she was that we were 'saving' her child's life. Moments like that remind me how far LEADPrep is from the bureaucracy that education so often is. It reminds me that the relationships we make with our students are more important than anything."

WHAT WE LEARNED ABOUT HIRING

When hiring and training teachers, we learned that we had to be clear on what we needed and expected. "Teacher" is a word that means different things to different people. Who teaches our children and how they teach is vital to the health of a micro-school. There are countless experts telling us contradictory things about how good teaching should look. In order to support our students, we needed to focus very intentionally on sorting out the exact teacher attributes required for our model. Sometimes, this was a painful process. We had to ask some teachers to leave, which was sad for our loving community. We saw some teachers who couldn't shift into a guide role and allow students to lead. Nice, soft-spoken people weren't always able to teach in our dynamic and active classrooms. People with the best intentions got stuck in old conventional methods of discipline and top-down lesson planning.

We also had to find a balance between being true to our LEADPrep vision as well as open to new ideas. Many other models have pieces that make sense in other contexts. For example, "smart" online learning creates uniformity in quality of instruction, and builds in personalization according to each student's progress. Online learning is touted by some who say it moves beyond traditional education's focus on test taking and uses the most advanced tool for delivering knowledge. Yes, perhaps that is true. But our LEADPrep model is a face-to-face community where our kids are seen, heard, and valued. How can we get the best of both worlds? If we can, we take components from other models, while remaining true to our mission. Within the classroom environment, we use online high school math courses, so students can learn at their own pace and be provided with regular diagnostics, pre-testing to jump ahead to new learning, and gap analysis to help re-teach any missing components. We also encourage all of our sophomores to take the college placement exam and try online English 101 as a group, with our support, in their junior year. We regularly take in new ideas, look for ways the relevant parts can be woven in to enhance options, and refine accordingly. It's exciting to see our newer teachers bringing new ideas to the table and doing the same refining process.

Another thing we've learned when hiring is that there are amazing "trailing spouses" surrounding larger international companies. In the overseas education world, families at our international schools frequently had one spouse with a job that brought them to another country. Usually, the other

---

When we lived in Hungary, I met a family where the husband worked with the US State Department and his wife, Jay, came along with the children. I was the high school principal on a different campus from my girls. My then second-grader Jadrian had always been quirky and creative. All kindergarten and first grade kids are goofy and unique, but Jadrian was becoming more and more of an enigma to her teachers and me. When the top-notch elementary school counselor began helping me unpack Jadrian's learning profile, I started to accept that there were specific differences in how my daughter thought and acted. I needed more information and expertise. Getting in line for a neuropsych evaluation back in the US during summer break was not viable. Enter Jay. Her doctorate was in educational psychology. She regularly did professional neuropsych evaluations in the US and had lots of time on her hands in Hungary. Not only did she diagnose Jadrian's attention deficit in second grade, she tutored Jadrian in third grade. She was a godsend and helped me learn new strategies to support my unique learner. Some learning tasks were agony for Jadrian, but Jay recommended strategies like having me do the writing (scribe) so that Jadrian could put her spelling words in sentences out loud. Afterwards, Jadrian would rewrite my notes. The result was not just a list of twenty sentences, but a weekly themed story with the spelling words embedded, and a child who was having fun instead of crying. Jadrian loved words; she just needed someone to help her brain take the steps in a way that made sense to her. Thank you, Jay!

---

spouse was trailing along, leaving a career behind. Although highly qualified and intelligent, these other parents were unable to work due to language barriers and visa regulations.

Trailing spouses are a gold mine of underutilized talent. During LEAD-Prep's Year Three, Bhavana, whose husband worked at Microsoft, became our aide and math assistant. Her bachelor's and master's degrees in science from India made her vastly overqualified. We were thrilled to have her on our team. She also added a rich cultural dimension, bringing in traditional food for the festival of Diwali, and explaining to our students how she refused an arranged marriage until after she went to college.

My daughter's college math tutor, Elif, joined us as a math teacher with advanced degrees from Turkey and Florida. Presently we have three international teachers, from Puerto Rico, South Africa, and India. Their international experience enriches our school in countless ways. Please don't overlook this resource as you are staffing your micro-school.

LEADPREP ACTION PLAN RESPONSES TO STEP 2

Who will run our school? I chose to use my school administration experience to run LEADPrep. Luckily, generous and knowledgeable business people joined our board and regularly fielded my questions and supported our business structure.

Who will teach our kids? As you can see, this has been an evolution. We let our model guide the qualifications we needed. Very few of our teachers have state teaching certifications, since Washington State private school law does not mandate this extra requirement. Each of our teachers has a bachelor's degree or higher. This means I can have amazing teachers without certification, like last year's math teacher who was actually a trained radiologist (and mother!).

How do we find these people? Here are some resources we've used: Craigslist, Indeed.com, NWAIS job site, word-of-mouth, parents scouting for us, and recommendations from other teachers. Get creative! Fantastic teachers are out there waiting to help your vision flourish. Your students will be enriched and inspired by everyone who contributes.

Take time now to add leadership and hiring ideas to your Action Plan and journal.

STEP 3

ENGAGE COMMUNITY COLLABORATORS

*There are times as a parent when you realize that
your job is not to be the parent you always imagined
you'd be, the parent you always wished you had.
Your job is to be the parent your child needs, given
the particulars of his or her own life and nature.*

—Ayelet Waldman

PARENTS AND GUARDIANS are our best collaborators and the core of our tribe. In many traditional schools, the parents are on the outside. For these parents, trying to be heard or to make sure that their children's learning and social needs are met can be incredibly frustrating. At LEADPrep, I prioritize communication with parents in order to understand and serve kids. Parents are the experts about their own children, and they bring many valuable insights. They also have an enormous investment in the success of their children. With parents on board, helping and getting the word out, our tribe of community collaborators grows and welcomes volunteers and other families much more quickly.

LEADPREP APPROACH TO COMMUNITY

Our school exists because our parents have actively and generously collaborated with us every step of the way. Our gorgeous website, logo, and branding is the work of parent volunteer Mark, who enrolled his son to be the first student in our school. He offered his Primary Blue Design company's resources. Mark's design contribution evolved over the years to include internal signage, a street corner sign, and personalized logos on our two vans. The vans were paid for by donations from generous parents at our school auction. Our school uses a custom-made Emotion Awareness Board for social/emotional learning and self-regulation check-ins. The emotion board was created by a mom who is an artist and writer, working in collaboration with our English teacher. Our school's speech therapy assessments and consulting were gifted by another generous parent. Auction planning? The work of more kind and talented parents. Word-of-mouth marketing? It happens all the time. Most new students come to our school after making a connection with another parent. The community of collaborators creates the synergy needed to start and maintain our micro-school.

At LEADPrep, we intentionally foster this sense of belonging from the start. Each parent encounter is an opportunity to community-build. We invite potential parents to contact specific LEADPrep parents before they enroll their child, to start creating meaningful personal connections. We have parent meetings where we listen and brainstorm together. We engage senior parents in the design of our graduation celebration. From start to finish, we invite community and collaboration. At our annual back-to-school potluck, our team and returning parents are on the lookout to make new teachers and families welcome. We use name tags all the time, so that parents can remember who the other parents are in relation to which student.

We use online resources to further this sense of community. We have two Facebook pages. One is our public page, which is our photo album of daily learning for families. We joke that since high school students no longer run home and shout, "Guess what I learned in school today," we needed to bridge that gap. This visual depiction of daily learning provides great family dinner conversation. The second Facebook page is private for only our parents. This page is run by parents and for parents, and the only parameter is that posts be positive. We consolidate parent communications into a weekly newsletter called "The LEADPrep Loop." We also have a parent at each campus who uses email to organize semi-official student social events and parent coffee groups.

OUR BIGGEST COMMUNITY SUCCESS

Our tribe has two circles of community that we count as our biggest success. First is our beloved all-in LEADPrep families, the amazing inner circle of our success. Second is the specialists they have recommended who have formed our Dream Team as we start Year Seven. Parents and guardians share our vision and help make it a reality. Offers of support from our parents and community remind us of their generous nature and commitment. If we have a new teacher moving here from the East Coast, he's welcome to stay in one family's backyard trailer while he finds his own place. If we need curtains to block light so that projected images can be seen in class, another parent volunteers to make them. When we need help navigating social media and adding Instagram, another skilled parent comes in to save the day. Want help figuring out how these donated robot kits might be used? Building shelves in the former preschool bathroom? Painting to prepare to move into your new school space? Running the auction? Forming a teacher appreciation team? Stocking the school library as a student-led project? Volunteers are on it! The generosity and creativity of our parents is deeply appreciated.

As they have embraced our vision, our parents have enthusiastically helped us extend how we serve students. Parent networking has led to the creation of what we call our "Dream Team"—a collaborative group of professional specialists who have joined the LEADPrep tribe to assist and consult at our micro-school.

At LEADPrep, we ask "what's best for our kids?" on a regular basis. If a kid has struggled in school before coming to LEADPrep, how can we give them all the support they need and deserve in this new environment? These kids don't need to be punished, lectured, or told to "try harder." They need adults who can see beyond challenging behaviors and identify the reasons behind them, as well as their individual strengths and learning styles. Students with learning differences need adults who can help understand the "why" behind their behaviors and struggles. Sometimes this requires the perspective of a skilled expert with advanced training, such as an occupational therapist (OT), a speech language pathologist (SPL), or a behavioral therapist. These experts can help us look at social communication needs, sensory or attention issues, and other influences on learning. They can review complicated student learning profiles and help our teachers understand how a child's specific attributes are affecting their learning in the classroom. Whether developmental or behavioral, each kind of specialist brings their own valuable perspective. Almost all students benefit from professional assistance, but this is particularly true for our anxious learners, reluctant learners, students with ADHD, and students on the autism spectrum. Ideally, specialists would see students within the school context to have first-hand data. Unfortunately, top specialists with these skill sets are in high demand, have long waiting lists, and are rarely able to visit students in a classroom setting.

Thanks to the synergy and enthusiasm of our tribe, we have accessed and formed a team of amazing specialists who are willing to help our micro-school. This is our Dream Team. LEADPrep has broken the paradigm of specialists working in isolation outside of school. Parents have networked with therapists, sharing their enthusiasm for LEADPrep. In turn, these generous specialists have embraced our students and our school model.

Our Dream Team includes experts from all the perspectives we desired: a compassionate, student-centered SLP focused on social/emotional skills and communication development, a top-notch OT looking at mind/body connections, and a brilliant behavior specialist who was actually trained by the daughter of B. F. Skinner (the founding father of behavioral theory). Our wise and fun teen counselor, shared with three other private schools, completes our team. This collaborative, transdisciplinary team of professionals is supporting not only the students but the teachers as well. They observe our students learning and our teachers teaching. They train us at professional development meetings and listen carefully to our teachers' questions and concerns. The staff and the Dream Team work together to think deeply about teaching strategies and individual support plans. Together we craft solutions that work for our wide range of learners. In order to get the most benefit from these wonderful consultants, we hired an enthusiastic full-time staff member (a former behavior technician) to be our "Dream Team liaison," and floating specialist co-teacher. When parents, teachers, and specialists work together in a micro-school, students get the attention they need in a meaningful setting where new skills can be learned and applied. Instead of being isolated, learning outliers are integrated. They can begin to experience trust, success, and happiness.

We are a wonderful collective providing support for our kids. The LEADPrep tribe of support has parents on the inside and now an outer circle of community experts. Volunteers and professionals bring a wide range of perspectives to our school. Regardless of our backgrounds, we are all focused on what's best for our kids. A caring, helping tribe is what each child needs and deserves, and that's the most important component of our micro-school community.

As I write this book (a summer turbo project before school starts again) and build the micro-school coalition, my tribe of parents and other supporters is yet again stepping up! LEADPrep's board president, Kester, is my chief contributing editor and collaborator. Our marketing guru, Joelle, is designing the cover, creating the web sites and associated social media platforms, and talking about driving traffic between them to generate enthusiasm for micro-schools. One of my daughters is helping with the back-end technology and the other one is working on citations and edits. Both of them are cheering me on. Our book consultant is a friend whom I have been able to informally coach as she has explored non-traditional school options. My business consultant has volunteered at LEADPrep, teaching students about the Myers-Briggs and their unique gifts. YES! This is the energy we need to create real change.

CHALLENGES WE FACED WITH COMMUNITY

In my experience, the biggest challenge in building a micro-school community is getting kids and parents to realize that an alternative school option may be needed. For kids, their willingness to look at new options often comes down to whether they have to leave friends at their old school. I've been told by parents, "I know my child has failed his first two years of high school, but he wants to stay there with his friends. And I want him to be happy." Argg!!! How happy will that boy be when his friends graduate and move away to college and he is left behind in a dead-end job!? And, truly, how happy is he to feel the sensation of repeated failure and lack of understanding? He is forming his permanent identity, and failure will become part of that identity.

In the midst of this emotional time, sometimes parents aren't able to step back and look at the big picture. When you look back on this time of life in a few years, how will middle and high school be if no changes are made? Will your child have graduated? Will they be thriving? Carl Allamby[85] was recently celebrated on CBS news. In his 40s he went from being an auto doctor (mechanic) to being a medical doctor. His perspective is one that would benefit these families in the midst of school problems: "I would hear people say, 'Carl, it's going to take nine years to become a doctor.' And I'd say, 'Well, nine years is going to pass anyway.' So, I'd rather be some place I want to be than some place that I could have been." Our children's school years are going to pass. It's my job as a school administrator to help kids get to the place they want and need to be.

I really appreciate it when a parent has a reluctant student visit our school for a day. That way, the student is at least open to seeing another possibility. After the visit, a student usually moves from catastrophizing (thinking attending a micro-school is the worst idea ever) to at least acknowledging there are students happily learning in other models. Even better are the families that insist their child try a micro-school for at least one semester before turning it down. Then the student has personal data instead of peer pressure informing a long-term school choice. Almost always, those reluctant students choose to stay at LEADPrep, where learning makes sense and they feel supported.

Coaching families through this process, I've come to realize that switching to a micro-school can be a tough paradigm shift for the parents as well as the students. Parents must be willing to look at learning from a vastly different perspective. Often, that means acknowledging for the first time that their child might be an outlier. This acknowledgment is complicated, and often fear-based or guilt-ridden. None of the pressures I felt as an administrator making big-ticket decisions for a large school could compare to the level of angst I felt as a mom making daily decisions about my girls' upbringing. *Was my divorce going to ruin how they viewed relationships when they grew up? Should I insist that Giana stay in the girls' choir as a lesson in honoring commitments, or should I let her quit to encourage free choice? Does Jadrian need an IEP, or would it be a stigma? Do I talk to other kids' parents about the social situation that exploded or let my daughter handle it on her own? Am I too involved? Not involved enough?* These are hugely personal issues. As micro-school leaders, we are often witnessing a parent's most vulnerable moments.

Parents might have to acknowledge their child's learning differences are substantial enough to require more school support. Our parental craving for our child to be "normal" is wired deep into us. We hope that if we don't give in to the differences, we can somehow transform our child into a "normal" kid. Of course, deep inside we know that normal does not exist and that we don't want to change our child. We just give them every chance for success and happiness. But we also fear our child will miss out on the fun we remember—dances, pep assemblies, clubs, or playing on sports teams. We project our definition of school fun onto our child's experience. Some parents refuse to see how mismatched their child is in the current situation. They blame systems or blame the child's behavior, lamenting about how poorly school is going without taking any practical steps to address the mismatch between school and student. But I've also seen many parents who are bravely choosing a different response. Their love for their child creates a willingness to adapt.

These parents embrace and celebrate their child's uniqueness with an intense determination to find or create a better school match for their beloved child.

Even if parents are motivated by the best intentions, their relationship with a micro-school can still be quite complicated once their student is enrolled. At LEADPrep, we know that the parent/school dynamic takes compassionate and intentional navigation. Parents often come with painful school experiences as baggage. In the years leading up to enrollment at LEADPrep, parents had to embody Mama Bear ferocity to try to get their child's needs met. I've met with parents whose despair has become rage because of injustices bestowed upon their children. In the past, their relationships with

Twice I have had parents respond to our solutions and progress with fury and withdraw their child from the school. One mom had an 11th grader with anxiety, autism, and depression. Becca was a shy, artistic, delightful girl. She began to attend school daily (for the first time in three years) and become more and more engaged. At the same time, her mother became more and more agitated, as if she were waiting for something to go wrong. Finally, Becca's mom demanded that her daughter get worksheets to complete at home, arguing that our personalized model should allow for this option. This went against our principles of relationship-building and seemed driven by the mother wanting Becca at home with her more than she wanted Becca to become healthier and engaged in school. We agreed to send packets home only until the end of the grading period, at which time the mom withdrew Becca. It was upsetting and sad to see a parent's own worries and unhealed pain derailing a student's education.

schools were adversarial, so they bring that background with them when they come to us. It takes time to build trust with them. We slowly help them let go of their fear and realize that LEADPrep is a positive tribe of support for their child.

Labels can also complicate our parent-school dynamics. If a student carries a diagnostic or behavioral label for a long time, that label becomes part of the belief system and identity of the student and parent. What was once a helpful diagnosis becomes something limiting. Some parents tell me, "My child has XYZ and therefore can't...." If teachers suggest an area for growth, sometimes a parent's first instinct is to resist and protect their child from being challenged. As a mom of girls with several different labels, at times I also found myself overly focused on those labels as a part of my story. I was conditioned to be a fierce advocate and that made me more focused on the dangers than the possibilities for growth. I wasn't always ready for others to say, "Yes, and...." My personal experience has given me great compassion for our parents who are caught in this aspect of parenting. Gently, we say,

"Yes, your child has this diagnosis AND here is how we will move forward toward deeper learning expectations." Sometimes, even a positive label such as "gifted" or "highly capable" can be limiting. In these cases, we have to say, "Yes, your child is highly capable AND they will benefit from extra help in this specific area." Every child is a unique individual, yet some parents experience huge resistance to the idea of breaking away from labels and writing a new chapter in their child's story.

Fortunately, these stressful situations are usually just a small speed bump on the road to parent partnership. The magic of LEADPrep truly shines when we are able to collaborate with parents, lessen the impact of limiting labels, and move students to new, deeper learning profiles. Most of our parents are very relieved to have a responsive school leadership that joins them in seeing their beloved child as a whole, valued, unique individual. At LEADPrep, a student's official diagnosis is far less important than the interests, relationships, and potential leadership capacity the student brings.

WHAT WE LEARNED ABOUT COMMUNITY

A lack of clearly defined roles, including who makes what decisions and how, can be a problem. It takes intentional planning to help parents be active in relevant and clear ways. Each micro-school has to ask how they will structure parent volunteering. Do we want parents teaching in the school? On the board? In a parent association? All volunteer projects need a clear sense of outcomes and parameters. Our mission and model guide our standards for volunteering. The more clearly you outline roles and how your tribe can pull forward as one unit, the better. Within this clarity, individual parents will have better tools to make a real difference and contribute in imaginative ways.

Just like in a homeschool community, whenever we can lean on parent and volunteer efforts, we have the opportunity for an enriched experience for our learners. At our school, we have had parents work in the school in exchange for tuition. Because of our service and field trips on Fridays, soliciting parent drivers was an early ask. Using a program such as *SignUpGenius* helps us put out requests and monitor involvement for activities such as work parties and potlucks. When it comes to marketing, we've realized that volunteers are wonderful at networking to prospective families because people trust a personal recommendation far more than a flyer or a yard sign. Our parents create an organic network for gathering resources and brainstorming solutions.

Other nonprofit organizations are also an important resource for us. The church I attend donated tablecloths and centerpieces for our auction and was a vital starting point in my search for volunteer teachers. Currently, LEAD-Prep has a valuable relationship with the Seattle Phinney Neighborhood Association and the Kirkland Teen Union Building. When our school first opened, we looked for local service opportunities right away. Our students help our landlords with grounds projects, clear blackberries at local parks, and regularly visit elders at a local memory care facility. Forging relationships within our neighborhood is an important part of our curriculum.

At LEADPrep, parents tend to be the most committed and motivated long-term volunteers. We have found that they make wonderful board members, honoring the three-year commitment more fully than people who don't have a direct investment. We have a "working board," where all parents on the board contribute in extra ways. In addition to our monthly meetings, we have a spring planning retreat. Our board also hosts a fall and spring parent gathering where the whole community discusses possibilities for our students. To be eligible to serve on our board, parents must have previously taken a leadership role in some aspect of our school. Thank goodness for our dedicated, helpful parents! We wouldn't be able to run our school without them.

LEADPREP ACTION PLAN RESPONSES TO STEP 3

2013 Action Plan for Operations (start-up draft)

Days and hours of operation: Monday-Friday, full-day classes to forge a community. Later start (9:00 am) to align with research on the sleeping pattern of teen brains.

Location: Downtown Kirkland.

Plan to meet legal requirements of: Washington State business license, state department of education private school approval, federal nonprofit 501(c)3 status.

Insurance plan: Join a nonprofit insurance cooperative.

Tribe leaders, teachers, and volunteers include: Two other mothers/educators and myself as leaders and teachers, asking parents to dive in as soon as they enroll their student; friends from my church and life.

Back-up contingency plan: The primary cost is rent, so we will work with the church to temporarily lower the rent, if enrollment levels are too low.

Action Plan for Operations (current version)

Days and hours of operation: Monday-Thursday, 9:00am-3:45pm, with Kirkland and Seattle campuses meeting separately. Fridays, 10:00am-3:00pm, are reserved for physical activities and expeditionary learning, with Kirkland and Seattle campuses joining together.

Location: Downtown Kirkland and North Seattle.

Plan to meet legal requirements of: Washington State business license, state department of education private school approval, federal nonprofit 501(c)3 status.

Insurance plan: nonprofit insurance cooperative, including car insurance for two vans. We needed an insurance broker to access this great deal.

Tribe leaders, teachers, and volunteers include: Myself as school administrator, Terry (Director of Learning), nine other full-time teaching staff, four part-time staff, and five consultants. An official school board with a president, secretary, treasurer, and marketing lead. A Parent Action Team/PAT that involved teacher appreciation team, auction team, parent tutoring volunteers, and social event coordinators.

Back-up contingency plan: Flexible staff members who can substitute teach any class. Also keeping myself available for subbing and to handle any issues that come up with students, staff, parents, and facilities. Two locations for redundancy and sharing school resources.

Spend a moment now adding reflections to your journal or specific ideas about community to your Action Plan.

STEP 4

GET THE WORD OUT

Speak to your audience in their language about what's in their heart.

—Jonathan Lister

I've learned that people will forget what you said, people will forget what you did, but people will never forget how you made them feel.

—Maya Angelou

WHEN I STARTED LEADPrep, I was deeply in touch with the "why" at the heart of my own story. That's the story I shared at the very beginning of this book. As a mom, I had raised two unique children who didn't fit into conventional public and private schools. As a career educator, I have always believed that all students deserve a humane, innovative education. As the founder of LEADPrep, I wanted to offer other kids the type of high school option I wish my daughters could have had. From the start, LEADPrep was designed to be a personal, inclusive micro-school for colorful, mismatched kids. As other parents joined me, this became our shared mission and vision. We saw a problem. We had a solution. We wanted to provide relief to other families. That was the "why" that connected us on emotional and practical levels. But how were we going to share our school's "why" with other families?

THE LEADPREP APPROACH TO MARKETING

In order to create momentum, we knew we needed to get in front of prospective families to enroll students. Once we had people face-to-face, we could share our passion and our mission. Raising awareness of our school became a major goal for the first two years. Without students, there is no school! We tried a variety of approaches, some more successful than others. We held several informational meetings in libraries in our school's greater area (the Eastside of Lake Washington). To encourage attendance, we posted flyers about these events everywhere. We launched a basic website to provide additional information about the school. Sometimes we held open house meetings that had no attendees. But still we persisted.

We tried a direct mail flyer to targeted zip codes, sending out postcards to 1,000 homes. I joined some small business networking groups and attended a variety of local networking functions. Although I'm not shy, I am an "introvert" on the Myers-Briggs scale. I'd rather have my nose down in a big project than attend a networking party to chit chat with strangers. But these networking groups led me to René, our fantastic founding school board president. He brought us that much-needed entrepreneurial wisdom during his three years' tenure at the helm of our board. These same networking meetings also led to a mom enrolling one of her daughters a few months after school opened, and then adding her second daughter the following year. This led in turn to the girls' grandmother volunteering as our exceptionally helpful and scrupulous bookkeeper and board treasurer. For LEADPrep, that initial networking effort built up our tribe in crucial ways.

Besides the direct mailers, the other print media tools we tried have been yard signs, brochures, magazine ads, bulletin board signs, and even pizza box ads. Surprisingly, our most successful physical ads have been the yard signs. And, of course, we make sure that our current school locations have sandwich boards out on the sidewalk and other promotional signage.

Our very first enrolled student came through the direct mail flyer. I was hesitant to try this method because of the cost and possible low return on investment. It turned out to be serendipity; our mailer was delivered to a father's graphic design business address. The postcard caught his attention, because he had just had a meeting with the public middle school his son attended. They had stated that their district didn't have a good high school fit for his son and had encouraged him to consider alternative schools. Good luck and good timing? We'll take it! This father went on to become LEADPrep's graphic designer and a valued board member.

Keeping our website relevant and updated has also been important for creating a public face for LEADPrep. When families become aware of us, the first thing they usually do is check the website, which shows them that we are a stable, functioning organization, and that we are doing what we say we are doing. We make sure we have our affiliations listed up-front in our "about" section, so people can see we are a 501(c)3 nonprofit school with formal accreditation. It's also important that people see that we have a 1:6 teacher/student ratio, since extra adult attention is a huge selling point for any micro-school. I personally keep the blog updated at least every month in order to show website visitors that LEADPrep is a living and growing community. We also make sure our enrollment phone number is in a banner at the top of every page.

No matter how much effort we put into print and online tools, face-to-face interactions have always been the mainstay of LEADPrep marketing. Our parent community is by far the most effective promotional resource. Committed LEADPrep parents are building strong relationships with families at other schools in their neighborhood and at schools their child previously attended. They are talking with families in their neighborhoods and workplaces. In fact, the majority of our current students came to us via word-of-mouth recommendations. I believe that's because prospective parents are drawn to the relationship-building aspect of our school. Personal recommendations create an emotional connection. Parents who previously felt alone in their struggles have found someone who understands what they are going through. They come to our school because they feel like our community accepts and cares about their child. Instead of hiding our families' difficulties and differences, our tribe of parents unpacks those difficulties, compares notes, and offers meaningful understanding. What a relief for parents to step into a community that supports all of our bright, fierce, quirky, unique, precious, shy, sweet, and questioning teens. Other people are hearing about our "why," and if it matches their own "why," that's when they enroll their kids.

OUR BIGGEST MARKETING SUCCESS

When it comes to promotion, our key success is that LEADPrep stakeholders have become very clear about who we are and what we offer. The ongoing conversations and campaigns to get the word out have allowed us to hone our message as our school grows and we settle into our core identity. We rely on each other to remind ourselves of who we are, and why we are here. This synergy among tribe members is priceless and creates many unexpected ben-efits. The kindness and openness among our parents is one of these benefits. Our parents candidly share their experiences with prospective families and answer these families' questions in a personal context. When parents are comfortable sharing their experiences about LEADPrep, it's a natural transi-tion to then invite other parents into the tribe. This creates the first part of our LEADPrep bridge, welcoming new students and seeing them for who they are in the present moment.

CHALLENGES WE FACED IN MARKETING

I would like to say that we found a way to get the word out and quickly fill our school. But, to be honest, marketing has been an uphill battle. It's hard to find bandwidth for marketing when you're starting a school because it's just one of many tasks that must be worked on simultaneously. I'm passionate about education and working with kids; I'm not passionate about advertising. As an educational leader, I want to get in there and work with my students and teachers! Yet as a business leader, I have to consider how to reach our target market—the parents who need our school and aren't yet aware it ex-ists. In business, it's often said that your product has to be seen ten times for a customer to consider a purchase. I'm not sure if that's true for other micro-schools, but I do know that LEADPrep is still under the radar of awareness for many families in our area.

As we already discussed in Part Two, many people feel reluctant about "selling" a product. When it comes to recommending LEADPrep, some par-ents love to be talkative about our school, but other parents feel more shy or uncomfortable. We discuss these feelings openly at our parent meetings, and parents share tips on how, why, and when to recommend LEADPrep. It's been especially helpful for parents to brainstorm talking points and encourage each other to use them. We recently welcomed an experienced marketing volunteer onto our school board, and her recommendation to parents is to just share in whatever way feels natural or comfortable to them. If someone isn't into face-to-face interactions, social media can be a great place to share. Another critical way parents can contribute is by writing positive reviews on Yelp, Google, and school-specific review sites. Hopefully, these digital messag-es lead to face-to-face meetings with other parents, or a phone call with me to start a meaningful discussion. Our school message is strongest when we dive into direct, personal conversations with prospective parents. A personalized education can only be demonstrated with personal stories and connections.

LEADPrep has been blessed in terms of parents who are skilled in graphic design and generous with their time. Year One we had a fantastic dad, Mark, who created beautiful logos and branding. He was an expert at font, color schemes, and all things graphic design. As we previously mentioned, his talent and effort morphed into our lovely website and signage. Just as he was stepping off the board (a few years AFTER his son had graduated), a new graphic design parent, Joelle, joined our board. She not only picked up where Mark left off, but she has training in marketing and social media. Her knack for promotions is impressive. She also has the back-end tech skills to create our Micro-School Coalition web page and drive our social media plan. This gives us many ways to market our school. We don't want our marketing to be pushy, but we need to remember that we are offering a solution to families' pain. Over the years, we've slowly learned what our prospective families are seeking, and we want to keep getting better at using all of the marketing strategies possible to explain how LEADPrep is providing real educational solutions.

Promoting alternative education can feel like an uphill battle when we are confronted with parent denial of special learning issues. As we discussed in the last section, many parents refuse to see the problems their child is having, or refuse to acknowledge that a micro-school might be a good option.

We face a different kind of challenge when parents come to us with very specific, preconceived ideas about what an alternative school should be. If a parent is desperately seeking a solution for their child, sometimes they have a very rigid idea about what teaching strategies we should be using. Occasionally, these parents get very upset when their proposed solution doesn't match our teaching model. We already know what our school mission is and we can't be all things to all people. For example, LEADPrep is not a 1:1 school, we are a group-work school. We can't accept students who are working below a certain academic level or students who are regularly defiant or hurtful to their peers. We aren't a democratic school, so students do have to go along with a teacher-led curriculum. We also require certain agreements from families in our school/student/family contract. If LEADPrep is not the right fit for a student, we work hard to help families find a good choice somewhere else—there are excellent 1:1 schools, special education schools, and democratic schools in the Seattle area. Most of these decisions are made in a positive spirit of collaboration, but occasionally a disappointed parent will channel their strong emotions into angry confrontations or anonymous bad reviews. Of course, these misunderstandings have been discouraging for me and the other teachers. With parent passions running high, anger is sometimes inevitable. Therefore, one of our marketing priorities has become giving a clear explanation of what kind of learning community LEADPrep is, and exactly what services it offers. Clarity up front can prevent heartache later.

We try to stay open minded and flexible about what kind of students we enroll, and which families will benefit from our community, but we also stick to our original plan to provide interpersonal, STEM-informed learning with an emphasis on making a positive difference in the world. Our newest print ad declares that we are "Collaborative, Experiential, and Student-Focused," and we encourage interested parents to "start a conversation," and join me for a 1-on-1 consultation and tour. When a family is the right fit, it's a wonderful feeling to welcome their child into our school. I've seen so many reluctant students come out of their shells and thrive at LEADPrep, so we're willing to take some risks in order to help as many kids as we can.

WHAT WE LEARNED ABOUT MARKETING

Truthfully, we've learned that marketing is the biggest challenge we have. My great team of teachers can create learning options that support a wide variety of students. I can collaborate with landlords, teachers, and parents. But it's hard for me to crack through the layers of resistance within prospective families. That's understandable; we want to protect our children, and our teenagers want to feel "normal." But this desire for normality sometimes forces parents and kids to miserably grind their way through traditional schools that aren't the right fit. We want parents and students to understand that we are a viable solution and that they are free to make a change today. So, on the one hand, we want micro-schools to be perceived as a safe, acceptable, stable option. On the other hand, we want micro-schools to be perceived as an exciting new option that challenges the status quo. This dual message requires a lot of marketing finesse, especially when you're trying to explain an innovative teaching model that people aren't familiar with. We've also learned that the families who need us the most don't know about us and probably aren't even looking for us.

What did we learn that was not effective? Print media was not effective for us. Magazine, newspaper, and pizza box ads did not generate any leads. Professional networking didn't build our numbers very well, but it did give us new resources and a greater understanding of many components of the business world. After gathering this perspective, I dropped out of the networking groups so I could put those daytime hours to more immediate use within our school.

What did we learn that was effective? We learned that the networking power of our tribe was the most powerful way to get the word out, with personal recommendations being the most productive source of new families. Parent comments on social media are helpful. Local counselors, consultants, and psychologists have been vital in getting the word out. Our web presence allows families to do an internet search and find us, which is an important link in the chain of communication. The most successful traditional marketing method has been yard signs. Yes, LEADPrep signs can be found mixed in with political campaign signs all summer long, and they've brought us several students.

As we've learned more about marketing, we have become clearer with the story we are telling. We know our key components and are slowly coaching all of our stakeholders on how to share the same message. One person tells another person, who tells another person, and those additional resources come to fruition as time passes.

Now let's take out our Action Plan (Appendix A) and travel back in time to when I was first doing market research. At this point, LEADPrep was a tiny nascent seedling—barely emerging from the idea phase. Before I started advertising my school to parents, I needed to make sure there actually was

---

Our marketing-savvy tribe members have explained that we need to brand everything, even our email signatures (the information that is automatically included at the bottom of each email.) Here is what we use:

Dr. Maureen O'Shaughnessy / Founder & Executive Director
Leadership Preparatory Academy
A **progressive middle/high micro-school** in North Seattle & Downtown Kirkland
425.298.6451 · maureen@lead-prep.org · **LEAD-Prep.org** · **Facebook** · **YouTube**

OUR MISSION
At LEADPrep we foster an educational community that cultivates *authentic voices* and strengths. We empower students to be *fearless* in their individuality and also *courageous* as local and global leaders.

Each member of our faculty and staff has the same signature below their name and title.

---

a potential market into which I could tap. And I needed to make sure I had the ability to fill that market. Doing a SWOT analysis (internal **s**trengths and **w**eaknesses, external **o**pportunities and **t**hreats) was an important part of my process.

Since I was the lone originator of the school and hadn't yet found anyone with whom to collaborate, I had to begin with the strengths I personally brought to the table. These included school and parent experience, advanced studies in educational innovation and systems, lots of energy, and a can-do attitude. For my weaknesses, I had to address my dislike of paperwork and number crunching. This inspired me quickly to get help from my accountant sister-in-law and CPA brother. Externally, I saw opportunities along the I-405 corridor near both Microsoft and Google campuses—STEM-focused communities. External threats included the gridlock of traffic and rising cost of Seattle area real estate. For LEADPrep, that meant looking at freeways and ease of access. It also meant looking for a location that had a variety of income levels. While we wanted to be socioeconomically diverse, we knew we needed some families who could pay full tuition in order for our school to be feasible. Most SWOT analyses for small businesses include competition as a threat. While we prefer to collaborate and don't believe we need to compete to fill an educational need, we also didn't want to be redundant by being located in a community with a variety of other learning options. All of these considerations played into my original plan for our opening location, model, and marketing plan.

As LEADPrep grows and evolves, we still do a SWOT analysis every couple of years. This helps us stay up-to-date on how the market has changed and how our resources have expanded to meet that market. To give you an idea of where we started, here is the SWOT and the marketing plan I created at the very beginning of our micro-school journey.

2013 Market Analysis of SWOT

Internal Strengths:

- My EdD in Educational leadership
- My parenting experience as the mother of two colorful, mismatched learning outliers
- Experience starting a micro-school in 1990, as a school-within-a-school, experience at both public and private schools, and experience running international micro-schools and online schools
- Supportive church community and family members
- Personal resourcefulness, determination, can-do attitude, and willingness to learn

Internal Weaknesses:

- My lack of knowledge in the legal and financial areas (no experience running a small business)
- My dislike of paperwork and bookkeeping
- Tribe of parents not yet gathered

External Opportunities:

- Huge unfilled need for schools that serve learning outliers
- Immediately available and innovative learning components such as flipped learning, STEM instruction, and project-based learning
- High-tech Seattle area rich in STEM businesses and start-ups, providing a technologically literate population who would be interested in STEM school start-ups
- Greater Seattle region growing rapidly and tech companies hiring, with more and more families moving in and seeking educational options

External Threats:

- Rapid growth, with freeways a tangle of traffic, so parents wanting options close to home (private schools draw from a large geographic area, so traffic could discourage families living a distance away from enrolling)
- Socioeconomic issues, possibly not enough families able to afford full tuition

Action Plan for Marketing

My market includes parents, usually those with students who are outliers or who want a small, inclusive school.

The market analysis tells me that a location near transit centers and freeway exits in the Bellevue-Kirkland-Redmond area would best serve potential families. It also informed me of the range of tuition charged by schools in this area.

Our plan for reaching prospective families and partners or donors began with tear-off signs on bulletin boards and a direct mail flyer to targeted zip codes. These signs and postcards invited families to various regional library information sessions and referred them to our website for details.

Outcomes we expect from getting the word out are new families enrolling students and becoming contributing members of our tribe. (We also ended up networking and gaining resources as people learned about us and wanted to help us get started.)

Is there a market for our school? Yes. At the time there were no day-long micro-schools for tweens and teens on the Eastside of Lake Washington. There were 1:1 options and a public alternative school, but not an inclusive micro-school.

What are the threats and opportunities we face? See SWOT above.

How will we get people interested? Look for publicity beyond our basic marketing. One of our early students had big aspirations and the local paper wrote up her story and how our school would support it; also, sharing personal stories face-to-face with other parents.

Before you continue, take a moment to update Step 4 of your Action Plan.

STEP 5

CHOOSE WHAT MAKES YOUR SCHOOL UNIQUE AND SPECIAL

*Your time is limited, so don't waste it living someone
else's life. Don't be trapped by dogma—which is
living with the results of other people's thinking.
Don't let the noise of others' opinions drown out
your own inner voice. And most important, have
the courage to follow your heart and intuition.*

—Steve Jobs

LEADPREP APPROACH TO MAKING OUR SCHOOL UNIQUE AND SPECIAL

BE FOREWARNED, my passion for educational innovation means this section is loaded with details. I'll be digging deep into a lot of powerful learning ideas here. You may want to skim this section for now, pausing on the sections that most closely align with your own micro-school's vision. However, these are the ideas that fueled our enthusiasm at LEADPrep, so they are an integral part of our school's history. After all, transforming education is what micro-schools are all about!

As we discussed in Part One, a single traditional model does not work for all learners.

Before starting LEADPrep, I researched local examples of schools that were successfully serving a wide variety of student types. Two of the programs I came to admire were the Puget Sound Community School in Seattle and the ORCA high school program at Everett Community College. A common factor in both these schools was experiential, project-based learning closely aligned with student passions. This same approach had been successful for me in creating a public high school-within-a-school in the '90s. I determined that this idea—student-centered, project-based learning—would be the foundation of our model.

Curriculum and instruction is my sweet spot. As a school administrator, I can handle the facilities and finances, but my true love is sorting out what goes on in the classroom. I've had extensive training in cooperative learning, habits of success, and curriculum mapping. I've also taught students of all ages (from kindergarten through college) and worked in one online school, six US schools, and seven international schools...oh, and two colleges! As you can tell, I'm hugely enthusiastic about expanding my horizons, and I've been fortunate to learn from many great educators around the world. I'm so grateful to all my mentors and co-teachers, and I've assembled their accumulated wisdom into our educational philosophy at LEADPrep.

Let's begin with the five structural features we combined to build our LEAD-Prep model. After that, I'll elaborate on our four primary teaching strategies.

LEADPREP STRUCTURAL FEATURES

Foster and Demand Inclusion

Our first, and overarching, structural component is being inclusive. Students need to be seen, heard, and valued. Period. We doggedly address the emotional climate at our school, intentionally fostering inclusion, self-regulation, and self-advocacy.

The rise of anxiety and depression in adolescence is alarming. The emotional demands of a large school can be overwhelming and exhausting, with students feeling invisible, undesirable, and rejected. If a student feels like they don't fit in, or if they feel like they have to work very hard to fit in, they're much more susceptible to feelings of worry and sadness. If a student gets the impression that they are the only colorful sock in a giant bag of white gym socks, that's a difficult feeling to live with every day. But it can be fun to be a colorful, mismatched sock when you're with a bunch of other colorful, mismatched socks. And the truth is that all humans are colorful and mismatched in certain ways. In order for kids to be happy, their differences have to be enjoyed and celebrated.

Attending an inclusive micro-school can change a student's life. A perfect example of this is one of our graduating seniors, George. When LEADPrep first started, a wonderful seventh grade boy named George visited our school. He was bright, curious, and had distinct passions. He was particularly interested in history, aesthetic design, and gender expression. George had been bullied in his previous school. When he joined our school, he began growing out his long curly hair and sharing his love of fixing antique clocks. George added creative and thoughtful elements to group projects. In his ninth grade year, he helped rewrite the ending of Romeo and Juliet. The students presented this play and George was one of the characters in drag. In tenth grade, he helped us form an LGBTQ club and one of the activities was a "heels day" where any student who wanted to could try wearing heels, as a way to get a new perspective on gender and culture. In eleventh and twelfth grades, George had dual enrollment, spending some of his time at our school, while taking college classes in advanced math, architecture, and sculpture. He was our resident musician, playing the piano at our annual auction. For the auction his twelfth grade year, George proudly showed up in full Victorian-era drag with a make-up look that took two hours (and his mom's help!) to prepare. His aesthetic was stunning, and he was thrilled to have such positive support. For graduation, he came again in drag—real antique 1920's flapper garb. After LEADPrep, he was accepted to multiple colleges. In his previous schools, George was anxious, bullied, and misunderstood, but during his five years at our micro-school George found the freedom to develop his academic and personal identity. On graduation night, his mom wrote, "Thank you, Maureen! LEADPrep has been just what George needed. A safe space to learn and become who he is. And he was surrounded every day in school by amazing and wonderful kids and adults alike. Tonight will be joyful and a little sad as well, as finish lines often are."

Inclusive schools build on students' strengths. We encourage LEADPrep kids to reflect on how they learn and where they excel. Looking through the lens of multiple intelligences, Harvard professor Howard Gardner's seminal work of categorizing nine types of intelligence[86], we celebrate the variety of "smarts" our students bring to the community. It's powerful to see students light up when their type of intelligence is validated. (What are these nine smarts, you ask? Naturalist, musical, logical-mathematical, existential, interpersonal, bodily-kinesthetic, linguistic, intra-personal and spatial.) One student who is reluctant to write (linguistic intelligence) is amazing on our camping trip. There he gets to use his naturalist intelligence to understand living things. He excels at reading nature, not a classroom textbook.

A micro-school like LEADPrep is also helpful for students who need less chaos and more safety within their school experience, or who simply need a few accommodations to feel comfortable. Need a quieter work space? Or to use voice recognition tools for writing? Or to give your presentation to a few students instead of the whole class? Inclusion means allowing students to self-advocate to get their needs met. The first step is actually listening to what students are seeking and paying attention to what's working on an individual basis. Our micro-schools can intentionally be an inclusive and welcoming place for all types of learners. In our community, we wished for a school like this, so we created it.

Teacher student relationships are special at LEADPrep. A few summers ago, our beloved science teacher, Terry, was surprised to find an email from her students:

"Hi Terry! I just wanted to wish you a super happy birthday!! I hope that you went out to a state park and went bird-watching or something else like that on your birthday. However, I am not the only one that wants to wish you a happy birthday. You see, a couple of the other students from LEADPrep also want to wish you a happy birthday. However, none of us could really say how much we wanted you to have a happy birthday, and, when we tried, we were only able to say a fraction of what we wanted to say...

However, we didn't let this get in the way. Instead, we combined all these fractions of a message, and then our message as a whole became more clear.

All of us—and even our dog Hank—wish you an amazingly happy birthday."

Putting the Adults Where the Learning Happens

Our second structural component is maximizing the student-teacher ratio at LEADPrep. Our goal is to have all the adults in our school *in* the classroom, where the students and learning are. In your micro-school's first year, it may be just one or two adults on your staff. You may need to streamline administration and rely on volunteers to support you outside the classroom. At LEADPrep, we have parents and volunteers taking on many of our extra roles—taking care of the website and social media, planning our auction, and buying and organizing food for our camping trip. Tech-savvy students and parents are our unofficial IT department. Because we're small and community-based, we don't need the myriad of full-time non-classroom roles that exist in most conventional schools. We share a school counselor with two other small schools, and we have a team of trusted outside language and occupational therapists consulting as needed. This helps the full-time staff concentrate on the classroom environment.

When it comes to adults in the classroom, a micro-school should have a 10:1 student-teacher ratio, or even less, if possible. Now that LEADPrep is larger, we have more full-time teachers. Funding full-time positions was an important financial goal that the school board continues to support. In previous years, our part-time teachers often had to juggle a second job, and the greater Seattle area is a pricey place to live. We make it a priority to pay our teachers competitively so that they can focus on just one job: LEADPrep learning. It has been a seven-year process (starting with my salary of zero) to transform our organization into a school that offers competitive salaries, retirement benefits, and medical insurance for our teachers. We prioritize teacher compensation by cutting back in other areas. For example, our space is shared and initially was rented instead of leased. For a few years, that meant setting up the tables and chairs each morning and packing up our classroom each afternoon. But, on a deeper level, it enabled us to focus on attracting and retaining great teachers and loading our classrooms with their supportive guidance.

With our full-time team, we use a co-teaching model. That means when a teacher is not leading their specialty subject, they are co-teaching the other subjects. Much of guiding learning is about helping students engage, stay focused, get back on track when there is a complication, and navigate peer relationships within group work. A skilled guide will ask students meaningful questions and help them break tasks down into smaller steps. That means a co-teacher doesn't have to be an expert on all subjects, they just have to be an expert on our kids—and they are! For example, our Spanish teacher, Nito, knows that 7th-grade Kyle loves to chat and socialize. During science class, Nito takes the co-teacher role. Instead of trying to discipline Kyle for talking, Nito makes sure to engage Kyle in friendly adult social interaction. He uses the conversation to redirect Kyle's cheerful energy toward the science activity in a positive, good-humored way. Nito didn't have to know the science content in order to be an effective co-teacher, he just used his natural ability to interact with kids. Afterward, during Spanish class, Nito switches his focus to leading the Spanish activity and answering questions about and in Spanish. Nito presents the lesson he planned while the science teacher, Terry, takes on the co-teaching role, gently encouraging the students who are less engaged. Our co-teacher model is highly effective, with the added bonus of fostering *esprit de corps* among our teachers. It's fun to see our teachers do things together, like simulate a game show, or model a Socratic dialogue. The kids love it when our teachers play off of each other's personalities to keep learning engaging.

At LEADPrep, our basic premise is that our resources need to be focused on the classroom and supporting individuals with their learning. When students get more assistance and have more personal support during the day, many of the non-instructional concerns go away. Kids don't have to be pulled out for special therapy or discipline. Instead, we coach kids in the context of an activity so they can learn and grow in a real-life situation.

Raise the Bar on Participation with Increased Student Agency

Focusing on student agency is our third structural component. We all want students to be empowered to take ownership of their learning. We refer to this ownership as having agency. Choice and student voice get lost in big systems. In our micro-school, we empower students repeatedly in small, daily ways.

The first step to nurturing student agency is to listen to their feelings and emotions. So many adults skip this important step. As we all know, tweens and teens often have strong emotions that seem to fill up their whole minds and bodies. Those emotions are important to them, and they are a valid part of the teen experience. Our LEADPrep teachers do their best to respect students' feelings, and never to minimize them or sweep them under the rug. At our school, we take time at the start and end of the day to do "check-ins" to build self-awareness and empathy. If a student is having a hard day because something sad happened, or an intense day because something exciting happened, our teachers use that awareness to interact with the students more compassionately.

Emotion Awareness Board. One of the tools we provide for our students is the Emotion Awareness Board.[87] This is a small magnet board printed with a colorful emotion wheel, designed by an artist who is one of our LEADPrep parents. The wheel has a wide range of emotion vocabulary words, arranged by intensity and positive or negative sensation. Students can use the board as a map to help them understand and express their feelings. For example, a student might be able to look at the board and say, "Hmm, I'm feeling angry and disappointed about something that happened at home. Maybe that's why I'm easily getting annoyed and frustrated with my project group members." A deep emotional language also helps with setting boundaries. We address emotions with students in order to communicate kindly and effectively: "Frank, I know you feel delighted and passionate about leveling up in your game. I was talking to Chris, so please let me finish and then I want to hear more about the game." If a conflict arises, we can use an Emotion Awareness Board to help students know that we understand their feelings: "When I asked you about your new glasses, I was feeling interested and curious. Now I realize that you thought I was feeling critical, and that made you feel embarrassed. I regret that I made you feel embarrassed and sad." At LEADPrep, we're deliberately creating a culture where emotions are an open topic of conversation. When students feel heard and understood on an emotional level, it makes them far more likely to self-advocate for their academic needs as well.

Design Thinking Model. Another way we support student agency at LEADPrep is through our design thinking model. Design thinking is the process we use to understand a problem, do research, and create a solution. If a student wants to see a change happen in our school, we don't just listen to what they have to say, we empower them to make that change a reality. All students are encouraged to identify specific issues in our school and use design thinking to propose meaningful solutions. Student-led changes at LEADPrep include all-gender bathrooms, creating quiet spaces ("calm caves"), and determining if a classroom pet would enhance learning.

Lunch Bunch. Some of our students are motivated learners who demand positive agency, while others are demotivated learners who use their agency in a negative way, to refuse engagement. At LEADPrep, one of the ways we raise the bar on participation is by not accepting "zeros." Students are not permitted to skip flips or project work. Our teachers provide "Lunch Bunch," a teacher-assisted lunch-time work session for students who are missing as-

Our projects begin with a driving question. For one of the STEM projects, we asked, "Can we build a device that will create enough electricity to light up a bulb?" Students had to use the design thinking process. At first students were confident they could build the device, but it proved much harder than they initially thought. Several students were very uncomfortable with PBL and complained that they just wanted me to tell them what to do rather than having to figure it out themselves. But they persisted. They started by creating some electrical energy by hand, making a coil of wire and moving a magnet back and forth through it. At that point we had to use a multimeter to detect any electrical current. Scaling up their prototype, one group of three students made a successful bicycle wheel generator. Other students built hand-crank versions. Unfortunately, the windmill version didn't generate enough electricity. But in the design thinking paradigm, students were not being evaluated on how well the project worked. Instead, they were experiencing first-hand how research, frustration, mistakes, and revision are all important aspects of problem-solving. It's not about teacher-led results, it's about student-centered experience.

signments. Yes, the threat of missing social time creates motivation, but, even more importantly, Lunch Bunch provides an extra burst of adult attention when a student is stuck. Lunch bunch is not a penalty, it's just a space set aside to catch up. This expectation breaks self-defeating patterns and lets students experience accountability combined with personal support. Nobody falls through the cracks at LEADPrep.

Full Participation. To experience the power of positive agency, students need to take the lead in their learning, with full participation. To create this emphasis at LEADPrep, participation counts for 50% of the students' grades. Group projects and discussions require the participation of each student. This learning structure requires kids to see themselves as important parts of a whole class effort. Our teachers don't have work packets and textbooks to send home. Learning at LEADPrep is active, with students being all-in on group-work projects. We explain this requirement up front to each student. We ask them to sign a participation agreement (Appendix D) prior to admission, to show that they will honor this commitment.

Leadership. Leadership is an important vehicle for student agency at our school. In our leadership class, students set personal goals, look at habits of success, and work on their "growth edges." We also have students propose and vote on their club activities. Student-led clubs let kids determine and lead their own activities, such as gaming, cooking, and hacky sack. We don't want LEADPrep students to be compliant and submissive; we want them to lead, design, advocate, and express themselves. Being active decision makers in their own learning journey is foundational to their success later in life.

Turning Six "Bosses" Into One

Reducing unnecessary demands is our fourth structural component. I don't believe our country's epidemic of teen executive functioning disorders is necessarily the biological diagnosis we have accepted as a society. Instead, I think adults are causing much of the problem by burdening our students with complicated and inefficient school systems. A lot of teen stress and dysfunction can be resolved when we stop expecting adolescent brains to deal with six or even seven different bosses each day. Our adult brains wouldn't be able to handle that many transitions or bosses in one day, so why expect it from our kids?

Early days, our high school students, with their typical creativity around work avoidance, explained that they could not stay for Lunch Bunch, because they had not brought a lunch from home. We quickly borrowed an idea from my daughter's alternative school experience and provided bread, peanut butter, and jelly. The PB&J idea didn't always go as planned. Once we found a middle school student eating our lunch supply of peanut butter by the spoonful. Other times, our high school students wasted the first part of lunch bunch by putting in restaurant orders with their peers going off campus. As teachers, we have to stay on our toes to make Lunch Bunch a time of effective accountability for our students.

Block Schedule. Within LEADPrep, we created many systems that streamline learning expectations. The first thing we did was create a block schedule. Instead of six or seven classes a day, we have three blocks on Monday/Wednesday and the other three blocks on Tuesday/Thursday. Here is an example:

LEADPrep Daily Schedule

	Monday	Tuesday	Wednesday	Thursday	Friday
9:00-10:30	HS Chemistry MS STEM	English	HS Chemistry MS STEM	English	
10:30-10:40	*break*	*break*	*break*	*break*	**10-1 Experiential Learning**
10:40-11:40	Math	Math	Math	Math	
11:40-12:20	*lunch*	*lunch*	*lunch*	*lunch*	
12:20-1:40	MS Earth Sci HS STEM	US History	MS Earth Sci HS STEM	US History	*lunch*
1:40-2:05	Clubs	Typing Club	Clubs	Toastmasters	**1-3 PE**
2:05-2:15	*break*	*break*	*break*	*break*	
2:15-3:35 Then clean/ close	Spanish	Leadership & Wellness	Spanish	Leadership & Wellness	

Since we are intentionally one community in two locations, our teachers teach their subject on alternating days on each campus. By having three blocks daily, students get to go deeper into each subject area, without as many transitions to handle.

Consistent Lesson Structure and Expectations. To keep expectations consistent, our teachers all share one standard lesson structure. Each of our teachers uses Google Classroom, where they post the flipped lecture the night before. We start each class with a "bell ringer"—a simple ice-breaker task that gets students actively engaged from the first minute of class. After varied project-based activities during the period, we end each class with an "exit ticket" question from the lesson, which assesses learning. The exit ticket question is more for the teacher's benefit than the students. We always want to check to see if our lessons are effective. LEADPrep grading rubrics all include the same emphasis on participation. During class, phones are locked in "phone jail"—no matter which teacher is leading the class, it's the same rule and the same expectation. Because our teachers prioritize consistency, students don't have to adjust throughout the day to meet a confusing variety of expectations. Research on decision fatigue[88] helps us understand that the more decisions we have to make, the less brain power we spend on other tasks. We want our students to spend their mental energy learning, not navigating through a swamp of miscellaneous rules and standards.

When kids are able to keep track of their work, it takes a lot of pressure off their parents as well. LEADPrep parent Margaret shares her family's story: "With our son, we worked as hard as we could with the public school teachers, getting on their homework sites, emailing them, having conferences with them. But we would get the same answers: 'He knows,' 'It's in his planner,' 'He should have the details,' and on and on. We were scared he would not pass ninth grade if we kept him in the public middle school. With LEADPrep, it was night and day. All students work at their own pace, towards goals set between the student and the teachers. We are so happy that our son is thriving and learning...At LEADPrep, you know right away if there are any concerns and the teachers step up to help where needed and keep us informed."

Our teachers collaborate to create one set of relevant learning expectations. By sharing expectations, they collectively become one boss. The result? Suddenly students with previous executive functioning issues are no longer experiencing those problems as academic deal breakers. This really can be a night-and-day difference for incoming students. Kids who were once distracted, anxious, or rigid begin to relax. They feel the calm security of understanding expectations and the satisfaction of being able to meet or exceed those expectations.

Get Flexible and Intentional with your Options for Grades, Credits, and Age Groupings

The fifth structural component is being intentional with our options in terms of grading, credits, and age groupings. When it comes to structural components, the options for micro-schools can be overwhelmingly diverse. At LEADPrep, knowing our state laws and the requirements of our affiliations (accreditation standards, etc.) was our starting place. We jumped in and researched graduation requirements, laws and codes, and the different rules for charter schools, home schools, and private schools. Washington State has alternative learning experience[89] (ALE) administrative codes that inform what non-traditional methods are allowed. Parameters are more flexible than we had first realized. We learned that we don't need to make up missed snow days, like public schools do. We could be governed by hours of instruction, instead of days of instruction. Along the same lines, we found out the specific number of hours and requirements a student needed to complete to earn an independent study credit. With growing online and homeschool learning, state education rules have flexed to address more than just the traditional brick and mortar scenario. We researched what was possible and let those possibilities inform our choices.

Grading. For grading at LEADPrep, we choose the pass/fail system for middle school students. For high schoolers who want a more traditional transcript, we primarily use letter grading. Regardless of whether students are using pass/fail or letter grades, all LEADPrep assessments are competency-based, with an 80% minimum level of competency required to pass. Any performance lower than that is revisited with teacher assistance until the student demonstrates a mastery level of 80% or higher. In math and independent studies, students can accelerate their learning or have added extensions. Many LEADPrep students work with teachers to design honors projects in English, history, science, or STEM. This is a wonderful opportunity for them to determine their own learning direction and follow their passions. Most of our 11th/12th grade students take at least one college (dual-enrollment) online class with our teachers' supervision and support. Our multi-age model means middle school students can work "up" and high school students can work "down." As a community, the kids support each other and there is no stigma to working at individual paces. Because of our inclusive culture at LEADPrep, our students understand that each person is unique and that their numerical age is probably the least interesting thing about them. Assigning course levels by the age of the student is perhaps the most fundamental error in the conventional school system. At LEADPrep, we promote and celebrate the idea that learning styles are far more complex and interesting.

Assessment. For the last piece of our grading model, our LEADPrep team deliberately puts more emphasis on formative assessment than summative assessment. We integrate daily learning check-ins to inform our teaching in real-time: a student who has mastered content can move on; a student with a gap can have it identified and filled in right away. This allows our students to learn at the right level, not waste time catching up or waiting for others to catch up. Formative assessment is greatly different from conventional summative assessment, which is waiting to tally points and grades until the end of a unit or semester. A summative assessment is often called a "post-mortem." Basically, a summative assessment is beating a dead horse. Because they are only used after the learning is over, they don't inform teaching or aid student learning during the class. We want our assessments to be part of the real-time, living experience of learning.

Narrative and Student-Led Reporting. Besides using ongoing in-class assessment tools, our LEADPrep teachers write extensive narratives twice a year to explain the grades on report cards. There are no canned "Is a pleasure to have in class" comments on our reports—each narrative is thoughtful, respectful, and identity-building. I get a little teary-eyed when I read these caring, personalized documents.

When mid-semester progress reports are released, we host bi-annual student-led conferences. Teachers are each in a station around the room. Students guide their parents through the stations, introducing them to each teacher, and leading the discussion about their learning. As a team, the student, teacher, and parents discuss the student's strengths, progress, and goals. These student-led conferences allow students to practice articulating their learning and personal goals to their parents, and to receive focused adult encouragement.

Our science teacher and Director of Learning shares this story with us: "At the beginning of a Biology course, Dallas told me he already knew a lot about Biology and didn't think he would learn anything from my class that year. Dallas was an accelerated learner who was studying a college level Biology text at the time, and he wanted to continue his reading during class time. I took this as a challenge and worked extra hard to create hands-on labs and activities for Dallas and all my students. At the end of each class I would ask Dallas what he had learned that day, and he surprised himself by always being able to tell me at least one new piece of learning." Terry and Dallas worked together to make small, in-class assessments a powerful tool for both teachers and students.

LEADPREP CLASSROOM STRATEGIES FOR LEARNING

Make Learning Project-Based

Real life is project-based. Project-based learning is one of our four primary learning strategies. Human beings constantly use a variety of mental tools to do things we want to do. We use a wide-ranging skill set to solve emerging problems and accomplish desired goals. In school, the best way to teach students is to let them use those skills in the context of project-based learning (PBL). Applying design thinking and knowledge to a situation or project makes the learning go deep. Important 21st-century skills (such as communication, creativity, and collaboration) are embedded. Project management skills are developed. Swiss child psychologist Jean Piaget put it this way, "Knowledge is a consequence of experience." This idea is echoed by the Chinese proverb, "Tell me and I'll forget; show me and I may remember; involve me and I'll understand." This wise adage aptly explains what brain research has verified: we need our students to have active experiences and take ownership in order for learning to sink in and become transferable.

Design Thinking. Encouraging students to have a voice in their learning is not always easy. After many years in a conventional school where students have been told to produce to the specifications of the teacher, a student might resist taking on the design work for themselves. One of our 11th grade students, Travis, would initially push back with, "Just tell me what to do and I'll do it!" Well, Travis, unfortunately we believe the students should be doing the thinking and then telling themselves what to do. At LEADPrep, we have had several students like Travis who rediscovered their curiosity and internal motivation.

As LEADPrep developed this teaching strategy, we found lots of resources and design thinking models to guide our project-based work. We especially like John Spencer and AJ Juliani's design thinking work. Their seven-step launch cycle[90] is posted on our walls and guides the design process we use in our projects. We subscribe to both John[91] and AJ's[92] blogs which give us many great ideas, such as classroom support for a Genius Hour of weekly creativity, where students can learn whatever they want. (Our corporate neighbor Google uses this model, encouraging their employees to spend 20% of their work hours on pet projects.)

Beginning the Launch Cycle. The first step of "look, listen, and learn" is where our flipped instruction comes in handy. Our teachers provide background content to support the project. The next three steps require students to slow down and use their 21st century skills of communication and collaboration. Impatient kids (and adults) often want to jump directly into creating a prototype, but first they have to ask questions (Step 2), understand the process or problem (Step 3), and sort out competing ideas (Step 4). Only then can the students create their prototype (Step 5). This delayed gratification is a challenge for all of us!

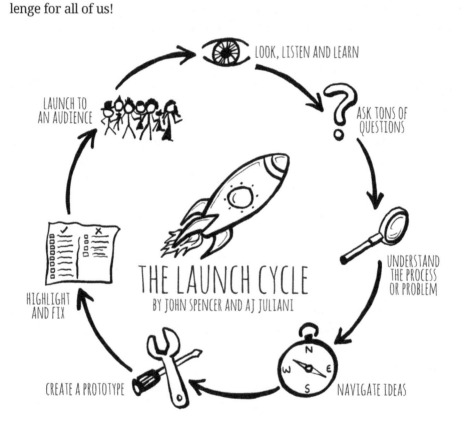

Least Favorite Step of the Launch Cycle. Step 6, "highlight and fix," is the revision step. This step is almost always a challenge for our students. Students who feel they did a good job usually don't want to go back and find areas to improve. Students who feel they did a bad job usually just want to throw the whole thing in the trash and move on. Revision keeps us flexible and challenges our rigid, black-and-white thinking. Depending on how the semester has been planned, this can result in many iterations of a project. Student debates in civics class last year were honed through multiple revisions. At first the students complained a lot ("Oh my gosh, this again? Can't we do something else!"), but in the end they enjoyed feelings of pride in their efforts and confidence in their product.

Final Step of the Launch Cycle. Working in cycles means there is no true starting or stopping point. Clarifying your audience before beginning guides the work and also determines your end presentation. An audience gives project-based work purpose and direction. For example, in Spanish II our students wrote children's books. Intentionally choosing an audience of age eight and younger helped them produce a successful product which they could be proud of regardless of their ability levels. Having an audience, even classmates, is the important launch step of the project. We work better knowing someone will see and appreciate our efforts. That's why our teachers build final presentation time into most class activities.

At each step of the process, we review team roles and what it means to be a contributing member of a team—that's a life skill most working adults wish their co-workers would improve!

Experiential Learning

The second learning strategy we count on is experiential learning. At LEAD-Prep, we extend this real-world application by getting students out of the classroom on Fridays, and by providing three Week Without Walls experiences throughout the school year.

Experiential Fridays. Hmmm...what do I remember most about my own high school experience in the late '70s-early '80s? My strongest memory isn't anything from within the four walls of the classroom. It was being a camp counselor for our school district's fifth grade camp program. Having a passel of eleven-year-olds relying on my mature 16-year-old guidance left a lasting impression on me. I had to use all of my skills to understand and address the needs of my hyperactive, homesick, shy, grumpy, or worried cabin members. I was using my mind, body, and heart—learning was relevant and I was making a positive difference. With that level of personal involvement, my teen self didn't mind working hard and having nights with little sleep. To put it simply, being a camp counselor engaged me on a deeper level than classroom studies.

At LEADPrep, we use our community-based Fridays to engage students deeply, and on multiple levels. One of our guidelines for planning Friday activities is to make sure we are giving our students a chance to engage with as many of Howard Gardener's nine multiple intelligences as possible. That way, students get to explore various ways to be "smart," and experience success in different areas of life.

At LEADPrep, there are four primary types of Friday activities. On Green Fridays, we experience nature and care for it. On Service Fridays, we give back, making a positive difference in our community. On Exploration Fridays, we go on field trips to learn more about the greater Seattle area. On Home Fridays, we invite guest speakers into our school to share their expertise. While we are located on two sites Monday-Thursday, Fridays are combined group activities where our whole community of students and teachers comes together to learn.

Our Friday rotation isn't exact. We tend to take more outdoor Fridays when there is a chance of sunshine—not something we count on December through March in the Pacific Northwest! We also sometimes have an excursion on a different day of the week, like when we were invited to a Thursday technical rehearsal of an orchestra. We are nimble and can adjust our schedule however we like. In LEADPrep's early days, our single full-time employee planned all the Friday trips and transported students with a few volunteer parent drivers. Now, through auction fundraising, we have two school vans. All of our teachers help with the planning and execution of our Friday learning experiences, which means our students have access to a wide-ranging network of connections and opportunities.

What are some activities we do on Fridays? For Service Fridays, we make quarterly visits to Aegis memory loss homes and do art projects with community elders; we sort thousands of pounds of pears at Northwest Harvest; we trim blackberry bushes at parks and do landscaping for our landlords. To support our homeless peers, we sell raffle tickets and serve at Friends of Youth's annual fundraising lunch. For Green Fridays, we collaborate with local organizations to help on trails; we take hikes; we garden; we learn orienteering, bird watching, and Tall Ship sailing. Our field trips and guest speakers draw on local resources that frequently align with our curriculum. For example, in early November we visited *Centro de la Raza*, a Seattle educational, cultural, and social service agency, centered in the Latino/Chicano community. We toured their display of altars (*ofrendas*) for the Mexican Day of the Dead. That expedition was preceded by a Friday guest speaker who spoke about the grief and loss process and helped us build our own altar.

For our LEADPrep *ofrenda,* students brought in and displayed artifacts that reminded them of the person or pet they had lost. With our guest counselor and caring teachers, the students felt safe telling classmates the stories behind the item. Ninth grade Sam had a jar of olives and a tiny fork. He remembered eating olives with his grandfather. Summer brought a cat collar from Mittens, her cherished pet. And sensitive Jordan brought a deck of cards. On each card he had written, "You are loved." He invited the students to each take one card. He bravely told us that his best friend had not felt loved and had committed suicide. He cried and told the class he wanted them to always remember they are loved. His vulnerability and powerful message came from real life and real community.

Most Friday afternoons, we factor in a PE activity. For high school students, this means they earn a half-credit of PE each year. We want these activities to be a sampler platter of movement options so that kids can find determine which lifelong fitness activities work for them. Karate, ultimate frisbee, and volleyball are big hits. Yoga hasn't been as well-received, even though the squirrelly boys who goof off in yoga classes are the ones who most need this mindful body awareness! That's okay, we're planting a seed that may grow into a tree later in life. Walking for fitness is also popular with kids who don't want to play in PE, and we have several exceptionally motivated hikers at our school. In our early days of LEADPrep, we had a kind mom who taught our students Jazzercise. Friday is the perfect day to loop in our talented, helpful volunteers!

Expeditionary Week Without Walls. When I worked internationally, our students often had a fall Week Without Walls (WWW) trip. These were powerful learning experiences because of the destination, and also because of the experience of preparing for the trip and building community with peers. I wanted to be sure that LEADPrep students had the chance for these weeks of intensive learning.

Year One we launched our first annual WWW service trip immediately prior to spring break. This week of outdoor service is a week guided by local nonprofit Mountains to Sound Greenway and focuses on maintaining and appreciating our Pacific Northwest forests. While middle schoolers work with Mountains to Sound Greenway, high school students have the option to travel. We make sure the trip aligns with our curriculum. The first year we taught World History, we offered a service trip to Guatemala. Three years later for World History, we planned a trip with WE (a global nonprofit formerly known as Free the Children) to build a school in Aguas Caliente, Nicaragua. During US History, we partner with Close Up Foundation and travel to Washington DC to experience the inner workings of our government and collaborate with other students from across the US.

Year Six we added a second WWW: a fall camping trip. Positioned in the third week of September, this experience builds a deep sense of community to start the year off right. We collaborate with a Seattle camping gear lending library to borrow tents and any other needed gear. A kind LEADPrep father takes a week off of work and joins us with his RV and camping expertise. A generous LEADPrep mother plans, buys, and organizes our meals in bags clearly labeled with the day and meal. Our team plans various activities, including reflective writing on the bridge over a river, campfire story hour, rock climbing with the YMCA, and varied levels of hikes.

As a high school principal in Budapest, I chaperoned the sophomore bus trip to the WWII concentration camp in Auschwitz, Poland. The students had studied World War II in their US History class and read *Night* by concentration camp survivor Elie Wiesel in English class. They had decided to fast one day of the trip for solidarity. That powerful experience and realization of a dark part of our history will be with all of us for a lifetime.

Of course, different students respond to this week in different ways. Some are thrilled to get a week in motion and nature. Others feel anxious and may even need to go home before the week is over. Whenever this happens, we celebrate the fact they showed up and participated. Even a small level of involvement is a victory for anxious students. When we get the kids and teachers out of the classroom we bond and learn to address new situations. Last year one sweet sixth grade student had his tent mates running to me for intervention after he announced, "I like to snuggle at night!" (Don't worry, we had a good conversation about boundaries and friendly affection.)

This shared experience increases students' connection to nature, their classmates, and teachers, and introduces them to skills they may not have previously explored. It also shifts the leadership dynamic among students. A classroom academic whiz may not be the kid who's skilled at hiking and camping. Taking turns leading and celebrating each other's strengths is a win-win that creates a new level of interdependence within our student group. The kids come back to school bonded by shared experiences, and with an enhanced sense of ease with peers.

Our third WWW experience will start this winter of Year Seven, when we will add a personal choice intensive week. The first step is to give our teachers the choice: what passion would you like to dive into for a week? Right now, our team of creative young adults (and older adults) are discussing intensives such as cooking, art, winter camping, technology, sports, and something to do with animals. The second step will be for students to select their top three choices, without comparing notes with peers or knowing which teacher is leading the intensive. At the end of our week-long intensive, we'll reconvene as a whole school, to share what we discovered and provide sample activities for our classmates. Experiential learning AND community: two focal points at our school.

Being progressive means we constantly question the status quo and deepen the ways we engage our learners. Being a micro-school gives us the flexibility to practice design thinking along with our students, making assessments and revisions along the way. At conventional schools, providing enrichment activities is considered the responsibility of parents and is often crammed into summer camps. At LEADPrep, we believe experiential, community-based, expeditionary learning is something each child should experience with their classmates throughout the year.

Flip the Classroom

Our third learning strategy—flipped classrooms—is the best educational paradigm shift of the millenium! This model flips the school on its head and makes learning dynamic. Teachers synthesize their lectures into the essential components and send them home as videos or slideshows in advance. After that, the whole school day is open for students to learn actively, not passively listening to teachers lecture.

I strongly encourage all educators to investigate the work of Jon Bergmann[93]. He is half of the Colorado teaching duo that brought this flipped model to the forefront of educational innovation. The Flipped Learning Global Initiative (flglobal.org) is trailblazing in a direction I strongly hope the micro-school movement will move. Jon is taking an important learning tool and making it available to many educators. When designing LEADPrep, I was deeply influenced by his vision and innovation.

Distinguished Teaching. To flip the classroom fully and put students in control of their learning is not easy for many experienced teachers. It might mean they have to give up their position of unilateral authority in the classroom. Yet research suggests this bold step is what truly delineates the average teacher from the excellent teacher. The rubric many schools use to assess teachers (Charlotte Danielson's Framework[94]) lists distinguished, top-ranking teacher lesson design in this way:

> The educator coordinates knowledge of content, students, and re-
> sources to design a series of learning experiences aligned to instruc-
> tional outcomes, differentiated where appropriate to make them
> suitable for all students and likely to engage them in significant learn-
> ing. The lesson or unit's structure is clear and allows for different
> pathways according to student needs.

As an overseas school director, I was trained by this smart, quiet, research-driven leader, when she trained educators in Bangkok. This level of planning Danielson demands for the gold star of distinguished teaching goes far beyond creating lectures with corresponding handouts and assigned reading. Learning experiences that differentiate and engage learners? That doesn't sound like lecturing, does it? Danielson continues by describing the resulting distinguished classroom experience: "Students, throughout the lesson, are highly intellectually engaged in significant learning and make material contributions to the activities, student groupings, and materials. The lesson is adapted as needed to the needs of individuals, and the structure and pacing allow for student reflection and closure."

Washington State mandates use of one of three evaluation rubrics (one of which is the Danielson Framework) and cites samples of this recommended distinguished level[95] to which we all aspire. Micro-schools are a much simpler setting for increasing the quality of instruction to align with the best practices the Framework encourages.

An unexpected bonus of our flipped classroom model and removal of hours of homework is parent appreciation. As every parent of a learning outlier can attest, the hours of agony over tedious homework eat up time and energy within the family. One mom told us, "Thanks to LEADPrep, I have my daughter back!" Instead of homework battles, they are now using the afternoons to exercise and cook together. This positive shift in the home dynamic builds emotional support and gives parents more bandwidth to help out at school in other ways.

Implement Personalized Learning Plans for All Learners

Personalized learning plans, our fourth and final learning strategy, is a work in progress for us. The first source of personalized learning is the close relationship between students and their teacher. This relationship allows teachers to coach students individually. Each student has personal goals in each class. In leadership class, we give students further tools for self-awareness and create processes for them to set big-picture goals. Now as our campuses grow from ten students to twenty or twenty-five, we are finding it helpful to create a more structured learning plan for some students. We are working with developmental therapy consultants to design and monitor individual plans with a common format.

SCERTS Assessment. Because we recognize the importance of social communication and emotional regulation in the classroom, we use the SCERTS model[96], developed by Barry Prizant, Amy Weatherby, Emily Rubin, and Amy Laurant. SCERTS stands for Social Communication, Emotional Regulation, and Transactional Support. This framework lets us understand how students are engaging and sustaining this engagement, and helps us track interactions between kids, teachers, and the classroom environment. With our social communication specialist, we use the SCERTS assessment tool to more easily identify social/emotional strengths and differences for each student. Then we work with the student and staff to create effective transactional support systems within the classroom. This model doesn't change our basic method, it just makes formal what we had previously been doing informally—keeping tabs on students who need help with social communication, emotional regulation, and the kinds of executive function assistance that teachers and peers can provide. Although originally created for students with autism, we've found the SCERTS model to be effective for a wide range of learning outliers. For example, individual SCERTS assessments help us look at the reluctant learner and understand why participation is such a challenge. They can also help us co-create plans with the student with anxiety, to determine in advance which strategies bring calmness and support learning.

Everyone has growth edges, and we encourage students to set achievable goals based on their own desires. We believe in each student and help them self-assess and take ownership of their learning. Often parents or outside counselors are a part of the planning and conversation. Our whole team of teachers has access to these goals/plans and the strategies we share to support each student. When everyone shares the same goals, this relieves the

Our science and STEM teacher Terry recounts: "My first week at LEADPrep I met 8th grade George. George was interested in every subject, but he had a unique gift for visualizing engineering solutions in his head and building objects in real life. I called him my Renaissance Student. He talked a lot about becoming an interior decorator, but I pointed out to him that with his math and engineering skills he might enjoy a career in science or engineering. After five years of a wonderful teacher-student relationship in science and STEM, George is headed to college to study design and architecture. I hope I had some influence in his choice to combine arts and engineering for his career."

student of the burden to explain himself to every single teacher or advocate for herself in every single class. At LEADPrep, we personalize to support our unique learners effectively.

OUR BIGGEST SUCCESS IN MAKING OUR SCHOOL UNIQUE AND SPECIAL

All of our successes are made possible by the fact that LEADPrep is a caring tribe with incredible buy-in from all stakeholders. This is not a place where kids are dropped off and parents don't feel a connection. Nor is it a place where students feel like they need just to keep their heads above the water and survive. Our teachers don't robotically slog through a list of procedures and external demands, with no voice in the process. We are an interdependent tribe of support. Parents reach out to each other and to prospective families. They fill our board with dynamic leadership. They add resources and ideas. They weed gardens and paint walls.

Students welcome new members of the learning community. They practice healthy conflict resolution and build meaningful relationships with each other. They knit handmade gifts for each other and send friendly texts to a student who is struggling to overcome depression and return to school. They care. Teachers love the kids, and they laugh as they share affectionate stories, like the one about the quiet girl who turned out to have a hidden talent of hip-hop rapping.

Our model—a responsive micro-school that meets the needs of a wide variety of sixth through twelfth grade learners—is a source of pride for us. We have researched current educational innovations and blended them together to form this learning model. Many smaller schools stick to the traditional model or have one single variation: a STEM focus, expeditionary learning, strong outdoor education, or support for learning differences. We went BIG and said, "We want it all!" Our teachers buy in to this big scope and have started asking, "Could we try this idea? Or how about this one?" Even more strategies are emerging every year. Teachers share ideas and observations to channel students' energy into new projects. They encourage children who feel left out. They proactively help the child with a history of self-harm be regulated and safe. LEADPrep teachers care deeply. Parents honor the hard work happening at school in many ways with thank-you notes, shared anecdotes, and meals and gifts from our recently-formed teacher appreciation committee.

Here is how we described our brand of "special" in one of our earliest flyers:

SPECIALIZED FEATURES

- **Personalized learning** applying learning styles and individual pacing

- **STEM Robotics** and Humanities focused on real-world application

- **21st Century skills** such as project management and creativity

- Ethical **leadership** and social **entrepreneur** (L&E) development

- **Flipped lessons** with video previews at home and hands-on learning in class

- Wednesday 2:15 pm **Toastmaster** (Eloquence Gavel Club) meetings to hone public speaking skills...*open to any interested area middle or high school student*

- **Individualized** electives and projects

- **9:00 am start times** and **off-campus Friday** projects

- Acceleration and **credit recovery**

CHALLENGES TO MAKING OUR SCHOOL UNIQUE AND SPECIAL

We avoided the challenge of being indecisive. We opened our doors with four clear pillars: Lead, STEM, Bridge, Flip.

- Lead (through self-awareness, growth, and service, with weekly Toastmasters practice)

- STEM (to help our students see context and interdisciplinary possibilities in this fast-growing industry)

- Bridge (between where the student was—learning gaps and all—and into college or work with our support)

- Flip the classroom (to keep students directly engaged with learning)

For our first year, we decided to be a high school, since that was my most recent background and where I found unacceptable options for each of my daughters. Late starts (9:00 am M-Th and 10 am Friday), and service/experiential learning on Fridays were no-brainers for us.

However, with our school's wide scope, we are a cautionary tale in limiting our instructional goals. Our student population is extremely diverse in needs and types. That diversity has spread us thin; but with our small size and big heart, we have made this challenge work. Not having a specific niche creates more challenges for our teachers, and it makes marketing more difficult since we can't summarize our school population in a single phrase. We accept all these types of students: ADHD, ASD, anxious, shy, gender-fluid, gifted, dyslexic, neurodiverse, twice-exceptional, reluctant, self-defining, and non-conforming (but willing to participate if they see the relevance). We do not take non-compliant students or those more than a few grade levels below their age group. With our fluid groupings and multi-age setting, this diversity is working for now, but we are constantly adding resources to support this wide array of learning profiles. In hindsight, limiting instructional goals might have been a wise choice, but I have a hard time choosing because I love all these students. If you want an easier path, avoid having too many goals in the early days. Count on being progressive to add more goals and widen your scope as you go along.

WHAT WE LEARNED ABOUT MAKING OUR SCHOOL UNIQUE AND SPECIAL

We have learned a great deal about creating an inclusive village. It started with our beliefs, pushing against what seemed inhumane and divisive in larger schools. Immediately, humane education tied into relevant learning and giving students a voice. When we embraced project-based and flipped learning, we found ourselves automatically aligned with the higher standards of the teacher evaluation tool; our teachers were given high marks in classrooms where the students direct their own learning. The PBL and flipped classroom model make achieving this goal much easier, since teachers do not take charge and lecture during class time. We quickly learned to monitor screen time and bring out the 1:1 Chromebooks only for very specific learning objectives and to put phones away during class time.

Another huge component of our inclusive emphasis has been learning to support mental health and social communication in a regular and ongoing manner. Mental health is vital topic to be addressed in secondary schools. We empower students with daily self-awareness practice so they can become adept at self-regulation: identifying needs and then asking to have these needs met. We watch for and encourage this self-advocacy. If a student feels distracted or feels she has too much energy, we want her to ask if she can take a break to run around the building before she starts math. Or if a student is feeling anxious and needs a break, we want him to know which tools work for him. Does he need to grab an ice pack? Move to a quiet space? Get some fresh air? We create the space and practice identifying feelings and needs and asking to have them met. Students are becoming skilled at using self-advocacy to ask their peers respectfully for what they need in our project-based team setting. This transfer of skills is wonderful to see.

Our colorful mismatched socks include a number of students who are gender creative, neurodiverse, and/or want hands-on learning and creativity. This variety allows us to acknowledge the many unique gifts and challenges our students bring. We get to learn from the diversity within our student population. Differences don't fit within a mass education model, but our LEAD-Prep students get to experience a rich tapestry of humanity and work on lifelong skills such as collaboration and communication within this context. While our inclusive model does take lots of work and vigilance, it is worth it. Switching from the conventional secondary model that focuses on subject matter almost exclusively, to this holistic, kid-centered model, requires us to constantly learn and adapt. For our students' sake, that is a responsibility we happily accept.

One of our students, Lily, is adopted and has the challenges of autism and anxiety. Self-harm is a concern. After a few months at our school, Lily asked if she could train and bring a support animal to school each day. I asked her for details on what it takes to be a support animal and a proposal on how it would work in our fledgling one-room Seattle space. She created a proposal. I approved, letting her know the next step would be to talk to the landlord, the rentals coordinator of this neighborhood association building. Lily asked for an appointment and was invited to bring her dog and meet with the coordinator. Lily self-advocated and had contingency plans for various scenarios. She was given approval. Now her dog Kira is our Seattle mascot. The students understand that when Kira is wearing a vest, the students may not touch her. But on breaks outside, when her vest is off, she is surrounded by animal-loving kids. Lily has agency and uses it at LEADPrep!

LEADPREP ACTION PLAN RESPONSES TO STEP 5

Learning will be inclusive, student-centered, and progressing over time.

Two or three learning tools we will use are project-based learning, flipped classroom with block schedule, and community-based experiential Fridays.

Specific learning goals include personalization for different strengths and learning styles, increased student agency and leadership, developing group-work skills, and design thinking skills.

We will impact learning by creating student buy-in to learning, encouraging goal setting and growth edges, and creating a sense of community between students and their peers and teachers. Students will be happier about school, as evidenced by parents. Students, parents, and teachers will all see improvement in students' personal well-being and academic ability, and an increase in confidence and personal interests.

We will measure the success of meeting these objectives by formative in-class assessments, Charlotte Danielson's Teaching Framework assessment, narrative grading with student-led parent-teacher conferences, ability of students to meet their own personal goals.

You made it through our story of Step 5! Be sure to add structure and strategy notes to your Action Plan before you continue reading.

STEP 6

GET CREATIVE WITH FUNDING

It is much easier to put existing resources to better use,
than to develop resources where they do not exist.

—**George Soros**

SORRY, but there is no way around it: starting any business requires capital. While we can get creative with volunteers and donations, money is also necessary. It's time to take your micro-school idea and ground it in reality. You need to be a solid business with fiscal responsibility, clear deadlines, and research-driven decisions to be successful. We will share our process and encourage you to engage the right tribe members or consultants to help you create a solid action plan to fund your school.

LEADPREP APPROACH TO CREATIVE FUNDING

Determination

Believing our youth are worth the effort, I dove in. With no outside funding, I was prepared to make a great deal of personal investment. This initial focused determination got LEADPrep running. Personally, I invested about $8,000 and worked three years without pay to start my micro-school. I took a job moonlighting at a local community college to fund this effort. It will take sacrifice to start your school.

The same determination that helps parents find ways to pay for a tutor, drivers' education class, or braces can create the funding needed to start a micro-school. We found creative ways to keep our operational costs to a minimum. Exchange of service agreements, where parents donate a service in lieu of tuition, can fill in a lot of gaps. For example, perhaps a student can have reduced tuition if the parent can design and maintain the website. Or perhaps a student can have tuition waived if the parent will serve as one of the teachers. Barter and get creative to fund your dream.

Major Costs

Your space and personnel are two major expenses. Sharing space is a wonderful way to reduce costs. As a daytime school, we didn't need our space on evenings or weekends, so a church for our Kirkland site and a theater lobby for the first year of our Seattle site worked well. The landlords used the space on evenings and weekends, and we used it during the day. For us, that meant we weren't allowed to keep the classroom set up from day to day, and we had to come up with creative solutions for safe storage in a shared space. But compared to the cost of commercial real estate, sharing a space was definitely a way we could economize. This choice kept our resources focused on teachers in the classroom and serving students.

Paying our teachers well has always been a priority. While we all started out volunteering, by the end of the first semester we were able to pay a lead teacher and part-time math teacher. At LEADPrep, we have two goals related to hiring teachers: (1) to recruit and employ teachers who are dynamic and caring facilitators of learning, and (2) annually increase wages and add benefits. It's important that our teachers feel valued and can afford to work in the Seattle area, where the cost of living is high.

Admissions Process

With tuition being the major source of income to pay for your space and salaries, it is vital to build and maintain enrollment. The admissions process will take much more energy than anticipated. Be very intentional with creating and implementing this process. We had to plan our message and find ways to communicate within our tribe and with potential families. We tackled questions such as, *How will we use existing families as resources to prospective and new families? How will we foster community with our parents at each school gathering? How do we tell our school's story and help it become the whole tribe's story?* At LEADPrep, our marketing communications are both internal and external. We use a parent Facebook page for parents to talk with each other. Our existing parents are always willing to talk to prospective families, so I frequently create email introductions between prospective parents and parents of students of a similar profile, such as age or geography. This allows us to use our internal group to welcome our external group. This cycle of inclusion and welcome reflects our values from the start.

Once families express interest, we are very deliberate in our screening and admission process to be sure to enroll students who are a good fit for our model. We encourage families to bring their child to a one-hour open house as the first step. The child participates in the class and gets an initial "vibe" of our learning community. During the open house, the parents meet with a LEADPrep parent, student, and me to discuss the school and their needs. Then we all tour the school and meet with a few of our students who share their story and field questions. Our friendly, confident students are always the best advertisement for LEADPrep!) The second step in the admissions process is for the prospective student to spend a school day participating with our students. Since participation is non-negotiable in our model, this visit shows us how the student might respond to our model. We know the visitor is probably nervous in this new setting and take this into account. We also do a simple math and writing assessment, instead of the external, high-pressure testing some other schools employ.

Finally, we do reference checks on the student and review records. We want to be sure we are creating a win-win situation. We know that taking a student whose needs are too big for us would have a negative impact on fully serving our existing students and put undue pressure on our hard-working teachers. We know taking a student just for the revenue is an unwise and unfair choice. We invest heavily in our admission process for the good of the prospective student, our community, and to assure a happy fit that will naturally allow a steady revenue stream.

OUR BIGGEST CREATIVE FUNDING SUCCESS

Our biggest funding success by far was creating a vision that others were willing to help fund. Yes, I made sacrifices to start LEADPrep. Then, in the first year, parents were willing to support our dream (and received 50% tuition discounts to reward their pioneering spirit). In addition to parental support, we attracted community support. Our trial year for our fledgling second campus in Seattle was in a theater lobby—a tiny, bright red theater lobby. Clayton, the owner of Pocket Theater, believed in community, inclusion, and our vision for alternative education. We told him we aspired to have ten students, which would give us enough revenue to pay the rent. He assured us that if we didn't start with ten students we could arrange for discounted rent until we got there. Wow! Talk about kind and supportive members in our village!

Paint your vision in bold colors and invite others to join in. The response we got was magical. Resources came from unimagined places. Bleak times were countered by an outside donation or kindness to our school. We learned to put one foot in front of the other, taking baby steps. We kept our eyes fixed on the horizon where our students were learning in dynamic and humane ways. The result of our consistent efforts is a LEADPrep tribe with a shared vision, sufficient funding, and an ever-improving micro-school where we serve our happy, colorful mismatched socks!

CHALLENGES WE FACED WITH CREATIVE FUNDING

Waiting for outside funding or spending inordinate amounts of time writing grants to get funding were the biggest pitfalls I was determined to avoid. Many people I have talked to have had momentum to start a micro-school, but lost this drive while waiting for someone else to step in with funding. I have also seen a school think it had enough volunteers and donations, and then not be able to keep its doors open for even the first full year, when soft promises did not materialize.

At LEADPrep, I have relied on an effective budget model called "zero-based budgeting." I picked this model up as a principal in Budapest and I've used it ever since. While many schools give each department a set amount of money to spend and a new textbook adoption every five years, zero-based budgeting is based on proven needs. In order for a teacher or a department to get money, they have to make a proposal for how they are going to spend it, and why. Gone is the spend-it-or-lose-it frenzy. Instead, teachers request with justification and receive the materials they need. For example, when we needed to regroup and pay new teachers mid-year, that became the need that drove our budget. Items that were not needs, but wants, were either wait-listed or were generously provided by parents. Zero-based budgeting actually builds trust between teachers and administrators because it increases the flow of communication and allows the administrator to encourage a teacher's plans and efforts.

Another funding pitfall we were warned about was having only one revenue stream. Tuition was the sole source of income for us. It was suggested by the NWAIS executive director that we look for additional revenue sources. An annual auction was added to our repertoire, but varied sources of income remain an ongoing challenge in our school. We do write some grant requests, but it requires serious man-hours to seek out and apply for grants, and they don't come with a guaranteed return or a multiple-year contribution, so they are a risky source of revenue. An ongoing goal of ours is to strike up a relationship with some of the tech companies in Seattle that might be willing to sponsor a small, neurodiverse STEM school. In the meantime, we cover expenses with the revenues we generate internally.

WHAT WE LEARNED ABOUT CREATIVE FUNDING

Before starting LEADPrep, I had been a principal and school director, so I had experience making budget decisions and had a good overview of the financial and employment aspects of a school. But in my previous schools there were trained employees managing those departments. I didn't have a masterful sense of all the layers of finance and human resource management needed for my own business. I learned to ask a lot of questions and get varied opinions. After many dead ends on finding how to insure my school, my networking led me to a connection with an insurance company that explained how I could qualify to be in a nonprofit insurance pool. Hooray! Being a part of a group pooling resources meant I got much better rates and gave me a great personal contact for insurance advice.

The ability to ask for help made all the difference when I was starting LEADPrep. While I want to serve and give, I also need help. The painful departure of the other two volunteer adults at the start of the school was compounded by one of these teachers taking her daughter and a few other students with her. She offered to homeschool them instead. This was difficult for me both emotionally and financially. Suddenly, I didn't have the revenue to pay the full rent price. After brainstorming with my kind board treasurer, Paul, I went to our landlord and asked if we could please pay a discounted rent amount until March. The landlord graciously agreed, and we had time to regroup and rebuild our enrollment. I also knew to hire a licensed and bonded payroll service. There was no way I wanted to mess up any of the tax compliance rules or teachers' salaries. By asking a myriad of questions and receiving guidance from my board, we were able to maximize the matched donation option that many of our parents' companies offer. In my experience, asking for help is absolutely necessary when you are starting a micro-school.

I also experience, time and again, that help is asking for us! Call it serendipity, guardian angels, or maybe a benevolent force in the universe. For example, a parent hosted our start-of-year family BBQ for Year Two, right after our board treasurer had stepped down to manage his own small business. Enter Sandy, the mother of our hostess and grandmother of one of our juniors. She informed me I needed an accountant and board treasurer. (I kept track of all financial transactions and was trying to teach myself Quick-Books.) Sandy explained that she was an accountant and was donating her services in both roles. Thank you, Sandy, and thank you, Universe! Although her granddaughter graduated a few years ago, we have fortunately been able to keep now-retired Sandy as our financial guru; I don't know where we would be without her.

Our Initial 2013 Action Plan for Finance

Estimated start-up costs: Basic marketing materials (flyers, mailers, etc.), affiliations (fees to register as a nonprofit, business licenses, etc.), and rent deposit were intial costs.

Monthly revenues needed: To stay operational, we needed money to cover salary and rent plus monthly insurance and materials costs.

Realistic monthly income: We would use any money we could bring in. We knew we were operating on sweat equity. Our goal was to enroll enough students to feel like a viable school and to increase revenues. With these dual goals and our mission of inclusion, not every new student was bringing in full tuition.

Tuition to cover expenses: These calculations provided a target for us, but they did not keep us from opening our doors since we had volunteers willing to work without pay. We were busy putting all of the pieces of the school model together while marketing and financing the school. Action and progress were going to help us attract more students and earn the revenues to pay our expenses.

Operating Expenses: Our cost was a daily rate for renting the church sanctuary. Soon we added salaries to our expenses.

How can we run our school with less money? We have had various parents and one student provide service in lieu of tuition. These students otherwise would not have been able to attend, so it would have been a loss for both the family and school. These services allowed us to have more classroom and technology support and run on less money.

How much tuition should we charge? Our market analysis included looking at a range of private school tuition, including religious schools (these often charge less than other private schools.) We knew we wanted to be affordable for public school students with families who hadn't budgeted for private school tuition. So, we chose to charge in the lower quarter of the range of tuition. Additionally, we explain the true cost per student to each of our families. The true cost of a LEADPrep education is about $5,000 higher than our tuition. We ask families with the means to consider making this $5,000 donation. Some families can, and if their business has a matched donation program (like Bank of America, Boeing, and Microsoft), we also get the matched donation. We raise tuition 3% each year to adjust annually for cost of living and avoid ever needing a drastic increase. This tuition process has worked well for our school so far.

Be sure to stop and update Step 6 in your Micro-School Action Plan.

STEP 7

LET THE MICRO-SCHOOL COALITION HELP YOU OPEN YOUR DOORS!

We can change the world and make it a better place. It is in our hands to make a difference.

—Nelson Mandela

LEADPREP BEGAN as an aspiration. It was my calling to dream courageously and then solve a problem. Other parents and educators joined me, and we were guided by envisioning these images: *Schools where teens are welcome and like attending. Schools small enough for each student to be seen, heard, and valued by multiple adults. Schools where the focus is on the whole human and community is created to support this holistic development. Schools where teachers and parents create a tribe to support varied learning styles and over-come challenges together.*

At the beginning of this journey, I went to a presentation by visualiza-tion guru Patti Dobrowolski.[97] She taught us a four-step process. We drew our present reality on the left side of a big piece of paper. Then we used visualization and all of our senses to imagine our desired new reality. We drew this new reality on the right side of the paper. Then we connected the two realities with action steps. Seeing that image on the wall of my house for the past seven years has given me momentum and purpose. I return to this process every time I need to update my dream and find that inner voice of inspiration. Visioning (and creating the visual images) is a powerful tool. I've shared parts of this process and her inspirational TedTalk with my students. I got bold and asked Patti herself to draw my latest visioning map, which is now hanging on my living room wall:

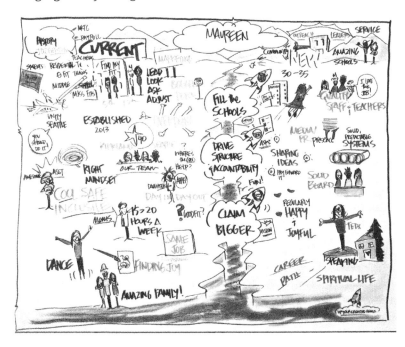

Take a moment. Visualize a picture of the school you want to create. How does it look? How do students feel? What are the colors and sounds? Sink into the potential future with all your senses. We invite you to get clear on your vision for our precious learners. How does it feel to be offering your micro-school? Experience the glow of your visualization. You are providing a vehicle to transform lives and empower our young. Access the deepest desires you have for the students for whom you care. Breath it in. See it. Realizing your vision is both thrilling and daunting, I know. Now, take out a sheet of paper and draw or paint the picture of your school. Transfer what you visualize in your mind into an image you see and touch.

Are you ready to make this dream a reality? Are you ready for a tribe of support to help you? Before we share how LEADPrep opened its doors, let me tell you what we are doing now to help YOU open the doors of your own wonderful school. We have created a collection of resources for you: the Micro-School Coalition.

HOW THE MICRO-SCHOOL COALITION WILL HELP

This micro-school primer you hold in your hands right now is a great starting resource. Following the process laid out in this book can lead you, step by step, on the path to begin to transform education in your community. This book is based on our tribe's vast collective experience in educational innovations—not just my experience, but our parents', teachers', and students' wisdom as well. Our experiences attending, teaching at, opening, and sustaining various micro-schools will guide your efforts. If you've read this far, chances are you are strongly thinking about how you can be a part of this learning revolution.

The **Micro-School Coalition**[98] **(MSC)** has been formed to provide resources for other micro-school founders. The MSC tagline is *Building Community to Transform Education for Today's Learners*. Let's collaborate while we are creating our micro-schools. Transforming education is a big task, but there's no need for each of us to reinvent the wheel and labor in isolation. The MSC will help you design and implement a new learning option for today's learners. The definition of a coalition is *an alliance for combined action*. Imagine our collective power to make a positive difference! Let's build that community together. I started LEADPrep by myself; it was lonely and hard. We don't want you to start your micro-school by yourself. Let the micro-school coalition help.

Imagine your vision backed by a coalition of support. A tribe to support your tribe! Welcome to the Micro-School Coalition. Here are the visualized images that guide the creation of this alliance: *Imagine a community of micro-schools and resources available to new and existing learning communities. Imagine the common goal to serve more children in a variety of new and evolving ways. Imagine collaborating to support others answering the same calling.* The MSC offers resources, training, and a real micro-school model.

MICRO-SCHOOL SUPPORTS

Online directory. On the MSC website you will find an online directory. This is a list of existing micro-schools. Our small-school cohort in Seattle has many schools on this list. Members in this directory are willing to answer questions from micro-school founders and parents. This list is based on the premise that collaboration wins over competition, because we know there are plenty of students to go around. The list is a starting point for those courageously beginning their own micro-school, a support to existing micro-schools, and a place prospective families can look for potential schools.

List of resources. The MSC site also hosts a list of resources for micro-schools. We will collectively grow this list of resources, sharing what we've found. Many of the resources are price-friendly teaching and administrative tools for your likely humble start-up budget. Relevant blogs—mine and other authors'—are on this site, as are recent micro-school articles to keep you informed of the impact innovative education is having on the world. We want you to have resources at your fingertips and a cohort model of collaboration through the process.

Group Training or Personal Consulting. The MSC also wants you to have direct support in your start-up journey. Group training means your tribe has support from other tribes who are also creating micro-schools. This was the cohort model Seattle University used when I was a doctoral student. Working in a cohort made learning much more dynamic and supported. I offer the same cohort opportunity to you.

The MSC cohort is small, and each micro-school leader completes prerequisites before becoming a cohort member. For this cohort, we need hard workers who are grounded in reality. Once started, there are monthly training sessions. Between these sessions, cohort members have support in completing the homework and Action Plan steps. There is also a private Facebook group to facilitate collaboration. The cohort supports our overarching goal for each participating start-up micro-school to have at least ten students and open their doors in less than a year. With the synergy of the group and step-by-step support, this training program can help innovators meet their goals.

If you're not ready to join the cohort, a personal consultation is a good place to start. As parents, when a subject is daunting or too much for our children to handle alone, we often engage a tutor or a coach, or sign them up for a class. When we want to lose weight or train for a marathon, enlisting personal support or coaching makes it easier. I am available to consult with you. Let's talk about your vision and see what you need for support. I provide a free initial consultation with at least three ideas on how you can proceed. Some founders

The hunger in our community for more school options is evident. As I form this coalition and get this book to the publisher, I am also coaching a micro-school founder through the seven steps. Her homeschool team in Snohomish county is planning a junior high micro-school. Their vision of providing dynamic support for twice exceptional tween learners (gifted students who also have specific learning challenges) is being supported by our seven-step process, the MIcro-School Coalition, and LEADPrep.

have just needed a few ideas or specific information. Others have worked 1:1 with me through the whole start-up process.

Unlike the cohort model and its tribe of support, the 1:1 route is more individualized and allows you to set your own pace. In addition to resources and consulting, we also encourage you to visit micro-schools in your area. Use the example of other micro-schools as a starting point to ask questions, clarify ideas, and envision how your micro-school will be similar or different. Each member in our micro-school directory is happy to field your questions and host your visit. It is easier to train for a triathlon, stick to a diet, or clean the garage with moral support and teamwork. Let the MSC be your partner as you open the doors of your micro-school.

Micro-School in Action: LEADPrep. Both our LEADPrep campuses in Kirkland and Seattle welcome visitors and questions. A picture is worth a thousand words. Remember our "virtual visit" at the very beginning of this book? We invite you to come visit in real-life and use our successful model as a springboard for the launch of your own wonderful micro-school. Our students will happily show you around and tell you why a micro-school is making a difference in their lives. Let our kids be the ones to inspire you to make a difference in the lives of other children.

Our new students were all welcomed cheerfully when they visited and joined LEADPrep. When families visit, we ask a few kids of similar age or background if they are willing to share their stories. (The fact that they're getting out of class *might* influence their quick willingness to help out.) Last spring, a couple who have a child in a residential treatment center (RTC) for anxiety visited our Kirkland campus. Two of our students, both of whom had been in a RTC the previous year, agreed to meet with the parents. Each candidly shared what hadn't worked in large public schools before the RTC, what they learned from their RTC experience, and how they apply it to find success at LEADPrep. After our students returned to the class, the parents told me how touched they were that our students spoke their truth with such poise and an obvious wish for their son to find a good fit. What a win-win: our students are empowered by sharing their authentic selves and being accepted, and potential families get to see the positive impact that's possible and feel real hope for their child's future.

LEADPREP APPROACH TO OPENING OUR DOORS

At LEADPrep we have accomplished something many micro-school advocates have not actually done: opened and maintained an actual micro-school, with no outside funding. Whew! This means that other individuals and parent tribes can do the same, if they are armed with creativity and fierce tenacity. The journey was a rollercoaster with many scary drops and exhilarating highs. Above all, we kept moving forward with a determination to never quit or give up. This foundation of transforming a creative idea into a hard-fought, sustainable reality gives us a unique position from which to support other micro-schools in their start-up. We can assure you that your Herculean efforts will transform kids' lives. On your journey, LEADPrep is like a big sister or brother, role model, and cheerleader for your own micro-school development process.

OUR BIGGEST SUCCESS IN OPENING OUR DOORS

At LEADPrep, our first—and ongoing—success has been **tenaciously holding onto this dream and keeping our doors open**. LEADPrep has seen two other Seattle micro-schools open and close in our brief tenure. One had private funding. One had a beloved local school leader at the helm. Neither was enough to keep the doors open. What has been different for us? We've had our share of adversity, but we refused to quit and learned quickly from our challenges. When things go badly, we regroup, learn from the experience, and try again. I know many people have said this before, but the journey to success is a marathon, not a sprint. No quitting allowed when the novelty wears off or when others let you down. If you're doing it for the kids you love, that's what gives you the motivation to return to the task again and again.

Our second success is our most important one, but could only happen because we kept our doors open through the start-up challenges. *LEADPrep has become a sanctuary that rebuilds the human spirit and mirrors back children's unique strengths and gifts.* Our community gives students a daily opportunity not only to be seen, heard, and valued, but to see, hear, and value their peers. These are kind, communal kids who feel empowered and are getting frequent chances to make positive differences in the world. What a wonderful gift, not just to these kids and families, but to our crazy, confused world. Maybe these students can be a model for our generation to create the "we" of a united community instead of the crippling "us vs. them" mentality that divides us and keeps us from serving the greater good.

At every step along the way, LEADPrep has honed our model and student expectations, adapting to new situations and opportunities. We kept it real and learned to not worry about having matching school furniture or other details that didn't directly impact student learning. We became excellent at asking these questions: *Are our students getting to learn in authentic ways? Do they feel seen, heard, and valued? Are they gaining confidence, skills, and a sense of purpose they can take out into the world? Are they kind? Are they being prepared to make a positive difference? Do we keep improving? Progressing? Innovating?* The answers to these questions assure us we are a successful work in progress. We want to help you ask the same questions, as a member of the growing micro-school community.

CHALLENGES TO OPENING OUR DOORS

As I mentioned previously, our biggest challenge has been marketing. We didn't have the ease of branding around a specific niche. Many families and students struggle to embrace the idea of being mismatched socks and seem stuck in angst, persisting in painful school settings. They are locked into the traditional model, settling for less-than-humane schooling. Despite our clear mission, our message via marketing did not result in convincing many of these parents to try our solution.

Our second challenge was internal—the hesitancy and discouragement that is part of any start-up venture. There were tears and *what-are-we-doing?* moments of doubt. Disappointments and discouragements result in some folks giving up, but our challenges made us dig our heels in and stand firm.

The real challenge we face every day is changing the paradigm while there's still time to help. Many children NEED a different learning experience, and they can't get it until we shift our education culture. This is not a minor pitfall; it is the deep crevasse in the present system into which our children fall, losing their passions and limiting their opportunities, forming negative self-images and habits of defeat. These are not little tiny cracks kids are falling through, but chasms. The pitfall is Grand Canyon deep. That's the fall students take when we don't find or create the schools they need.

WHAT WE LEARNED ABOUT OPENING OUR DOORS

We have learned to be unapologetically a work in progress. Are we perfect? Heck no! Do we make mistakes? Heck yes! Do we revise and keep going? Absolutely. LEADPrep lists "progressive" in our mission statement. We apply the same design thinking process (mistakes and all) that we want our students to use. We are nimble and constantly striving to improve. The following are milestones from our first six years and the lessons we learned in each year.

Year One. We opened our high school, added eighth grade, and attracted a former Microsoft techie to volunteer-teach STEM. **We learned** to expect the unexpected, especially teachers and students joining and leaving at odd times. We also learned to accept setbacks and refuse to quit in the hard times.

Year Two. We hired a full-time lead teacher, added seventh grade, took our students on an international service trip for 12 days in Guatemala, fully implemented the flipped classroom model, added a hands-on science teacher shared with a homeschool co-op, held our first annual auction, became accredited, and joined the independent school association. **We learned** that others wanted to help: a Seattle teacher led our Guatemala trip, as he had for his public school students for over a decade. A parent guided us to our wonderful science teacher, Terry, whom we shared with a homeschool co-op for two years and now employ full-time as our wise and kind Director of Learning.

Year Three. We added sixth grade, Digital Storytelling classes with an outside film company, and rented an office space that finally gave us storage. **We learned** that being the first sixth grade student can be lonely and that outside companies, like Cherry Street Films, can be partners toward our vision and a wonderful real-world boost for our learners.

Year Four. We moved into leased space that didn't have to be disassembled nightly and gave us more room and a place to display student work, added a Washington DC Close-Up (educational travel) offering, and became a WE service school for global community. **We learned** that increasing student enrollment is a much slower process than we anticipated and that perseverance is the solution.

Year Five. We moved our part-time science teacher to full-time, added a medical insurance stipend for our teachers, piloted opening our second campus (and temporarily shut it, shuttling Seattle students to the Kirkland campus, while we worked out some operational kinks), and took students on a Nicaragua Free the Children/WE service trip. **We learned** that we can't renew contracts for kind, well-intentioned teachers who don't actually follow our model. This determination to align with our mission meant making some difficult staffing decisions and deciding to part ways with teachers we respected, but who weren't the right fit for LEADPrep.

Year Six. We increased our full-time team to seven. We added an IRA matched retirement plan for our full-time teachers. After a lengthy process, we were approved to be hired by public school districts as a non-public agency. We also added a week of camping in the fall. **We learned** that having a team, while necessitating much more communication and supervision, was wonderful. The synergy, collaboration, humor, and variety of personalities serving our kids was very positive. Year Six felt like the right LEADPrep team was formed.

LEADPREP ACTION PLAN RESPONSES TO STEP 7

What's the timeline for this project? Our timeline was eight months. We began building the school in January of 2013 and opened in September.

What's holding us back? With nothing except an idea and my experience, lack of knowledge on how to create a micro-school made my path more difficult. But I chose to not spend energy on doubts and to use daily small actions (baby steps) to keep moving forward past hesitancy and being overwhelmed.

How can we make this plan a reality? Meeting Washington's private school application requirements gave me concrete actions in the beginning. Attending networking meetings helped me see the varied components that go into a business and how others are addressing the various aspects of being a business.

What are three steps I will do within a week to take action? I like to reverse-engineer. I set goals for where I planned to be at the end of each month and then worked backward with weekly and daily steps toward the goals. The timeline in your Action Plan is a great place for you to do the same.

Your Action Plan and journal should have lots of notes by now. Take a moment to review both. Think about the progress you have made and clarity you have created as you have looked at your micro-school through the lens of these seven steps. Congratulations on the hard work you have already completed.

MAKE THE DIFFERENCE,
ONE MICRO-SCHOOL AT A TIME

I wouldn't change you for the world,
but I'll change the world for you.

—Unknown

THERE IS AN ELEPHANT in the room that most of our society is refusing to acknowledge. The K-12 educational model is broken. When I studied California's High Tech High model and watched their *Most Likely to Succeed*[99] documentary, I realized that others were willing to point out that elephant. A broken system is producing broken results as our high drop-out rates and levels of teen anxiety demonstrate. ***Ignoring the signs of our failing education system is parallel to not heeding the multitude of signs of global warming.*** For decades, our society has ignored the signs and symptoms of climate change. Even now, with raging fires, catastrophic hurricanes, and unseasonable cold streaks and heat spells, global warming is derided as a myth by many people. This is the ostrich-in-the-sand approach—if we hide from a problem and ignore it, maybe it will go away. Our society is also ignoring the fact that our current K-12 learning model is harming many of our children. We claim there is no problem, and all the while our youth population is being decimated by conforming to a system that destroys as often as it educates. We have huge broken systems that our country and our fellow citizens are not acknowledging. Is this the world we want to leave for our grandchildren? The vital mission of micro-schools is to create change for our kids, not to replicate broken systems.

We are creating this needed change. We are gathering the powerful tribe that supported LEADPrep and is now supporting the Micro-School Coalition. A cycle is building of parents supporting each other, parents caring about each other's children, and parents supporting new educational options. Tribes support micro-schools, and, in turn, micro-schools support and inspire each other. The snowball effect happening is a wild success that takes my breath away. I am inspired to dream in even broader strokes. *What if our colorful rainbow of outliers were accepted as the majority, and then caring tribes forming micro-schools became a normal part of our country's culture? What could setting this standard of interpersonal connection and focus on service and strengths mean for our society, as our youth become adults and take on government and other leadership positions?* The seeds we plant in our middle and high schools could change the direction of our entire world. See what I mean about breathtaking?!

Remember our call to action in the introduction? It was a call to take our love for our kids and demand more for them: more learning, more joy, and more understanding. My intention was to help you see that now is the time to act. You can create a micro-school where all of our colorful unique kids thrive. This book provides four of the five needed ingredients:

1. We have affirmation of parental angst at the struggles our teens are enduring.

2. We have a solution of seven clear, thorough steps to launch a micro-school.

3. We have an example of a school that has followed these steps and has been providing an inclusive and innovative learning community for students since 2013.

4. We have a coalition to support you every step of the way.

The missing fifth ingredient is YOU. We need your passion and determination to join the work of this coalition of micro-schools. With creativity and grit you can add your own transformational learning community to the options available for our children. The time is now.

Our children don't get a second chance at their K-12 education or at forming their identity. Transform your passion for more and better learning options into viable solutions. Talking and lamenting alone will not change the educational landscape. Your hard work and commitment will. This conclusion is brief so that you can stop reading and take action!

Together we can make schools that celebrate our drawer full of colorful, mismatched socks. Let's make learning work for ALL of our students! Calling all fed up and courageous parents...let's go!

ACKNOWLEDGEMENTS

So many mentors and muses have blessed me with the support that has been foundational in creating and serving in four micro-schools. I extend my sincere gratitude to the following people who made this book possible.

—Mentors and muses: My school teachers, Dennis Martinen, Vicki Swartz, Sue Lombard, students and teachers of my first micro-school: Connect, Bob Sills, and my myriad of wise spiritual directors

—Present-day supporters: Seattle Unity prayer chaplains and the LEAD-Prep community

—The amazing book contributors who took on my "summer project" challenge to craft this book in July and August and deliver it to the publisher before the school year began:

—Kester Limner for her belief in LEADPrep and this coalition. Her hours upon hours as contributing editor make this book sparkle and invite!

—Joelle Chizmar for simultaneously creating visual magic in our book cover, coalition website, overall branding, and social media presence

—Editors who real-time edited in Google Docs: Karen Lynn Maher of LegacyONE and Richard Sine, with volunteer editors Giana O'Shaughnessy-Ross, Jadrian O'Shaughnessy-Ross, Marilyn O'Shaughnessy, Gloria Wall, and Nicole Wall. Talk about an amazing tribe!

—My precious family: Pat and Marilyn—parents who modeled grit, servant leadership, and deep faith, while blessing me with roots and wings; Jeff Robinette—my fun, adventurous, encouraging husband; and my beloved Jadrian and Giana—for remedial and intensive training on parenting unique teens and being the ultimate muses, transforming my frustration into a fierce commitment to be that change we sought so hard for both of you. Your journeys and teachings inspire me daily.

APPENDICES

Appendix A

Action Plan Outline

Our seven-step process will guide you through creating a plan to open your micro-school. As you read each step in Part Two, stop and fill out that piece of your Action Plan. Jot additional notes as you get more ideas in Part Three. This document, along with notes and reflections you keep in your journal, will give you a place to keep track of your ideas and plans.

STEP 1: Begin with the Mission

School Name:

Learning Model:

Our graduates can

Students we serve

Affiliations we choose are

Our Mission:

Step 2: Recruit Energetic and Committed Trailblazers

Business Leader:

BL Responsibilities:

Educational Leader:

EL Responsibilities:

Step 3: Engage Community Collaborators

Action Plan for Operations

Days and hours of operation

Location

Plan to meet legal requirements

Insurance plan

Tribe leaders, teachers, and volunteers include

Back-up contingency plan includes

Step 4: Get the Word Out

Market Analysis of SWOT

Internal Strengths:

Internal Weaknesses:

External Opportunities:

External Threats:

Action Plan for Marketing

My market includes

The market analysis tells me

Our plan for reaching prospective families and partners or donors is

Outcomes we expect from getting the word out

Step 5: Choose What Makes Your School Special

How learning will be

Two or three learning tools we will use are

Specific learning goals include

How we will impact learning

We will measure the success of meeting these objectives by

Step 6: Get Creative with Funding

Action Plan for Finance

Estimated start-up costs are _____ (explain) _____

Monthly revenues needed to stay operational are _____ (explain) _____

Realistic monthly income is _____ (explain) _____

Tuition for ten students needs to equal _____ to pay expenses

Step 7: Open Your Doors!

Timeline to Open our Doors in a Year or Less

Month	Goal	Person Responsible	Expected Outcome and Date of Completion	Notes
Month 1				
Month 2				
Month 3				
Month 4				
Month 5				
Month 6				
Month 7				
Month 8				
Month 9				
Month 10				
Month 11				
Month 12	Our micro-school is open and serving color-ful mismatched kids!			

Telling Our Story

Mission Statement and Web Presence Worksheet (Step 1)

Part One: Our Vision

1. **What does the graduate of our school look like?** List ten descriptors for the profile of a student who successfully completes your school. Now rank the top four.

2. **Who will we serve?** List the grade levels you will offer. Determine if you will start with all grades or add grades over time. Note the learning profile of your ideal student. To create clear boundaries, list student profiles that you will not be able to serve.

3. **How will we serve them?** Determine if you plan on using a traditional space and schedule. Note if your model will be blended (partially online) and the attendance expectations.

4. **What affiliations do we want?** Determine if your school will be public or private. Nonprofit or for-profit. Then decide if you want state approval and/or accreditation.

5. **What legacy will we leave?** Visions are big. Write a sentence describing how your school transforms learning.

Part Two: Our Name and Mission

1. Look at the notes you took while reading through the list of school options.

2. Look back at the mission statement samples in Step 2.

3. Review how you answered the five questions above.

Now write three sentences or less that introduce your micro-school and uses the information above. Design a name that describes and helps people understand your school or location. Take your time. Revisit your draft. Get input. Let it shift as you look at details.

When your mission feels complete, review it. Ask three questions based on each facet of your mission statement draft: one question to test basic understanding, one personal question, one outward facing question. LEADPrep values being an educational community. Our board spent a meeting asking: *What kinds of people make up our "educational community?"* (checking for clear understanding). *Who is the most important person in our educational community right now?* (our personal question). *Explain why having an educational community is important to us.* (This final question reflects who we are out to our prospective tribe members.)

Do the same with the facets of your mission statement. Let the answers to these questions guide you in creating a mission statement that tells your story.

Part Three: Web Presence

Now that you have a name and mission, it is time to create your web presence. Every decision you make begins to create your brand. Think of the impression you want to make. Here are some steps and considerations.

1. Choose your domain name. If you are a nonprofit, you will probably want a site ending in *.org*. If you are a for-profit school, a *.com* site is more common. There are many other choices, but uncommon endings may not enhance your brand. You can purchase a domain name at sites like GoDaddy, Name.com, and Domain.com. Each of these sites has a search feature so that you can find available domain names. Buy your domain and possibly other domains with similar names in order to take them off the market and avoid confusion.

2. Create a simple website. Schools are businesses. They need to be easily searchable online. You need a website.

3. Provide email addresses for staff. We choose to use the Google Suite, since we use Google Classroom. You want to purchase email and link it to your domain name. All school emails sent should be sent from **yourname@yourschool.org** to show your official affiliation.

4. Link a Facebook page to your website. Also, consider if you want to add an Instagram account. These two sites enhance your search engine optimization (SEO) efforts.

5. Set your style. Create a common logo image and tagline. Choose your colors and font. Consistently apply this style and messaging—your brand—to all of your social media and marketing projects.

Now you are telling your story and beginning to attract your ideal tribe.

Sample Micro-School Job Description
(Step 2)

Job Description Template
Leadership Preparatory Academy
2019-20

LEADPrep is a progressive grades 6-12 micro-school with a North Seattle campus. We are seeking a _____ teacher. Our dynamic, personalized model includes project-based learning with co-teaching support.

DUTIES

Preparation

- Create hands-on (specific subject area) learning experiences aligned with interests/learning styles, using design thinking, exposing students to real world connections and interdisciplinary activities/lessons

- Prepare corresponding syllabi and first quarter "lessons" prior to September

- Prepare fully (including supplies) and load on curriculum map and Google Classroom (GC)—two flip video mini-lessons and the following week's activities—by Friday at 3 pm

- Design two blocks of sub-lesson plans before the start of the school year; refresh after using

Teaching

- Arrive at 8:30 and stay until 4:15 M-Th; 9:30-3:15 Fridays (with off-site prep)
- Provide project-/problem-based instruction
- Be mindful, proactive, and focused on engagement with students when in the school
- Facilitate student reflection/self-advocacy when needed; expect respect and kindness
- Assist in specialist teaching, break/lunch supervision, and co-curriculars, as needed

Other:

- Provide prompt, excellent customer service to parents
- Take the lead in one key school project or program
- Serve as "expert" and share new educational/technology ideas to infuse into the learning
- Welcome and interact with guests; model and encourage student hospitality
- Provide 1:1 advising to students on your advising list (TBD in October)
- Participate in teacher goal setting and evaluation (Danielson model)
- Contribute bi-monthly to the parent newsletter
- Provide regular (twice a week) Facebook photo updates
- Use GC for mapping, grading, homework reports, and attendance; create students' quarterly progress reports
- Promote the school to other service providers/customers
- Add content to the school YouTube channel
- Set up and attend events: OHs, BBQ, BTSN, Nov conferences, auction, WWW, and graduation
- Supervise daily facility cleaning by students
- Other duties as assigned, including being current on First Aid/CPR training
- Aim for AMAZING!

In exchange for these services:

- (List salary and benefits here)

Sample Family-School-Student Commitment Form (Step 3)

Leadership Preparatory (LEADPrep) Academy
Covenant for Excellence
Student &Parent/Guardian Commitment
2019-2020 School Year

Student Name:

Parent/Guardian Name:

We agree to bring our best selves to this learning community. We are asking all players to commit to being intentional and doing their best this year!

Our LEADPrep team is all in! We commit to:

- Preparing quality bell-to-bell teaching with flip lessons posted at least two days in advance of class

- Responding promptly to parent communication

- Personalizing learning and continuing to learn more ways to make learning relevant

- Knowing/honoring each student, seeing the strengths, and nudging on "growth edges"

- Collaborating as a team to maximize synergy and interdisciplinary opportunities

- Having FUN as we serve our students!

We ask each student to commit to:

- Participating fully, with excellent, punctual attendance

- Checking in with themselves and self-regulating

- Going beyond "doing assignments," maximizing time with bell-to-bell learning; if finishing early asking "How can I extend my learning?" and "How can I make a positive difference right now?"

- Asking respectfully for what they need; empowering themselves/taking responsibility for making all aspects of their learning work well

- Completing all work due prior to the corresponding class; 30 minutes of homework each night

- Avoiding behaviors that limit own or others' learning

- Setting and working toward meaningful goals

- Completing 20 service hours annually

- Assisting LEADPrep in developing to its potential; actively marketing and promoting the school

We ask each parent/guardian to commit to:

- Helping their student process situations and empower her/him to deal directly with the situation

- Trusting the student to take responsibility for her/his learning and needs; collaborating with teachers to empower student ownership

- Creating routines that support healthy teens, including nightly scheduled homework, considering screen time to end an hour before bedtime and no devices in the bedroom at night (Chromebooks will stay at school: one less device!), breakfast and healthy lunches provided, students well-rested for school

- Spreading the word about LEADPrep in person and on social media

- Communicating regularly and proactively with school personnel

- Assisting LEADPrep in developing to its potential; actively marketing and promoting the school. We welcome the names and contact information of potential families

- Submitting timely registration/tuition and fee payments

- Forming a new and enhanced definition of school-home collaboration

- *Serving forty hours (40) of volunteer time per family* per school year. This helps us form a village of caring adults who know our students, by getting everyone involved with our school and each other. It also helps keep our tuition lower. Through organized "work parties," "friend raisers," and school activities, our families become an embraced part of the LEADPrep community in a short time. All adults in the student's support circle may serve: grandparents, neighbors, family friends...let's extend our village! How might you help?

__ Garden work party	__ Construction team	__ Driver/Chaperone
__ Classroom help/art	__ Auction team	__ Open house liaison
__ Welcome team	__ Year-end clean up team	__ Other, specify: _____

Know you can always ask "How may I help?" or "I have three hours, what needs to be done?" or share ideas for new projects.

LEADPrep is dedicated to each student's success and will work closely with parents and students to make this happen.

I agree to the above-stated commitments and the expectations in the school handbook.

Student Signature: _____   Date: _____

Parent/Guardian Signature: _____   Date: _____

Appendix E

Elevator Speech Template
(Step 4)

Writing and practicing your elevator speech is helpful for clarifying the key components of your micro-school and getting to a succinct description. Steps to take:

1. Start with an introduction of who you are. Give your name and explain your role in the formation of the micro-school.

2. Explain your concern or how the need impacts you personally and why you are invested in being a part of the solution.

3. Provide a summary of what your micro-school provides.

4. Explain what you want from your audience. Clearly state if you are looking for a building or prospective families or other resources.

5. Finish with a call to action. This is the "buy now" moment. You want to use enthusiastic words and ask for a specific action to be taken. Express how they will benefit. A call to action could be, "Hand out these flyers to five friends with children. Let's be sure your friends have an opportunity to join this great micro-school."

6. Take your time and make it conversational. Be sure to ask them about their school experience or that of their children.

7. Practice to gain confidence.

You have a valuable resource to offer. Taking time to get clear on your "why," what you are offering, and your "ask" or call to action is critical.

Checklist of Business Decisions
(Step 5)

This is a partial list of steps and information to guide your business decisions.

Business Type

LLC/for-profit or nonprofit. Decide which and register your business with your state. Then you will have a business registration number. You will need to determine what city business license you need, once you have determined where your school will be located. You will also need to register your nonprofit with the IRS to obtain an employer identification number (EIN). Finally, you will need articles of incorporation and bylaws, to complete your application for nonprofit 501c3 status.

Affiliation

- State-approved

  Type in "approved private schools" and your state. You will find the state agency that approves private schools. Work with their timeline and criteria to become approved and posted on their state list.

- Church- or other special affiliation

  Work with any other special group that aligns with your mission to meet their criteria.

Banking and Credit Cards

You will want to open a business bank account. Consider if you also want a business credit card.

Insurance

You will need to be sure that you have insurance that protects your students, faculty and staff, board members, and property. If you are a nonprofit, there may be a nonprofit insurance pool available with better rates than traditional insurance. This resource can be found at microschoolcoalition.com.

Other Considerations

Are you allowed to operate a school on your chosen site? While the private school approval process will likely address these, be sure that you are following the zoning laws for your city.

City or county approval may also be needed. Does the health department need to inspect your space and assure safety standards are met? Is a sign-off needed from the fire marshal?

Expense and Revenue Template
(Step 6)

Let's take a comprehensive look at your expenses. List the specific expenses for each category.

Start-up Costs

Advertising and promotion: _____

Borrowing costs: _____

Equipment (furniture, computers): _____

School and office supplies: _____

School space deposit: _____

Insurance: _____

Incorporation, license, and permit fees: _____

Monthly Operational Costs:

Employee expenses (typically up to half of the budget): _____

Monthly rent: _____

Taxes (business, employment…): _____

Technological (wi-fi, computer support and maintenance) expenses: _____

Utilities: _____

Website hosting: _____

Now fill in start-up and monthly costs on your Action Plan for Finance. Knowing these expenses, what does the tuition for ten students need to equal to pay your expenses? If you need $30,000 to start-up and $10,000/month for ten months, you need $130,000 in revenues and a cushion ($20,000?) or $150,000 in revenues. So each of the ten students would need to pay an annual tuition of $15,000 to cover your costs. (If you have other funding sources, the tuition will be reduced accordingly.) Add this calculation to your Action Plan.

Fundera.com, the SBA, and other sites can provide more ideas on costs. Existing micro-schools in the coalition are also a good source of information.

Appendix H

Executive Summary Template (Step 7)

Putting it all together, you will want a one-page summary to introduce your school to prospective families, employees, and funders. Here are components to include in your executive summary:

- Tagline/Mission

- Why you are compelled to create this school

- Your purpose

- Summary of market analysis (There is a need—explain it.)

- Description of how your school meets the need from the market analysis

Appendix I is the executive summary we created for the Micro-School Coalition.

Micro-School Coalition information (Step 7)

Micro-School Coalition Executive Summary

The **Micro-School Coalition** (MSC) is *Building Community to Transform Education for Today's Learners* (tagline). The Micro-School Coalition is an alliance of existing and potential micro-schools determined to transform education, creating more and better learning environments for our children. With synergy and collaboration, our combined efforts support the launching and sustainability of dynamic micro-schools that redesign the learning experience (mission).

Transforming education is a big task. Starting LEADPrep was lonely and difficult. There is no need to reinvent the wheel and labor in isolation. We choose to create an alliance with other collaborative micro-schools to be an example, catalyst, and resource for those bravely starting their own micro-school (purpose).

We see the increase in neurodiversity, dropout rates, and climbing mental health issues within our youth population. We also see brave micro-school founders close their doors because they did not understand the complexity of starting a micro-school and were not equipped to be sustainable. These statistics are a cry for help, and we are answering their call (market analysis).

The MSC will help you design and implement more learning options for today's learners. With a directory of micro-school contacts, their shared ideas, resources, and available coaching in a cohort or individually, our coalition wants to become a part of your micro-school tribe. Let us support your courageous undertaking. We can help you build a foundation to open your doors within one year, with ten or more students...and then provide support to keep your doors open.

ENDNOTES

PART ONE

1. Denizet-Lewis, Benoit. "Why Are More American Teenagers Than Ever Suffering From Severe Anxiety?" *The New York Times*. October 11, 2017. Accessed August 08, 2019. https://www.nytimes.com/2017/10/11/magazine/why-are-more-american-teenagers-than-ever-suffering-from-severe-anxiety.html

2. Sugarman, Joe. "The Rise of Teen Depression," *Johns Hopkins Health Review* 40, no. 4 (2019). Accessed August 08, 2019. https://www.johnshopkinshealthreview.com/issues/fall-winter-2017/articles/the-rise-of-teen-depression

3. Came, Deb. "Graduation and Dropout Statistics: 2018 Report to the Legislature," Washington Superintendent of Public Instruction. Accessed August 08, 2019. https://files.eric.ed.gov/fulltext/ED583136.pdf

4. Swick, M.D., Susan D., and Michael S. Jelnick, M.D.. "Failure to Launch Can Happen to College Students." *MDedge Pediatrics*. April 01, 2019. Accessed August 08, 2019. https://www.mdedge.com/pediatrics/article/194363/mental-health/failure-launch-can-happen-college-students/page/0/1

5. Gonser, Sarah. "Students Are Being Prepared for Jobs That No Longer Exist. Here's How That Could Change." NBCNews.com. April 12, 2018. Accessed August 09, 2019. https://www.nbcnews.com/news/us-news/students-are-being-prepared-jobs-no-longer-exist-here-s-n865096

6. Morton, Neal. "Washington's High-school Graduation Rate Holds Steady at 79 Percent." *The Seattle Times*. March 07, 2018. Accessed August 09, 2019. https://www.seattletimes.com/education-lab/washingtons-high-school-graduation-rate-holds-steady-at-79-percent/

7. Rowe, Claudia. "Report: Washington's Dropout Rate Is High for Students with Learning Disabilities." *The Seattle Times*. May 16, 2017. Accessed August 09, 2019. https://www.seattletimes.com/education-lab/report-washingtons-dropout-rate-is-high-for-students-with-learning-disabilities/

8. Richter, Ruthann. "Among Teens, Sleep Deprivation an Epidemic." News Center. October 8, 2015. Accessed August 09, 2019. https://med.stanford.edu/news/all-news/2015/10/among-teens-sleep-deprivation-an-epidemic.html

9. "Chapter 2 Shifts Needed To Align With Healthy Eating Patterns." A Closer Look at Current Intakes and Recommended Shifts - 2015-2020 Dietary Guidelines. Accessed August 09, 2019. https://health.gov/dietaryguidelines/2015/guidelines/chapter-2/a-closer-look-at-current-intakes-and-recommended-shifts/

10. Sandoiu, Ana. "Teens Get as Much Physical Activity as 60-year-olds, Study Shows." *Medical News Today.* June 19, 2017. Accessed August 09, 2019. https://www.medicalnewstoday.com/articles/317975.php

11. Hansen, Michael, and Diana Quintero. "Analyzing 'the Homework Gap' among High School Students." Brookings. August 10, 2017. Accessed August 09, 2019. https://www.brookings.edu/blog/brown-center-chalkboard/2017/08/10/analyzing-the-homework-gap-among-high-school-students/

12. Parker, Clifton B. "Stanford Research Shows Pitfalls of Homework." *Stanford News.* April 16, 2016. Accessed August 09, 2019. https://news.stanford.edu/2014/03/10/too-much-homework-031014/

13. Horowitz, Juliana Menasce, and Nikki Graf. "Most U.S. Teens See Anxiety, Depression as Major Problems." Pew Research Center's Social & Demographic Trends Project. February 21, 2019. Accessed August 09, 2019. https://www.pewsocialtrends.org/2019/02/20/most-u-s-teens-see-anxiety-and-depression-as-a-major-problem-among-their-peers/

14. Schrobsdorff, Susanna. "Teen Depression and Anxiety: Why the Kids Are Not Alright." *Time.* October 27, 2016. Accessed August 09, 2019. https://time.com/magazine/us/4547305/november-7th-2016-vol-188-no-19-u-s/

15. "College Students' Mental Health Is a Growing Concern, Survey Finds."Accessed August 09, 2019. Monitor on Psychology. https://www.apa.org/monitor/2013/06/college-students

16. Shapiro, Margaret. "Stressed-out Teens, with School a Main Cause." *The Washington Post.* February 17, 2014. Accessed August 09, 2019. https://www.washingtonpost.com/national/health-science/stressed-out-teens-with-school-a-main-cause/2014/02/14/d3b8ab56-9425-11e3-84e1-27626c5ef5fb_story.html?noredirect=on&utm_term=.711c7d0783c6

17. Neighmond, Patti. "School Stress Takes A Toll On Health, Teens And Parents Say." NPR. December 2, 2013. https://www.npr.org/sections/health-shots/2013/12/02/246599742/school-stress-takes-a-toll-on-health-teens-and-parents-say

18. Szczerba, Robert J. "Experience What Autism Might Feel Like." *Forbes Magazine*, Accessed August 09, 2019. https://www.forbes.com/sites/robertszczerba/2016/06/07/experience-what-it-feels-like-to-have-autism/#199f49924cb0

19. "Sensory Differences." Autism support - leading UK charity - National Autistic Society. Accessed August 16, 2019. https://www.autism.org.uk/about/behaviour/sensory-world.aspx

20. "Data & Statistics on Autism Spectrum Disorder | CDC." Centers for Disease Control and Prevention. Accessed August 16, 2019. https://www.cdc.gov/ncbddd/autism/data.html

21. "Understanding Gender." Gender Spectrum. Accessed August 09, 2019. https://www.genderspectrum.org/quick-links/understanding-gender/

22. The Williams Institute, n.d. https://williamsinstitute.law.ucla.edu/visualization/lgbt-stats/?topic=LGBT#density.

23. Human Rights Campaign. "Growing Up LGBT in America: View and Share Statistics." Human Rights Campaign. Accessed August 09, 2019. https://www.hrc.org/youth-report/view-and-share-statistics

24. "Adolescent Connectedness Has Lasting Effects | Adolescent & School Health | CDC." Centers for Disease Control and Prevention. Accessed August 09, 2019. https://www.cdc.gov/healthyyouth/protective/youth-connectedness-important-protective-factor-for-health-well-being.htm?s_cid=hy-carousel-035

25. Sirois, Martie. "'Gender Creative' Is Not the New 'Hipster'." HuffPost. January 03, 2017. Accessed August 9 2019. https://www.huffpost.com/entry/gender-creative-is-not-the-new-hipster_b_586ada7fe4b04d7df167d6c6

26. Gray, Eliza. "PHOTOS: Meet the New Generation of Gender-Creative Kids." *Time*. May 18, 2015. Accessed August 10, 2019. https://time.com/3743987/gender-creative-kids/

27. Solutions, Starlight. "The effect of High-Functioning Autism on Sexual Orientation and Gender-Identity." Accessed August 10, 2019. http://programme.exordo.com/autismeurope2016/delegates/presentation/305/

28. Mayo Clinic Staff. "Teen Depression." Mayo Clinic. Mayo Foundation for Medical Education and Research, November 16, 2018. https://www.mayoclinic.org/diseases-conditions/teen-depression/symptoms-causes/syc-20350985

29. Mayo Clinic Staff. "Generalized Anxiety Disorder." Mayo Clinic. Mayo Foundation for Medical Education and Research, October 13, 2017. https://www.mayoclinic.org/diseases-conditions/generalized-anxiety-disorder/symptoms-causes/syc-20360803

30. Kennedy-Hill, Saoirse. "Mental Illness at Deerfield." *The Deerfield Scroll,* February 1, 2016. http://deerfieldscroll.com/2016/02/mental-illness-at-deerfield/

31. "Children and Teens." Anxiety and Depression Association of America, ADAA. Accessed August 10, 2019. https://adaa.org/living-with-anxiety/children

32. "Anxiety and Depression in Children | CDC." Centers for Disease Control and Prevention. Accessed August 16, 2019. https://www.cdc.gov/childrensmentalhealth/depression.html

33. "Data and Statistics About ADHD | CDC." Centers for Disease Control and Prevention. Accessed August 10, 2019. https://www.cdc.gov/ncbddd/adhd/data.html

34. "The Brown Model of ADD/ADHD: Brown ADHD Clinic: United States." Brown ADHD Clinic. Accessed August 16, 2019. https://www.brownadhdclinic.com/the-brown-model-of-add-adhd

35. Silver, Larry. "Executive Dysfunction, Explained!" ADDitude. August 2, 2019. https://www.additudemag.com/executive-function-disorder-adhd-explained/

36. Board, ADHD Editorial. "ADHD Statistics." ADDitude. August 2, 2019. https://www.additudemag.com/statistics-of-adhd/

37. "Teens with ADHD More Likely to Drop Out." *Futurity,* October 7, 2010. https://www.futurity.org/teens-with-adhd-more-likely-to-drop-out/

38. Fremont, Wanda P. "School Refusal in Children and Adolescents." American Family Physician, October 15, 2003. https://www.aafp.org/afp/2003/1015/p1555.html.

39. Fish, Jonathan. "5 Facts About Childhood Cancer Survivors." St. Baldrick's Foundation, June 10, 2018. https://www.stbaldricks.org/blog/post/5-facts-about-childhood-cancer-survivors/

40. "Cognitive Late Effects in Childhood Cancer Survivors." Together. Accessed August 10, 2019. https://together.stjude.org/en-us/life-after-cancer/long-term-effects/cognitive-late-effects.html

41. Peterson, Tanya J. "Diabetes and ADHD: The Correlation Is High." HealthyPlace. Accessed August 10, 2019. https://www.healthyplace.com/diabetes/mental-health/diabetes-and-adhd-the-correlation-is-high

42. Marien, Hania. "Adverse Childhood Experiences and Chronic Absenteeism." Oregon Educator Network, February 6, 2017. https://www.oregonednet.org/groups/tribal-attendance-pilot-project-tapp-public-blog/posts/adverse-childhood-experiences-and

43. "About Adverse Childhood Experiences |Violence Prevention|Injury Center|CDC." Centers for Disease Control and Prevention. Accessed August 10, 2019. https://www.cdc.gov/violenceprevention/childabuseandneglect/acestudy/aboutace.html

44. Brown, Nicole M, Suzette N Brown, Rahil D Briggs, Miguelina Germán, Peter F Belamarich, and Suzette O Oyeku. "Associations Between Adverse Childhood Experiences and ADHD Diagnosis and Severity." Academic pediatrics. U.S. National Library of Medicine, 2017. https://www.ncbi.nlm.nih.gov/pubmed/28477799

45. Wright Edelman, Marian. "Children and the Opioid Crisis." Children's Defense Fund, June 20, 2019. https://www.childrensdefense.org/child-watch-columns/health/2017/children-and-the-opioid-crisis/

46. "Our Mission." Children's Defense Fund, April 9, 2019. https://www.childrensdefense.org/about/who-we-are/our-mission/

47. Pallarito, Karen. "School Performance in Kids of Opioid-Addicted Moms." WebMD. WebMD, January 16, 2017. https://www.webmd.com/children/news/20170116/kids-born-to-opioid-addicted-moms-seem-to-fare-poorly-in-school#2

48. Ornoy, A, V Michailevskaya, I Lukashov, R Bar-Hamburger, and S Harel. "The Developmental Outcome of Children Born to Heroin-Dependent Mothers, Raised at Home or Adopted." Child abuse & neglect. U.S. National Library of Medicine, May 1996. https://www.ncbi.nlm.nih.gov/pubmed/8735375

49. Zill, Nicholas, and W. Bradford Wilcox. "The Adoptive Difference: New Evidence on How Adopted Children Perform in School." Institute for Family Studies. Accessed August 10, 2019. https://ifstudies.org/blog/the-adoptive-difference-new-evidence-on-how-adopted-children-perform-in-school

50. Marien, Hania. "Adverse Childhood Experiences and Chronic Absenteeism." Oregon Educator Network, February 6, 2017. https://www.oregonednet.org/groups/tribal-attendance-pilot-project-tapp-public-blog/posts/adverse-childhood-experiences-and

51. "Perfectionism Linked to Anorexia, Bulimia in Women." WebMD. February 5, 2003. https://www.webmd.com/mental-health/eating-disorders/news/20030205/perfectionism-linked-to-eating-disorders

52. Hamzelou, Jessica. "Anorexia Is a Metabolic Disorder as Well as a Psychiatric One." *New Scientist*, July 15, 2019. https://www.newscientist.com/article/2209883-anorexia-is-a-metabolic-disorder-as-well-as-a-psychiatric-one/

53. Suarez, K. "Stress and the Sensitive Gut." *Harvard Health*, August 2010. https://www.health.harvard.edu/newsletter_article/stress-and-the-sensitive-gut

54. McDonald, Kerry. "Questioning the Back-to-School Default." FEE. August 9, 2019. https://fee.org/articles/questioning-the-back-to-school-default/

55. Konnikova, Maria. "The Limits of Friendship." *The New Yorker*. June 20, 2017. https://www.newyorker.com/science/maria-konnikova/social-media-affect-math-dunbar-number-friendships

56. "Empowering Future Leaders and Change-Makers." WE Schools Landing. Accessed August 10, 2019. https://www.we.org/en-CA/our-work/we-schools/

PART TWO

57. Weber, Sam, and Connie Kargbo. "Black Families Increasingly Choose to Homeschool Kids." PBS. Public Broadcasting Service, April 22, 2018. https://www.pbs.org/newshour/show/black-families-increasingly-choose-to-homeschool-kids

58. Ladner, Matthew. "Teacher-Led Micro Schools, ESAs Create Opportunity in Native American Education." redefinED, April 15, 2019. https://www.redefinedonline.org/2019/04/teacher-led-micro-schools-esas-create-opportunity-in-native-american-education/

59. "What Is SEL?" Casel. Accessed August 10, 2019. https://casel.org/what-is-sel/

60. Ascd. "WHOLE CHILD." ASCD Whole Child Initiative. Accessed August 10, 2019. http://www.ascd.org/whole-child.aspx

61. "Alternative Private School Where Teens Thrive-LEADPrep ." Leadership Preparatory. Accessed August 16, 2019. https://lead-prep.org/

62. Trackers Forest School. Accessed August 16, 2019. https://trackerspdx.com/forest-school

63. "Innovations Academy / Welcome." / Welcome. Accessed August 16, 2019. https://www.k12northstar.org/domain/4109

64. "Our Mission & Values." Peace Valley School, January 17, 2018. Accessed August 16, 2019. http://peacevalleyschool.org/about-us/our-mission/

65. "Simon Sinek." Simon Sinek, n.d. https://simonsinek.com/

66. Nelson, Jane, and Lynn Lott. "Classroom Management with Positive Discipline." Classroom Management | Positive Discipline for Teachers. November 29, 2008. Accessed August 19, 2019. https://www.positivediscipline.com/teachers

67.   Raleigh, Meghan F., Garland Anthony Wilson, David Alan Moss, Kristen A. Reineke-Piper, Jeffrey Walden, Daniel J. Fisher, Tracy Williams, Christienne Alexander, Brock Niceler, Anthony J. Viera, and Todd Zakrajsek. "Same Content, Different Methods: Comparing Lecture, Engaged Classroom, and Simulation." *Family Medicine.* February 2018. Accessed August 19, 2019. https://www.ncbi. nlm.nih.gov/pubmed/29432624

68.   McLean, Sarah, Stefanie M. Attardi, Lisa Faden, and Mark Goldszmidt. "Flipped Classrooms and Student Learning: Not Just Surface Gains." Advances in Physiology Education. March 2016. Accessed August 19, 2019. https://www.ncbi. nlm.nih.gov/pubmed/26847257

69.   "K-12 Education." BUCK. Accessed August 19, 2019. https://www.buckinstitute. org/education/k-12/

70.   "Education Program." Mountains To Sound Greenway Trust. Accessed August 19, 2019. https://mtsgreenway.org/get-involved/education/

71.   "Expeditionary Learning Schools." Wikipedia. August 05, 2019. Accessed August 19, 2019. https://en.wikipedia.org/wiki/Expeditionary_learning_schools

72.   "Poster: Habits of Success Pyramid." Summit Learning Store. August 16, 2019. Accessed August 19, 2019. https://summitlearningstorefront.com/product/poster-habits-of-success-pyramid/

73.   Silver, Harvey, Richard Strong, and Matthew Perini. "Integrating Learning Styles and Multiple Intelligences." Integrating Learning Styles and Multiple Intelligences - Educational Leadership. 1997. Accessed August 19, 2019. http:// www.ascd.org/publications/educational-leadership/sept97/vol55/num01/ Integrating-Learning-Styles-and-Multiple-Intelligences.aspx

74.   The Myers & Briggs Foundation - MBTI® Basics. Accessed August 23, 2019. https://www.myersbriggs.org/my-mbti-personality-type/mbti-basics/home. htm?bhcp=1

75.   Glasser, Howard. "Nurtured Heart Approach: Emotionally Nutritious Words." Www.ChildrensSuccessFoundation.com. Accessed August 23, 2020. https://ncjtc-static.fvtc.edu/resources/RS00008799.pdf

76.   "21st Century Skills." Wikipedia. July 17, 2019. Accessed August 23, 2019. https:// en.wikipedia.org/wiki/21st_century_skills

77.   Fetsch, Emily. "Six Ways Non-Profit Entrepreneurs Are Distinct from 'Traditional' Entrepreneurs." by Emily Fetsch | Kauffman.org. Kauffman Foundation, May 21, 2019. Accessed August 23, 2020. https://www.kauffman. org/currents/2015/03/six-ways-non-profit-entrepreneurs-are-distinct-from-traditional-entrepreneurs

78. Otar, Chad. "What Percentage Of Small Businesses Fail — And How Can You Avoid Being One Of Them?" Forbes. August 21, 2019. Accessed August 23, 2019. https://www.forbes.com/sites/forbesfinancecouncil/2018/10/25/what-percentage-of-small-businesses-fail-and-how-can-you-avoid-being-one-of-them/#7e8b726b43b5

79. Griffith, Erin. "What Do Failed Startups Have in Common?" Pando. July 23, 2013. Accessed August 23, 2019. https://pando.com/2013/07/23/what-do-failed-startups-have-in-common/

80. Projects, Contributors To Wikimedia. "Scottish Mountaineer and Writer." Wikiquote. July 03, 2018. Accessed August 23, 2019. https://en.wikiquote.org/wiki/W._H._Murray

81. Ibrisevic, Ilma. "The Ultimate Guide to Writing a Nonprofit Business Plan." Nonprofit Blog, July 16, 2019. Accessed August 23, 2019. https://donorbox.org/nonprofit-blog/nonprofit-business-plan/

82. Ark, Tom Vander. "7 Ways Microschools Help Communities Innovate." Forbes. July 11, 2019. Accessed August 23, 2019. https://www.forbes.com/sites/tomvanderark/2019/07/11/7-ways-microschools-help-communities-innovate/#284d50657aff

PART THREE

83. "Private Schools." Welcome to SBE. Accessed August 23, 2019. https://www.sbe.wa.gov/our-work/private-schools

84. Bauermeister, Rylan. "Helping Them Help." PNA, n.d. https://www.phinneycenter.org/

85. Hartman, Steve. "Auto Doctor Fulfills Childhood Dream and Becomes a Medical Doctor in His 40s." CBS News. August 09, 2019. Accessed August 23, 2019. https://www.cbsnews.com/news/auto-doctor-fulfills-childhood-dream-and-becomes-a-medical-doctor-in-his-40s/

86. Ascd. "Integrating Learning Styles and Multiple Intelligences." Integrating Learning Styles and Multiple Intelligences - Educational Leadership. Accessed August 21, 2019. http://www.ascd.org/publications/educational-leadership-sept97/vol55/num01/Integrating-Learning-Styles-and-Multiple-Intelligences.aspx

87. Emotion Awareness Board, n.d. http://kesterlimner.com/emotion/

88. Tierney, John. "Do You Suffer From Decision Fatigue?" *The New York Times*, August 17, 2011. https://www.nytimes.com/2011/08/21/magazine/do-you-suffer-from-decision-fatigue.html?mtrref=undefined&gwh=0E3F262FDA6DA7487D1C9 4ED303003AF&gwt=pay&assetType=REGIWALL

89. OSPI, n.d. https://www.k12.wa.us/student-success/learning-alternatives

90. Spencer, John. "Get Started with Design Thinking." John Spencer, April 23, 2019. http://www.spencerauthor.com/designthinking/

91. "Blog." John Spencer, n.d. http://www.spencerauthor.com/blog/

92. Juliani, A.J. "Homepage." A.J. Juliani, January 10, 2019. http://ajjuliani.com/

93. "Flipped Learning Simplified." n.d. http://www.jonbergmann.com/

94. "A Vision Of Excellence." The Danielson Group, n.d. https://danielsongroup.org/framework

95. Danielson, Charlotte. "PDF." Princeton, NJ, 2011. https://www.k12.wa.us/sites/default/files/public/tpep/frameworks/danielson/danielson-framework-for-teaching-evaluation-instrument-2011.pdf

96. "The SCERTS® Model." The SCERTS Model. Accessed August 23, 2019. http://scerts.com/

97. "Up Your Creative Genius." Patti Dobrowolski. June 21, 2019. Accessed August 23, 2019. https://pattidobrowolski.com/

98. "BUILD." Micro. Accessed August 23, 2019. http://microschoolcoalition.com/

99. "Most Likely to Succeed Trailer HD." YouTube, August 10, 2016. https://www.youtube.com/watch?v=JE5XRrfetu4

ABOUT THE AUTHOR

Maureen O'Shaughnessy, EdD, is a career school innovator with over 30 years of transforming learning in schools to better serve all students. She is the founding director of Leadership Preparatory Academy, a nonprofit progressive micro-school in Washington State. With a master's degree in educational administration and a doctorate degree in educational leadership, she has an extensive understanding of the components needed to transform the education system.

Dr. O'Shaughnessy has served as head of school and principal internationally in countries such as Kuwait, Hungary, and Ecuador. Weaving in a strong emphasis on service and leadership at each school, she has been an educational change agent across the globe. Dr. O'Shaughnessy has dedicated her career to promoting compassionate, innovative, and responsive learning models so that all students can thrive. She is happily married and has two wonderful adult daughters who are muses and teachers along her journey.

Made in the USA
Monee, IL
20 July 2020